# The Prehistory of Korea

# The Prehistory
# of Korea

JEONG-HAK KIM

*Translated and edited by*
RICHARD J. PEARSON AND KAZUE PEARSON

**The University Press of Hawaii** ✗
*Honolulu*

The publication of this book has been subsidized by a grant from the Joint Committee on Korean Studies of the Social Science Research Council and the American Council of Learned Societies.

Originally published by Kawade Shobo as the first half of *Kankoku no Kokogaku*. Copyright © 1972 in Japan by Jeong-hak Kim.

Translation copyright © 1978 by The University Press of Hawaii

Manufactured in the United States of America

# Contents

# Figures

# Plates

# Tables

# Introduction

Korean archaeology has a long tradition dating back over many decades. In the period of occupation by Japan, when the later historical periods were particularly favored, the excavation of the Chinese Han Dynasty garrison of Lolang, which lasted from the first century B.C. to the fourth century A.D. in the area of P'yŏngyang, and the excavation of the Silla Tombs of Kyŏngju provided particularly outstanding results. In contrast to historic archaeology, however, prehistoric studies developed much more slowly. From the mid-1950s, with the economic reconstruction of the north and south, prehistoric archaeology developed swiftly, although the results have been largely unknown outside of Korea. In the north, detailed excavations of sites such as Kungsan and Chit'am-ni have been described in monographs in the series *Yujok Palgul Pogo,* while short research articles were published in the journals *Kogo Minsok* and *Munhwa Yusan.* In the south, active field survey, coupled with some excavation, was undertaken by the National Museum, Seoul; Korea University; Seoul National University; Pusan National University; Yonsei University; and other colleges. The past decade has witnessed an efflorescence of journals and articles from Seoul and Pusan.

Many published materials, however, are of limited distribution and very little is available outside of Korea. Even in Japan, where there has been a recent revival of interest in Korean studies, few of the publications can be found. Professor Jeong-hak Kim (Jŏng-hak Kim in the McCune-Reischauer system of Romanization) has made a great contribution in gathering together the materials from recent excavations and synthesizing them along with the earlier Japanese materials. It is from his publication in Japanese, *Kankoku no Kokogaku,* published in Tokyo in 1972, that we have translated the sections which comprise this book. Grateful acknowledgment is offered to the original publishers, Kawade Shobo; to Mr. Keizo Fukuda, the editor; and finally to Professor Kim, for giving permission to undertake the translation and for assistance throughout the project.

Recent economic development in Korea has spurred the destruction of sites. The reader will notice that many finds in both the north and south occurred in the course of construction of new agricultural, industrial, and transportation facilities. In some cases, major projects such as the building of dams near Seoul were undertaken with no salvage archaeology at all. It is vital, therefore, that all sites which have survived should be protected. A further problem concerns the role of commercial dealers, who pirate ancient tombs all over the country, later offering their finds to competing antiquarians (even university museums), who purchase objects for which no contextual information may be available. In addition, the extensive erosion which occurred at the end of the Yi Dynasty and during the Japanese occupation, with the deterioration of the Korean environment through faulty land management, has taken its toll. Sites are often completely washed out or else covered with eroded debris. Finally, it appears that the original number of sites may have been relatively small. An indication of this would be the fact that in the construction of the Seoul-Pusan highway very few sites were reported, while similar lengths of road in Japan produce innumerable remains.

The significance of Korean archaeology can be assessed from a number of standpoints. With the growing development of Asian studies, Korea has come into its own. Westerners are amazed to find that a country as large as England or France, rapidly increasing in economic and diplomatic importance, is virtually unknown to them. It has been estimated that from the hundreds of thousands of Americans who spent time in Korea during the Korean War, only a dozen or so became fluent in the language. A comprehension of Korea, however, is requisite for the study of the development of the culture of Japan, and for the appreciation of ancient relationships between various parts of east Asia.

Korean prehistory is important not only in the realm of comparative culture history, but also for the contribution it can make to archaeology in general. The peninsula is comprised of a number of ecological zones, from subtropical broadleaf forests in the south to montane coniferous forests in the north. At the same time, its geography fosters communication in specific directions. Mountain ranges along the east coast and in the southern portion have had their particular effect on the development of Korean culture. Communication from Siberia to the northwest, from the Soviet Pacific coast to the northeast, from China to the P'yŏngan-Hwanghae region, and from Japan and the Yangtze to the southern coast are all evident in the archaeological record. The process of diffusion from these areas and the effect of various ecological zones wll be of interest to scholars of anthropology in general. In addition, the formation of various early Korean states, whose roots lie in the Plain Pottery Period, will be of interest to students of cultural evolution. At this point, these states do not seem to have been pristine centers of Bronze Age civilization. Their development makes an interesting comparison with areas of northern Europe, from which new archaeological data and the recent second revolution in radiocarbon dating have led to rethinking about the originality of their development and reevaluation of their antiquity. From the present book similar ideas may develop about Korea.

Korean archaeology is also of vital importance in the establishment of a Korean national identity. After a bitter period of Japanese colonial rule, Koreans are anxious to assert a new image in world affairs as an independent ethnic entity. For this reason, Korean ancient history and archaeology are of great interest to a wide audience. These studies show that the modern political states of Korea and Japan had little meaning in ancient times: rather, we can see a continuum of small communities, some of which later became states, stretching from the continent to the offlying islands.

At present, Korean archaeology is preoccupied with groundwork—the documentation of site and artifact distributions and the establishment of classes and types—with the basic purpose of building a chronology. The establishment of an initial outline has only been possible in the past five years, and the gaps are obvious. The work is complicated by lack of funds, limited excavations, and a high rate of destruction of sites, as mentioned earlier. The reader will find that detailed, problem-oriented archaeology has not yet been developed in Korea. For instance, we know almost nothing about changes in climate and vegetation. Coordinated studies of these problems lie in the future.

From Professor Kim's book it can be seen that Korea was probably inhabited by the Fourth Glaciation. In fact, the excavators of both of the major Palaeolithic sites have suggested even earlier dates for human occupations. The lower layers of Sŏkchang-ni have produced artifacts which have been compared to Choukoutien Locality 1, while a Middle Palaeolithic position has been suggested for Kulp'o-ri. It seems safe to suggest that early *Homo sapiens* first occupied Korea; it may even be that Neanderthal or Neanderthal-like individuals also inhabited Korea in the past. The Sŏkchang-ni site has also yielded some evidence of Upper Palaeolithic habitation remains and early art. A pebble tool industry and a later flake-blade industry can be recognized. However, the exact relationships of these technologies is still a problem. From recent evidence in Japan, where these two kinds of industries have been termed Early and Late Palaeolithic, there appears to be a chronological overlap. Perhaps two kinds of technologies were used by the same groups of people for different activites or in different environments for a period of time. Clear similarities exist between Korean Palaeolithic assemblages and those of Japan, the Soviet Maritime Province, and China. However, the significance of these correspondences still needs to be worked out. When we consider that ten years ago almost nothing was known of the Palaeolithic Age of Korea, the progress which has been made seems remarkable indeed. In the future archaeologists can hope to learn about the physical characteristics of the early populations of Korea and their connections with other parts of the Asian mainland. People with many varied interests in archaeology will want to know how the Palaeolithic inhabitants of Korea are related to modern Koreans as well.

The succeeding culture of Korea, which is separated from the Palaeolithic by a long hiatus, has been termed the Geometric Pottery Culture. In translating, we found it difficult to decide on consistent terms for cultures and periods; therefore we use the term *culture* very loosely, as if to comprise a group of similar artifact assemblages that appear to have similar distinctive characteristics. Geometric Pottery is sometimes termed Neolithic on the basis of the presence of polished stone tools and the ceramics—even though the presence of food production cannot be precisely determined. There is some controversy over the origins of early pottery in Korea, as exemplified in the discussion of the stratigraphy of the Tongsam-dong site near Pusan. Some scholars feel that the earliest pottery in Korea was undecorated or, at the most, embellished with only a few appliquéd strips of clay. In the south particularly, this early form of pottery seems to resemble the extremely old earliest pottery from Japan. This would suggest that the Geometric Pottery Period, in its entirety, might be extremely long, and that internal developments within it might be of great interest. On the other hand, some scholars feel that this interpretation is based on a misreading of the stratigraphy of Tongsam-dong. If this is the case, it is suggested that ceramics began relatively late in Korea, perhaps as a result of influences from Siberia via the Pacific coast or from coastal northeast China.

Korea is situated between Japan, from which archaeological pottery has been documented well over twelve thousand years ago, and China, where the oldest ceramics are tentatively radiocarbon dated to over ten thousand years before the present, at the cave of Hsien-jen-tung, Wan Nien, Kiangsi. It seems that the ceramics of Siberia, Japan, and Korea are all related, and stand somewhat apart from the ceramics of China. Further research on this period will be of great interest, since the oldest dates at present for Geometric Pottery in Korea run about 3000 B.C. From present indications, we might place the Geometric Pottery Period in the time slot from about 4000 B.C. to 1000 B.C. Yong-nam Kim, a well-known North Korean archaeologist, has suggested that the fifth millennium B.C. might be considered the most likely date for the beginning of the Neolithic Age of Korea, and that 4000 B.C. should be considered as a beginning date for Geometric Pottery. The scholars in P'yŏngyang, in keeping with Marxist orthodoxy, believe that the matrilineal clan system reached a peak in this period, and was followed by a patrilineal system in the development of bronze-using cultures.

It is remarkable that archaeological chronologies have been built up for the Geometric Period with so little reliable stratigraphic evidence. The entire chronology is a little like a house of cards. The methods that have been used to achieve an internal ordering of sites are the analysis of motifs of manufacture and decoration, and the shapes of the vessels. Virtually no quantification has been attempted, and the samples are not very reliable. For the earlier time span, at least, there are few guideposts to be found outside of Korea for comparison. At present, function of vessels, which may vary in a different manner from decoration, has not been examined separately, and regional synchronic variation between sites remains to be explored. Almost all variation in ceramics, finally, is viewed as chronological. Yet from other studies of material culture, we know that there are many other dimensions along which objects can differ from one another.

A word should be said about the problems of crossdating Korean archaeological cultures with Chinese counterparts. When Professor Kim wrote his book, there were no radiocarbon dates available from China. He suggests that the Early Plain Pottery Culture, with its stone knives and burnished pottery, might be directly related to the Lungshanoid cultures of the China coast or the Yangtze region. In particular, he suggests that the stone artifacts of Sinhŭng-dong resemble those of Ching-lien-kang. Recently radiocarbon dates from this area show that the Lungshanoid cultures are earlier—perhaps as early as the fourth millennium B.C.—and certainly as early as the third millenium. It has been suggested by Professor Kim that the stone knives of the Korean peninsula are derived from the Yang Shao and Lungshan of China. Again, there are problems in dating and in pinpointing the sources precisely, since the Lungshan and Kiangsu and Shantung appears to be earlier than the Plain Pottery of Korea, and the manifestation of both Lungshan and Yang Shao in the areas of Liaoning and Manchuria are relatively weak. However, Lungshan-like sites from the second millennium B.C. such as Shuang-t'ou-tze in the Liaotung Peninsula, suggest that some styles did persist long enough to influence the Plain Pottery of Korea. These later sites require more study. There are still many problems in the selection of Lungshanoid cultures as reference points in the discussion of the Plain Pottery Culture of Korea; these can be resolved in part by further work on the internal chronology of this period within Korea itself.

It must also be kept in mind, of course, that time is not the only dimension along which variation can occur in ceramics. We know nothing of the sociological significance of various ceramic styles within Korea, except to distinguish certain regional variants. As yet, we have little rigorous information on the degree of variation that occurred within one layer of a site, or even within one region during a short span of time. The suggestion that Chit'am-ni must represent a period of chronological overlap between Geometric and Plain Pottery within the site must be carefully considered as *one* possible explanation to be substantiated by using all lines of evidence.

From current evidence, pottery seems to have spread from the east coast of Manchuria into the northwest of Korea, then moved gradually south. A number of Japanese archaeologists, however, doubt the early radiocarbon dates for pottery in northeast Asia in general. They would suggest that Korean ceramics began later than 4000 B.C., the date cited earlier in this section, and that Japanese ceramics began about 3000 B.C.

Even in the early stages of the Geometric Pottery Period, regardless of its absolute date, local diversity is clear. Decorative motifs and vessel forms vary among the centers of the northeast and northwest, and among those of the Han River, Pusan, and the southern coastal islands. Evidence from Tongsam-dong also shows that trade with Japan took place.

The lack of suitable lithic materials, such as obsidian or fine flint, throughout most of the peninsula is said by Kim to have had a drastic effect on the diversity of stone tool types. Woodworking tools and hunting tools are clearly represented. Whether any stone tools were used for cultivation remains a problem. It has been suggested by Yong-nam Kim *(Kogo Minsok* 3 [1966]: 1–11) that cultivation can be inferred from Layer II of the Sŏp'ohang site, which Kim considers to be Early Neolithic. He suggests that cultivation was well developed in the north by the early fourth millennium B.C., and that stone hoes are identifiable in the archaeological assemblage. At the same time, cut whale bones from Sŏp'ohang Layer II indicate use of marine resources of various kinds.

In all probability, the cultivars were millets and other grains in the north, and rice in the south. At this time cultivation was practiced in China, and there was cultivation of an incipient kind in Japan by the end of the Geometric Period. The more precise circumstances of food production in Korea cannot be outlined until more work is done on ancient environment and climatic change.

In correspondence, Professor Kim has stated that rice cultivation in the south may have begun considerably later than the cultivation of grains in the north. It may have started, he suggests, with the development of the Plain Pottery Culture. Direct evidence for rice cultivation is extremely scanty at this time, and its chronology and development can only be guessed at.

By the subsequent Plain Pottery Period, which lasted from about 1000 B.C. to 200 B.C., or to the first century B.C. in the south, a stable pattern of food production was well developed. Bronze artifacts and other luxury goods appear with dolmens and other elaborate forms of burial which required coordinated labor and the central authority of a tribal, or perhaps a chiefly, organization. At this time, it seems, an increase in population also occurred.

The new ceramics, as outlined by Professor Kim, show some continuities with the Geometric Pottery in vessel shape; however, the consistency of the clay and the decoration are new. The earliest occurrence seems to be in the north, with two different styles appearing in North Hamgyŏng Province and North and South P'yŏngan Provinces. Particularly in the Taedong River Basin of South P'yŏngan Province, proximity to China seems to have been important. New forms of Plain Pottery, with flat bottoms and relatively straight sides, and the presence of some painting and polishing or burnishing, reflect influence from the northeast of the China area. The overlapping of this culture with the previous Geometric Pottery Culture, as well as the exact nature of the transition, is difficult to document given the lack of undisturbed, stratified sites and the dearth of ecological information. New forms of stone artifacts appear, including some circular disc-shaped adzes, perforated in the center, which may be weeding tools. It would be of great interest to carry out detailed studies of site distribution within particular valleys and in relation to vegetation zones and river courses, in an attempt to develop hypotheses which can be tested through excavation.

For a variety of reasons, Korean archaeologists have been keenly interested in the study of bronze artifacts. In the thirties, the Japanese found a number of swords and mirrors in Korea, and assumed that they were either of Chinese manufacture or produced in imitation of Chinese objects from the Yellow River Plain. It was stated that they were of late Warring States origin—perhaps dating from the third century B.C. Also, the polished stone daggers found in Korea were thought to be imitations of bronze prototypes either brought directly from China or dispersed through the large Han colony of Lolang, near the present city of P'yŏngyang. These theories have been unpopular with the Koreans because they were thought to exaggerate the "borrowed" nature of their own culture while depicting them as colonials lacking any local originality. It was particularly hard for them to accept this theory from the Japanese, who were occupying their country and suppressing their culture. At that time, Chinese archaeology was in its infancy, and very little was known of the areas of Liaoning and Manchuria.

With the rapid development of the chronology of the Chinese Bronze and Iron Ages in the fifties and early sixties, the excavation of important sites in the Liaoning area, and the accumulation of new data from Korea, the case can be made for a local development of bronze artifacts based on prototypes from Liaoning, Sui Yuan, and ultimately southern Siberia. Professor Kim eloquently presents this case for the first time to a general audience. At the same time, the earliest forms of the controversial stone daggers can be derived from stone spearheads, although the later forms seem clearly to be copies of bronze artifacts.

Some scholars have made a case that the origins of the present-day Koreans are to be found in the area to the northwest of Korea—the area which produced the early bronze prototypes. They suggest that the Wei Mo tribes, as they are called in early Chinese documents (Ye Maek in Korean), migrated into Korea from Liaoning. Their relations to earlier indigenous tribes of the peninsula, and to the peoples of the south who were later to become the Han tribes of Korea, deserve our future attention. The diversity of burial forms in Korea during the first millennium B.C.—cist coffins, dolmens, pit chamber tombs, and jar burials—may reflect different ethnic or social groups in addition to chronological divisions. Their interrelationships will be of great interest in the study of the formation of early states in Korean history.

Although, beginning in the later forties, there have been other resumés of Korean archaeology, Professor Jeong-hak Kim's work was chosen for translation because it was the most complete. It is particularly important for its wide selection of illustrations and photographs. It provides a base line or starting point, giving the most important distributions. It attempts, in the face of many obstacles, to establish typologies for major classes of artifacts and to arrange them chronologically. The rapid accumulation of new data will make such a synthesis very difficult in the future. To investigate the interrelated causes or correlated factors for the distributions of artifacts outlined by Professor Kim, both spatially and temporally, and their occurrence in particular sets, is the complicated task which lies ahead.

Some of the more than sixty radiocarbon dates available to prehistorians of Korea are presented in the text. For a more complete listing, with recalibration according to the bristlecone pine sequence, the reader may consult "The Study of Korean Archaeology," by R. Pearson, in a guide to Korean studies, edited by Han-Kyo Kim, forthcoming from The University Press of Hawaii.

Some mention should be made of some of the technical aspects of this book. The style of Romanization is the McCune-Reischauer system. Korean place names usually include the *gun* or county, and a village (*li, ri,* or *ni,* depending on the sound at the end of the preceding word), a group of villages *(myŏn),* or a division of a city *(dong).* For Japanese names we have used the Hepburn system of Romanization, with few modifications, and for Chinese names, the Wade-Giles system, which remains the style most familiar to most archaeologists. A glossary of Korean place names, with their Chinese characters, appears at the end of the text.

The original version of Professor Kim's book in Japanese appeared in late August 1972. We began the translation of the first half of the book several months later, completing the first draft in the summer of 1974. The latter portions of the book, which deal with the Three Kingdoms, were not attempted because they lay outside of our area of immediate interest, the prehistoric period of east Asia. This work was undertaken in connection with a larger project to examine the prehistory of Korea, Central China, Japan, and the Ryukyus. Support is acknowledged from the Canada Council, the Wenner-Gren Foundation, the Joint Committee for Korean Research of the Social Science Research Council and the American Council of Learned Societies, and the University of British Columbia. Particular thanks are offered to the Japan Foundation for support in the final stages of preparation of the manuscript. During the summer of 1974, I held visiting positions at Keio University and the Institute of Humanistic Studies, University of Kyoto. At that time, Professor Teruya Esaka and Professor Yutaka Tani were of continued assistance. Particular thanks are offered to Professor Tadao Umesao, National Museum of Ethnology, Japan, for active support on many occasions. During the autumn of 1975 when revisions were being made on the manuscript, I held a visiting position at the Institute for Humanistic Studies, University of Kyoto. Thanks are offered to Professor Tatsusaburo Hayashiya, director, for hospitable assistance.

RICHARD J. PEARSON

Kyoto, November 1975.

# CHAPTER I
# Preceramic Industries

## NATURAL ENVIRONMENT

Very little research has been done until now on the preceramic sites in the [Korean] peninsula. The Tonggwan-jin site on the Tuman River was reported as a Palaeolithic site before World War II, and excavations took place at the Kulp'o site at the mouth of the Tuman River after the war. The Sŏkchang-ni site on the Kum River near Kongju has also been reported. There are differing chronological and cultural interpretations for these sites, and more evidence from such ancillary sciences as geology and palaeontology is needed as well. In areas adjacent to the Korean peninsula, such as China, Mongolia, Siberia, and Japan, many Palaeolithic sites are known; although only a few sites have been found in Korea, there is no doubt that it was inhabited in Palaeolithic times.

What was the environment like during this long span of time? Traces of glaciation in the peninsula have been found on Mt. Paektu and the Kwanmo Range in the north, but these glaciers were very localized. Moreover, none of the larger continental glaciers extended to Korea; a relatively mild climate, therefore, is thought to have prevailed. A characteristic geological feature of the end of the Pleistocene in Siberia, Mongolia, northern China, northeastern China, and the Korean peninsula was the deposition of loess. According to R. F. Flint, loess is derived from siltlike components, and there are many cases in which small quantities of sand and clay occur. Usually dull yellow in color, it can become grey through weathering. The current consensus is that most of the loess was accumulated and carried by wind. This kind of material is thus derived from plains, and its distribution is closely related to the distribution of dry, arid conditions. Siberian loess is generally derived from glacial silt or from fine alluvial sands; such yellow sand layers, for instance, can be seen in Kuranoyarsk, the southern basin of Minusinsk, Irkutsk, and the southeastern part of Baikal. Most of the loess was deposited along the river basins and lakeshores in the Pleistocene. The Mal'ta and Afontova sites, in which Palaeolithic artifacts were found, were formed on the typical loess of these areas.

Northern China possesses a famous loess belt accumulated at the end of the Pleistocene. J. G. Anderson, one of the early scholars concerned with the loess and prehistory, follows the theory of Richtofen that the Chinese loess was made of the accumulation of sand and dust carried from the desert areas; he thinks, however, that the soil of northern China itself also contributed to the formation of the loess. The quality of the clay of the Tertiary appears to be very close to that of the loess. Anderson says that there was almost no evidence of earlier Pleistocene glacial activity; a simple glacial provenience, therefore, is not likely. According to him, most of northern China in the period of accumulation of loess was a rather dry grassland; thus, vast amounts of sands and dust were wind-carried and accumulated particularly in the valleys or basins where local winds were not so strong. Over a long period of time, the sand formed a yellow layer as thick as several tens of meters.

Shui-tung-kou in the Ordos and Djalai-nor in Mongolia are Palaeolithic sites in loess areas, and the Ku-hsiang-t'un site in northeastern China also occurs in loess. The excavators of the Tonggwan-jin site, which is on the Tuman River, report that the loess found at the site is very close to that of Manchuria.

## PRECERAMIC COMPLEXES
### TONGGWAN-JIN SITE

The site, which is on a Pleistocene terrace of the Tuman River, was found in 1932 when railway construction cut through the terrace and rhinoceros teeth were found. The next year, Tamezo Mori excavated in the same location and found remains of several kinds of fossil animals and two objects thought to be made by ancient man. In 1935, Shigeyasu Tokunaga and Tamezo Mori excavated this terrace and found human artifacts together with abundant remains of fossil mammals. Beneath the surface there was a first loess layer extending to a depth of 3.5 meters on the north cliff and 2.0 meters on the western cliff, then a blackish loess layer, 2.4 meters and 2.8 meters thick respectively. Below this was a second loess layer 2.8 meters deep overlying a layer of mixed sand and pebbles, which was 1 meter deep. The bottom of the site consisted of a pebble layer. From the yellow loess layer in the northern cliff, a considerable number of fossils, such as *Myosphalax, Citellus,* and *Cervus elephas L.,* were found, and from the first loess layer on the western cliff many fossils, such as *Hyena,* mammoth, *Rhinoceros,* and *Bos primigenius,* were obtained. At the same level which produced these fossil remains were two obsidian objects, definitely human artifacts according to the reporter, as well as many tools of bone and antler.

The layers that contained the previously mentioned remains were loess layers; the loess of northeastern China and the Korean peninsula, however, are perhaps not primary loess but consist of redeposition over primary deposits by wind or water. The loess layer of Tonggwan-jin was deposited in a layer about 10 meters thick over the present alluvium and is clearly differentiated from the latter.

It is difficult to be clear about the faunal assemblage, because the sample is small; one might speculate, however, that *Elephas primigenius, Rhinoceros antiquitatis,* or other extinct mammals such as *Hyena* and *Megaceros* existed after the middle of the Pleistocene epoch, and that these were slightly later than those from the Ku-hsiang-t'un site of northeastern China.

Cultural remains consisted of two lithic and numerous bone and antler artifacts. Both of the stone artifacts were small and made of black, shiny obsidian. The reporter said that one of the stone artifacts had a substantial cutting edge near the tip.

The five antler artifacts were fabricated from the first or second branches, cut and shaped into tools.

The bone artifacts were made of the bones of wild horses or large deer such as *Megaceros*. Some were made of wild horse ulna or tibia split lengthwise, while others were modified into a long strip shape from the shoulder blades of large animals. These artifacts comprise the total complement from Tonggwan-jin. Unfortunately, few of the tools possess unmistakable Palaeolithic features. Are the bone artifacts, which are similar to those found at Ku-hsiang-t'un, indicators of a Late Palaeolithic manifestation? Ku-hsiang-t'un has been regarded as Late Palaeolithic; recently, however, there has been some doubt expressed concerning this attribution. The same reservations should be kept in mind in considering the Tonggwan-jin site. Ryosaku Fujita has expressed his doubts about the assignment of Tonggwan-jin to the Palaeolithic. Sueji Umehara agreed with Fujita's reservations and stated that it would be too hasty to conclude any close association among the artifacts themselves or the faunal assemblage, since the terrace on which the site occurs has been used for Neolithic burials, and microblades and bone artifacts from modern fauna have also been found.

In the report by Tokunaga and Mori, however, the stratigraphic relationships are clearly described, and they mention that Neolithic artifacts are scattered on the surface of the terrace. There appears to be no question, therefore, as far as stratigraphy is concerned. It is likely that Fujita and Umehara based their opinion on the report of the artifacts by Nobuo Naora, probably without seeing the latter report by Tokunaga and Mori. More investigation from various angles, including geology and palaeontology, should be carried out on Tonggwan-jin.

## KULP'O-RI SITE

This site, located in Kulp'o-ri, North Hamgyŏng Province, consists of a shell mound on the slope of a low mountain, situated in a flat area 300 to 400 meters long. Probably sea level occurred near the site in ancient times. Excavation took place in 1960, and two cultural layers, of Neolithic and Bronze Age, were ascertained. In the second excavation during the same year, one marble chopper was found from the bottom of the Neolithic Layer. During the third excavation in 1963, stone tools made of hornfels, quartzite, and granite gneiss were found; some similar specimens were found in the surface collection. In the fourth excavation, carried out in the same year, a workshop area was reported. At this locality were scrapers, quartz flake points, and a quartz nucleus.

The stratigraphy was as follows: Layer I (15 cm) consisted of top soil. Layer II (40 cm) was composed of dark brown fine sand; Layer III (25 cm) was of bluish dark brown sandy clay; Layer IV (6 cm) was yellowish brown clay, and Layer V (about 40 cm) was dark black clay. The clay in this final layer contained fine gravels, and from this layer an artifact of hornfels was found, in addition to a marble chopper. Below Layer V was a clay layer of pebbles and gravels about 90 centimeters thick. After Layer VI, the earth became harder and there was a 110-centimeter layer of clay and pebbles (Fig. 1).

The reporter of the excavations said that the Palaeolithic manifestation consisted of a slightly more recent layer which contained stone implements mainly of hornfels and an older layer which contained artifacts mainly of quartzite. All of these artifacts were regarded as belonging to the Palaeolithic and have been termed the Kulp'o-ri Culture. The whole culture can be divided into Period I (Layer VI) and Period II (Layer V), according to the stratigraphy of the site. One of the three artifacts made of hornfels found in the third excavation was bifacial (Fig. 2:1), the second was unifacial (Fig. 2:2), and the third was finished all on one side while the other side was flaked only on part of the edge (Fig. 2:3). A stone core and a chopper made of granite gneiss were found in the layer assigned to Period I, and it is said that the blade of the chopper showed evidence of use. In the fourth excavation, numerous quartz chips of various sizes were found and there were some stone implements and stone cores of apparent human workmanship. Also on the same level was an anvil stone with more than 50 quartz chips beside it. In 1964 a fifth excavation yielded more stone artifacts, including a quartzite chopper.

Stone artifacts of Periods I and II are said to be made by the prepared platform technique. As proof of this, the author cites the presence of completely altered artifact surfaces (no cortex remaining) and the presence of stone core tools. The choppers are stated to be unifaces. Although bifaces persist in Period II, unifaces appear to be predominant.

The reporter on Kulp'o-ri looked for similarities with

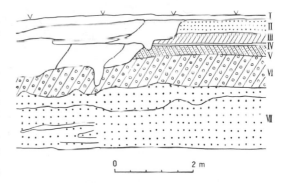

Figure 1. Profile showing the stratigraphy of the Kulp'o-ri site

I    surface soil layer
II   dark brown fine sand layer
III  sandy clay layer
IV   yellowish-brown clay layer
V    dense black clay layer
VI   clay and cracked pebbles
VII  angular gravel and clay in alternating layers

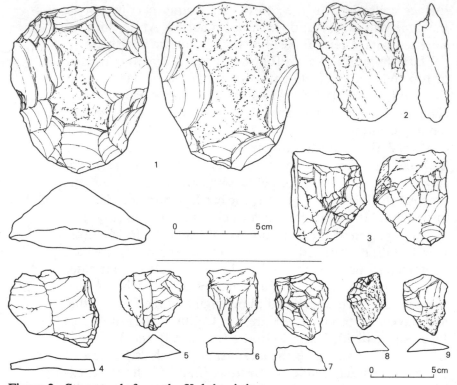

Figure 2. Stone tools from the Kulp'o-ri site

Chou-K'ou-tien, K'o-ho, Ting ts'un, and Shan-ting-tung, which all produced unifacial assemblages. He suggests that the bifacial hand axe in the Ting ts'un Culture is an exception; the bifacial technique seen in Kulp'o-ri Period II therefore represents a departure from the main current.

The reporter assumed that Kulp'o-ri I was Late Lower Palaeolithic—that is, that it was comparable with Mousterian in terms of typology and that Period II was much later. However, Period II also seems to fall within the Later Lower Palaeolithic.

The basic criterion for distinguishing Mousterian from earlier Palaeolithic culture is the presence of bifacial hand axes and particular kinds of flake tools. In the oldest Mousterian there are numerous small hand axes, which disappeared in the mid-Mousterian as flake tools appeared.

In the description of Kulp'o-ri stone tools, there were unifacial and bifacial stone tools, the unifaces being predominant. In this regard, Kulp'o-ri appears to be comparable to the Mousterian of Europe. However, typology and chronology are not well understood in the Palaeolithic cultures of east Asia, and it is difficult to make comparisons solely on artifact typology; more work should be done on geological and stratigraphic problems at Kulp'o-ri.

## SŎKCHANG-NI SITE

The site is on the upper reaches of the Kum River about 6 kilometers from Kongju. Stone artifacts were first found in the eroded river bank. Excavations were initiated by Yonsei University and have been carried on for a number of years. No final report has been published; the account given here is based on newspaper coverage, reports by the excavator, Professor Pow-key Sohn, and on-the-spot observations of the site.

Seven excavation areas were opened by 1968. At Pit No. 1, bedrock was reached 11.34 meters below the surface. Professor Sohn divided the 11 meters of deposit into 27 strata, 11 of which were considered to be definite cultural layers, while 3 more were somewhat uncertain (Fig. 3). A number of cultural layers were singled out for description [Table 1].

The description of layers below these has been omitted, since they need more work. Professor Sohn regards each layer as belonging to a different cultural period, suggesting that the lowest cultural layer could be as old as the Lower Palaeolithic. Thus, Lower, Middle, and Upper Palaeolithic are thought to be included in this site. In a recent article about the sixth cultural layer, Professor Sohn classified the stone artifacts as follows: 2 hand axes, 11 chopping tools, 3 choppers, 18 side scrapers, 9 end scrapers, 10 points, 9 cleavers, 4 blades, 1 point. These were classified as tools for general use. In addition, tools used in the production of other tools include: 2 hammer stones, 4 hammering tools, and 1 pecking stone. Within the category of general use, core tools comprised 40 items (about 60 percent) and flake, 27 (about 40 percent); with the predominance of the former, it was considered a "core tool" assemblage. (Fig. 4.)

All the core tools of this cultural layer were small, and flakes were produced by the cylinder hammer technique. Manufacturing techniques appear to be close to those of the

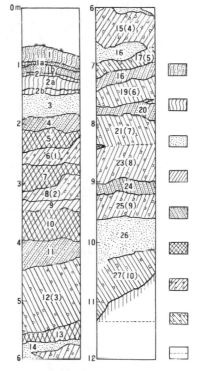

Figure 3. Stratigraphy of the Sŏkchang-ni site
(from top)
    surface layer
    humus layer
    fine sand
    clay
    sandy clay
    hard clay
    angular gravel
    water-worn gravel
    wood charcoal

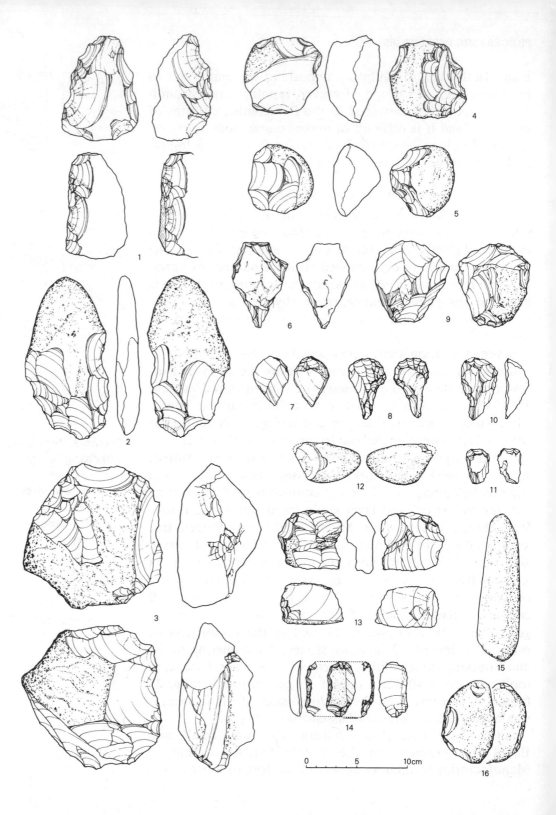

0        5        10cm

Table 1. Contents of Cultural Layers of the Sŏkchang-ni Site

| Cultural Layer | Contents |
|---|---|
| 1 | Pebble and flake tools, including a number of composites; porphyry dominant material |
| 2 | Primarily quartzite artifacts, many small tools, such as side scrapers, end scrapers, some large flake tools |
| 3 | Flake tools and core tools from quartz and granite gneiss |
| 4 | Small tools of porphyry, quartzite, and obsidian; flake points made by simple flaking of small stones; tools on retouched blades |
| 5 | Pebbles with simple flaking and zigzag bifacial chipping |
| 6 | Large core tools, quartz chips; flake points, burins, scrapers, hoe (?); also tools used for fabrication, such as hammer stones, pecking stones, and anvils |
| 7 | Small tools of quartzite predominate, including small flake tools; some small tools similar to flake points from Shui-tung-kou in the Ordos. |

Clactonian or Mousterian, suggesting to Sohn a Middle or Upper Palaeolithic date.

The difficulties of grouping Palaeolithic typological units into a chronology are well known. In addition, problems arise when we try to apply European criteria to the Palaeolithic cultures of eastern Asia. There must, of course, be some common features in the development of the Palaeolithic in Europe and Asia; specific differences are also clear, however, and the Sŏkchang-ni material must be examined in this light. Of particular interest is the chronological position of each of the strata. Special attention should be given to the accumulation of the river deposits. There are many ways for increasing the precision of interpretations from the site, and it is to be hoped that Sŏkchang-ni will yield further results at the hands of its ardent excavator.

Figure 4. Stone tools from the Sŏkchang-ni site

# CHAPTER 2
# Geometric Pottery Culture

The oldest pottery found in Korea can be termed "Geometric." This has been called "Comb-Pattern" hitherto. Before World War II, the so-called *mumun* or Plain Pottery was considered by some to be older than Geometric Pottery. However, after the war, an earlier stratigraphic relationship was demonstrated for Geometric Pottery.

Comb-Pattern Pottery was first named by Ryosaku Fujita in 1930, on the basis of similarities between the Korean pottery and the *Kammkeramik* in northern Eurasia. He defined it as pottery with designs incised by a comblike instrument. He also described it as Stone Age pottery decorated in parallel wavy designs, parallel dots, and rows of small circles, applied on the half-dried, unglazed ceramic with something like a comb.

*Kammkeramik* was the name applied to prehistoric pottery in northern Eurasia, such as Russia and Finland. From recent excavations, however, it is clear that the cultures in this region were far from homogeneous, and the term *Kammkeramik* or "*Kammkeramik* Culture" has become inappropriate. Particularly in Siberia, many excavations carried out by A. P. Okladnikov and others show that the prehistoric culture in this area was quite complicated and differed from that of northern Europe in many respects.

There can be little doubt that the decorated pottery in the Neolithic Age of Korea was influenced by the prehistoric pottery of northern Eurasia and, geographically, the relationship between Neolithic Culture in Korea and prehistoric Siberian cultures should be regarded as important. Prehistoric culture in Siberia, however, was quite different from that in northern Europe, as mentioned earlier. The Korean Neolithic pottery is quite different from that of either northern Europe or Siberia. Thus the single term *Kammkeramik* is inappropriate in all areas from northern Europe to Siberia.

Tsugio Mikami was not satisfied with the term "Comb-Pattern Pottery" either, and used simply the term "decorated pottery." Tatsuo Sato followed this custom. Neolithic pottery in Korea varied depending on the area and period; in many cases it is not close to Comb Pattern. Therefore, I have adopted the term "Geometric" or "Geometric-Designed Pottery."

Studies of Geometric Pottery in Korea include the prewar work of Ryosaku Fujita and the postwar studies of Arimitsu, Mikami, Sato, and To. I have also worked on these ceramics as well.

Postwar excavations have yielded many new materials; in particular, stratigraphic information has been significant. The representative site for Geometric Pottery in the central part of the peninsula is Amsa-ri, Kwangju. The site was found before the war; most of the materials discussed here, however, have come from more recent excavations. The same is true of the site of Nongp'o-dong (Yup'an) in Chongjin.

I have tried to look at Geometric Pottery "Culture" as a totality, including all of the other artifacts found with the ceramics. For this purpose, representative sites are examined in their entirety.

It goes without saying that the characteristics of the Geometric Pottery Culture can be clarified by comparison with the Plain Pottery Culture. Another enlightening comparison can be made with the prehistoric cultures of Siberia and northern Europe. A third comparison can be made with the Jōmon Culture of Japan and prehistoric cultures of northern China.

To study the variations of Geometric Pottery Culture, it is convenient to divide the Korean peninsula into four areas—northwest (North and South P'yŏngan Province, Hwanghae Province), northeast (Hamgyŏng Province), central (Kyŏnggi, Kangwŏn, and Ch'ung ch'ŏng provinces) and southern (Kyŏngsang and Chŏlla provinces). (See Fig. 5.)

## CENTRAL AREA
### *AMSA-RI SITE*

Although many sites have yielded the remains of Geometric Pottery Culture, most have only been surface collected or test pitted; almost none has undergone intensive excavation.

The Amsa-ri site was exposed in the large flood of 1925, yielding a huge amount of remains. Collections were made by Shozaburo Yokoyama and Ryosaku Fujita. However, no detailed report was made by the collectors; only fragmentary accounts can be found. Arimitsu described the site recently in his "Study of the Comb Pattern Pottery of Korea" (1962) and provided abundant plates. He did not use Yokoyama's collection, however, but used rubbings of them from the present National Museum of Korea and photographs collected by Sueji Umehara. Wŏn-yong Kim also wrote an article, "The Pottery and Stone Implements of the Amsa-ri Site," using the collections and notes donated to the National Museum by Yokoyama. Both works by Arimitsu and Kim were based on prewar materials.

According to the present administrative divisions, Amsa-ri in Kwangju is called Seoul Special City (Metropolitan Seòul), Amsa-dong, Song-tung Ku. However, the historical name Amsa-ri, Kwangju seems more appropriate in this kind of exposition.

Situated on a sandy deposit of the Han River, the site yielded mostly Geometric Pottery; other forms were found, however, including reddish-brown plain pottery, grey-stamped pottery, and even iron wares in small quantities. The site has been a dwelling area ever since the Neolithic, and some areas show that disturbance occurred between the various occupations.

I surveyed the site six times between 1960 and 1964, and conducted trial excavations in one area. In 1967, with Ki-ung Kim, I excavated two areas, and in 1968 I took the responsibility for a five-university joint excavation. Most of the

Geometric Pottery contains mica, and a very few examples were made of clay mixed with asbestos. In this site, all of the Geometric Pottery has a sandy texture; apparently local clays were used. The mica in the clay appears to be a natural component; however, the asbestos must have been mixed in artificially. In other areas, talc and various other tempers were used.

Most of the bases in a sample of 44 vessels were pointed, while a few were round (Fig. 6). Among the round examples, five were almost flat; they appear to be indistinguishable from the body sherds, and represent a transition from the round-bottom to the flat-bottom type. From complete examples found in other areas, it seems that the round bottoms belonged to low bowls. All of the total sample of rims were straight. Once again, from complete or restored vessels it seems that the predominant shape was a hemisphere with pointed bottom, round-bottom vessels being rare.

Most of the vessels had geometric decoration from the rim to the bottom. Two vessels had plain bottoms, one being perforated. It appears that this omission of decoration was deliberate, and that the bases could not be confused with those of Plain Pottery. This latter point is clear from the paste, since Plain Pottery found in this site or on a nearby hill was made of a sticky clay (Plates 1, 2).

The decoration was mostly incised or impressed, and many vessels had different patterns arranged from the mouth to the body. The most popular rim design (74 percent of the 315 rim sherds) was composed of short slant parallel lines (Fig. 7:1–3). The next most popular design (5.1 percent) was composed of small arcs (Fig. 7:18). Next was a decoration of tiny circles (1.3 percent) probably pressed into the clay with a broken bird bone (Fig. 7:24). It is similar to the pit-marking decoration of Phase II of the Neolithic in northern Europe. A similarity can be noticed in the technique of two alternately applied designs in the Neolithic Phase III of northern Europe and in Amsa-ri. The short slant parallel and tiny circle motifs were applied alternately on the rim of the Amsa-ri examples (Fig. 7:17). From the mouth, there was a band of short slant parallel lines, followed by a line of tiny circles; the two kinds of design were repeated once more; then the slanting line motif was doubled and the concentric circle

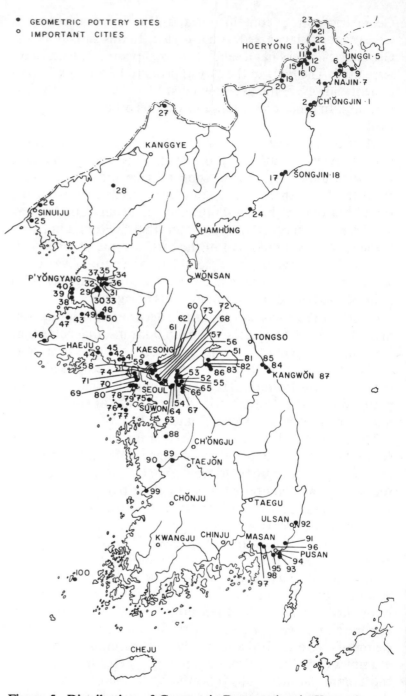

Figure 5. Distribution of Geometric Pottery sites in Korea (prepared especially for the translated edition)

*Numbered Sites*

North Hamgyŏng Province
1. Chongjin City, Songsan
2. Kyŏngsŏng-gun, Yŏngsong-myŏn, Nongp'o-dong
3. Och'on-myŏn, Wonsudae
4. Punyŏng-gun, Kwanhae-myŏn, Yujin-dong
5. Unggi-gun, Unggi-myŏn, Songp'yŏng-dong
6. Unggi-gun, Unggi-myŏn, Yongsu-dong
7. Kyŏnghŭng-gun, Najin-up, Haesangumi
8. Kyŏnghŭng-gun, Sinan-myŏn, Najin-ni
9. Kyŏnghŭng-gun, Nosŏ-myŏn, Chosan-dong
10. Hoeryŏng-gun, Pongui-myŏn, Namsan-dong
11. Hoeryŏng-gun, Pyoksong-myŏn, Hukgubong
12. Hoeryŏng-gun, Pyoksong-myŏn, Soch'on-dong
13. Hoeryŏng-gun, Hoeryŏng-up, O-dong
14. Hoeryŏng-gun, Hwap'ung-myŏn, Saeul-dong
15. Hoeryŏng-gun, Undu-myŏn, Unyŏn-ni
16. Hoeryŏng-gun, Undu-myŏn, Sugup'o
17. Haksŏng-gun, Hangnam-myŏn, Ssangp'o-dong
18. Sŏngjin-gun, Sŏngjin-up, Haeng-jŏng
19. Musan-gun, Musan-up, Chilsŏng-dong
20. Musan-gun, Upnae-myŏn, Musan
21. Chongsong-gun, Haenyŏng-myon, Chigyŏng-dong
22. Chongsong-gun, Namsan-myŏn, Kanp'yong
23. Chongsong-gun, Namsan-myŏn, Pangwon-dong

South Hamgyŏng Province
24. Sinch'ang-gun, Sokhu-myŏn, Kangsang-ni
25. Yongch'on-gun, Yongamp'o-up, Chunghung-dong
26. Miju-gun, Sujin-myon, Misong-ni
27. Chunggang-gun, Chungdok-ni
28. Chunggang-gun, Changsŏng-dong

South P'yŏngan Province
29. P'yŏngyang, T'osong-dong
30. P'yŏngyang, Sog'am-dong
31. P'yŏngyang, Sa-dong
32. P'yŏngyang, Oya-dong
33. P'yŏngyang, Sŏngyo-ri
34. Taedong-gun, Imwon-myŏn, Ch'ongho-ri
35. Taedong-gun, Imwon-myŏn, Kŭmtal-li
36. Taedong-gun, Ch'uelmi-myŏn, Mirim-ni
37. Taedong-gun, Sŏch'ŏn-myŏn, Sop'o-ri
38. Yonggang-gun, T'osŏng-myŏn, Yondo-ri
39. Yonggang-gun, Haeun-myŏn, Yongban-ni
40. Yonggang-gun, Haeun-myŏn, Kungsan-ni

Hwanghae Province
41. Yŏnbaek-gun, Soksan-myŏn, Yongdong-ni
42. Yŏnbaek-gun, Sŏksan-myŏn, Ugok-ni
43. Anak-gun, Sŏksan-myŏn, P'ano-ri
44. Haeju, Haeju-up, Namsan
45. Ongjin-gun, Masan-myŏn, Chŏmam-dong
46. Changyon-gun, Hacan-myŏn, Monggŭm-p'o
47. Unyul-gun, Nambu-myŏn, Kungyang-ni
48. Pongsan-gun, Tongsŏn-myŏn, T'osŏng
49. Pongsan-gun, Munyong-myŏn, Songsan-ni
50. Pongsam-gun, Munyong-myon, Chit'am-ni

Kyŏnggi Province
51. Yangju-gun, Kuri-myŏn, Saro ri
52. Yangju-gun, Kuri-myŏn, Kureungsan
53. Yangju-gun, Mikŭm myŏn, Chikŭm-ni
54. Yangju-gun, Mikŭm-myon, Susŏng-ni
55. Yangju-gun, Wabu-myŏn, Tongmak-dong
56. Yangju-gun, Pyolnae-myŏn, T'oegewon-ni
57. Yangju-gun, Kuji-myŏn, Mangu ri
58. P'aju-gun, Kyoha-myŏn, Tayul-li
59. P'aju-gun, Imjin-myŏn, Toksŏ-ri
60. P'aju-gun, Chori-myŏn, Pongilchŏn-ni
61. P'aju-gun, Chunae-myŏn, Paeksŏng-ni
62. P'aju-gun, Wolrong-myŏn, Tŏkŭn-ni
63. Seoul City, Kwangju, Kuch'ŏn-myŏn, Amsa-ri
64. Seoul City, Kwangju, Tongbu-myŏn, Sŏn-ni
65. Seoul City, Kwangju, Tongbu-myŏn, Misa-ri
66. Seoul City, Kwangju, Tongbu-myŏn, Kusan-ni
67. Seoul City, Kwangju, Sobu-myon, Ch'ungung-ni
68. Seoul City, Sŏngdong-ku, Wangsip'-ni, Ungbong
69. Kanghwa-gun, Hwado-myŏn, Tongmak-ni
70. Kanghwa-gun, Hwado-myŏn, Sagi-ri
71. Kanghwa-gun, Hwado-myŏn, Tojang-ni
72. Koyang-gun, Sindo-myŏn, Obuja-dong
73. Koyang-gun, Wŏndang-myŏn, Kasi-dong
74. Koyang-gun, Pyŏkje-myŏn, Chiyŏng-ni
75. Sihung-gun, Kunja-myŏn, Oi-do
76. Puch'ŏn-gun, Tŏkjŏk-myŏn, Soya-do
77. Puch'ŏn-gun, Tŏkjŏk-myŏn, Sŭngbong-do
78. Puch'ŏn-gun, Pukdo-myŏn, Si-do
79. Puch'ŏn-gun, Pukdo-myŏn, Sin-do
80. Puch'ŏn-gun, Pukdo-myŏn, Changbong-do

Kangwŏn Province
81. Ch'unsŏng-gun, Sindong-myŏn, Hakgok-ni
82. Ch'unch'on-gun, Sinbuk-myŏn, Ch'ŏnjŏn-ni
83. Ch'unch'on City, Kyo-dong, Pongŭi-san
84. Ch'unch'on City, Soksa-dong
85. Myongju-gun, Sach'on-myŏn, Pangdong-ni
86. Myongju-gun, Ungok-myŏn, Yŏngjin-ni
87. Kangnŭng-up, T'osŏng

South Ch'ungch'ong Province
88. Ch'ŏnan City, Pongyong-dong
89. Kongju City, Changgi-gun, Sŏkchang-ni
90. Puyŏ-gun, Kuiam-myŏn, Nabong-ni

South Kyŏngsang Province
91. Yangsan-gun, Sŏsaeng-myŏn, Sinam-ni
92. Yangsan-gun, Kangdong-myŏn, Muryong ni
93. Pusan City, Yŏngdo-ku, Tongsam-dong
94. Pusan City, Yŏngdo-ku, Yongson-dong
95. Pusan City, Sŏ-ku, Tadep'o-dong
96. Pusan City, Pusan-jin ku, Kŭmgok-dong, Yul-li
97. Kimhae-gun, Chuch'on-myŏn, Yangdong-ni
98. Kimhae-gun, Chuch'on-myŏn, Nongso-ri

North Chŏlla Province
99. Kunsan City

South Chŏlla Province
100. Muan-gun, Huksan-myŏn, Taehuksan-do

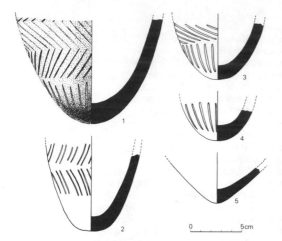

Figure 6. Bases of ceramic vessels from the Amsa-ri site

motif tripled. Neolithic Phase III ceramics in northern Europe have alternating punctate and comb impression; however, these designs were applied to the whole surface of the pottery. The method of applying the design seems to be similar, although the area of design is different. A lattice, checkered pattern occurred on the rim and mouth (Fig. 7:21). This design was also applied on the body; however, it occupied 4.1 percent of the rim designs as well. The design was incised with comblike tools of either single or double teeth. Irregular space between the checks suggests that a single-toothed tool was probably used.

Herringbone design was predominant on the body of the ceramics; however, as a rim design it occupied about 5.4 percent (Fig. 7:9). This pattern, which consists of incised parallel slanting lines, goes under various names, such as "cryptomeria design," "feather design," or "parallel incisions." Termed "herringbone" by the American archaeologists, it can be seen in New World prehistoric ceramics.

An intermittent comb design also occurred at Amsa-ri (Fig. 7:10). The dotted lines were impressed on the surface of the pottery with a comblike instrument; this design can be seen on many ceramics from the early periods in northern Eurasia. This is the so-called *Kammkeramik;* however, it was actually a rare motif in Amsa-ri, being restricted to the mouths of the vessels. In northern Eurasia, comb marking was applied all over the surface of the pottery.

Rim decoration includes punctation, using something like a pointed wood or bamboo stick (Fig. 7:15). Depending on the technique, some look like pitting, while others look like comb marking. In our collection there was one example with twelve lines of punctate design extending from the tip. The decoration is quite effective, alternating triple and single lines being punctated from different directions.

Herringbone is the most widespread form of body design, occurring on 1,821 sherds from a total of 2,184 (83.4 percent). This motif was rare in the early period of northern Eurasian ceramics but increased considerably in the later period. Both horizontal and vertical application of the herringbone design occurred. In some cases, triangular or rhom-

Figure 7. Rubbings of rim sherds of Geometric Pottery vessels

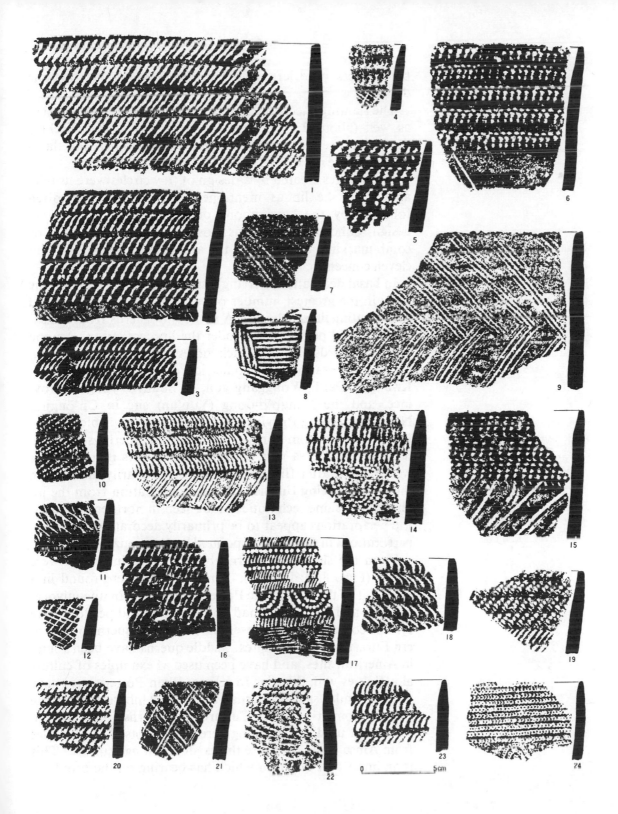

1 2 3 4 5 6 7 8 9 10 11 12 13 14 15 16 17 18 19 20 21 22 23 24

0 _____ 5cm

boid spaces were left open between zones of herringbone
design.

The slanting checkered pattern was seen in the body design
as well (about 2.2 percent). In some cases, the checkers
themselves were of irregular sizes, while in others the slanting lines were not drawn perfectly straight.

Double arcs created by a design of tiny circles were usually
applied to the lip as mentioned before, and were often
followed by the herringbone design beneath it. The arc
design found in this site was mostly made by tiny circles or
comb marking, and most of the arcs ranged from double to
eleven concentric lines.

In basal decoration, herringbone design extended from the
body in the greatest number of cases; a few were decorated
with slanting lines (Plate 4). A number of sherds from Amsa-
ri had round perforations under the lip decoration. Among
290 rim sherds, 23 had such holes. (See Plates 5, 6, 7.)
Similar perforations in Geometric Pottery occur at Misa-ri,
Kwangju; Pal-li, Yonggang-gun, in South P'yŏngan Province, and the Nongp'o-dong (Yup'an) site in Ch'ŏngjin,
North Hamgyŏng Province. Since this trait is visible in Neolithic ceramics from northern Europe and Siberia, some connection with Korea may be found. It appears that the holes
were pierced after firing; the hole was primarily made from
the outside, being finished off by a penetration from the interior. The same technique can be seen in northern Eurasia.
Lip perforations appear to be primarily decorative; however,
perforations in the body or pointed base are puzzling.

From the site of Amsa-ri, about seven grindstones were
found (Figs. 8, 9; Plate 8). Three of them were found in a
house pit of the Geometric Pottery Culture in an unequivocal
context, and all of them had both mortars and pestles (Plate
9). The concave mortars resemble the saddle querns of northern Eurasian Neolithic sites. Saddle querns have been found
in American sites, and have been used as examples of cultural affinities with Siberia. In Korea, Plain Pottery sites have
yielded similar saddle querns—apparently inherited from the
earlier Geometric Pottery Culture. The querns are thought to
have been used for grinding cereals or roots. Do examples
from Amsa-ri demonstrate the existence of agriculture? This
is an important question which has bearing on the problems

Figure 8. Stone tools from the Amsa-ri site

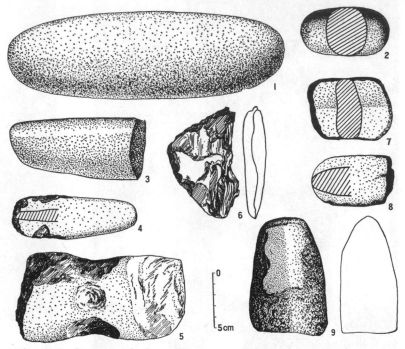

Figure 9. Stone tools from the Amsa-ri site

of Korean agricultural origins. In the materials which we have examined, there were no stone tools which specifically might have been used for agricultural purposes besides adzes (Fig. 9:5) or scrapers (Fig. 9:6). Since the site was on a sandy dune area along the Han River, the inhabitants may have been primarily fishermen without agriculture. From this site as well as from Misa-ri, also on the Han River, which also yielded Geometric Pottery, chestnuts *(Aesculus turbinata)* were found (Plate 3); therefore, the grindstones may have been used to grind these nuts.

However, from the site of Chit'am-ni, Pongsan-gun, Hwanghae Province, excavated in 1957, grain was found inside a round-bottomed comb pattern vessel in Dwelling 2, Area 2. The excavators identified the seeds tentatively as millet *(Setaria italica)* or hi *(Panicum crus-galli)*.

This site will be discussed later; it is important to note here that from the Geometric Pottery Layer in Area 2, lithic artifacts such as arrowheads, spear points, grinders, plows, sickles, and celts were found in association with the ceramics. Stone sickles appear for the first time with the

Plain Pottery Culture. Since the Plain Pottery Culture follows that of the Geometric Pottery, it appears that the site belongs to the end of the Geometric Pottery Culture and had already been in contact with the succeeding culture. Therefore, the grain appears to be from the very end of the Geometric Pottery Culture. My opinion is that cultivation was not practiced at the time of the Geometric Pottery components of either Amsa-ri or Misa-ri.

In our materials there are a few sinkers made of stone or clay. The stone sinkers are small, oval-shaped pebbles, with chips removed from the middle of the ends, while the clay examples are hollow cylinders. These sinkers suggest that fishing was the primary subsistence activity of the groups who created Geometric Pottery. Many arrowheads of various shapes were reported, their provenience is not clear, however, since they were surface finds. This site not only had a Geometric Pottery component, there were also plain and cord-marked ceramics from later occupations. The latter were different from those of the Japanese Jōmon, since cord marking is derived from paddle impressing, which is similar to the process used in ancient China as well. From the area which we excavated, no stone arrowheads were found. However, from the occurrence of arrowheads on other Geometric Pottery sites, we can assume that the groups producing the Geometric Pottery of Amsa-ri lived primarily by fishing and also by hunting.

## MISA-RI SITE

The site is also situated on sand deposits along the river bank, and was found through the erosion of the Han River. It is the first Geometric Pottery site to have been found after World War II; it has been surface collected but not excavated. Survey of the site was carried out in 1960 and 1962. The ceramics are similar in shape and decoration to those of the Amsa-ri site . The pottery bases were mostly pointed and round (Fig. 10); some are of a transitional style showing a change to a flat bottom. As in the case of Amsa-ri, mica and asbestos were mixed with the sandy clay. Some decorations were composed of multiple rows of tiny circles arranged in consecutive S or U or herringbone formations (Fig. 11). There were also variations of double semicircles or consecutive semicircles. In addition, rim perforation can also be ob-

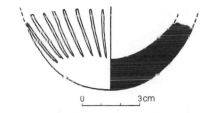
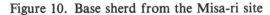

Figure 10. Base sherd from the Misa-ri site

Figure 11. Pottery decoration from the Misa-ri site

served. No stone artifacts were collected by us; however, according to other reports, stone celts, scrapers, sinkers, and "sticklike" artifacts were found. It is noteworthy that the stone celt and scraper were made by chipping and flaking. The sinkers had the same form as those of Amsa-ri. From traces of abrasion on one side, it appears that the sticklike artifact was used for grinding, as a pestle.

Amsa-ri and Misa-ri are the major Geometric Pottery sites in the central region. In addition, surface collections were made from the islands of Changbong and Si-do off the west coast, and Yangdo-ri and Tojang-ni off Kanghwa Island, which were surveyed after the war; however, only surface collections have been made so far. From this universe of sites, only Amsa-ri has thus far yielded settlement information; we would recommend that it be designated as the type site in the central region.

Some artifacts surface collected from Amsa-ri do not seem to belong to the Geometric Pottery Culture: for example, the polished stone tool and the undecorated pottery in the collection of the National Museum, Seoul. In our surface collection, a polished stone celt was recovered; also, from Area 2, the excavation of 1967 produced some undecorated pottery, similar to examples in the prewar collections of the National Museum, Seoul, in which the diagnostic characteristics include the flat bottom, expanding shoulder, and out-turned rim. The National Museum collection includes a polished, crescent-shaped knife, which no doubt belonged to the Plain Pottery component, judging from examples of other areas. Since these restricted artifact categories from the Plain Pottery Culture can be segregated on comparative grounds, the Geometric Pottery components may be considered as a type locale.

The house remains of Amsa-ri did not yield any remains of posts; however, in the excavation of 1968 we found one hearth in each of the three dwellings (Plate 10). The fireplace was surrounded by pebbles and cut stones in a square formation; each example was in well-preserved condition.

## NORTHWEST AREA

The Geometric Pottery Culture of the northwest was known in the Japanese occupation, from surface collections and test pits in Hwanghae and P'yŏngan Provinces. After liberation, the northwest area has been one of the most extensively excavated, and abundant new materials have been recovered. Important sites are Chit'am-ni in Pongsan-gun, Hwanghae Province, and Kungsan in Onch'ŏn-gun, South P'yŏngan Province. Two sites in North P'yŏngan Province are important examples for the end of the Geometric Pottery Culture.

The Chit'am-ni and Kungsan site reports have been translated or summarized in Japanese. I summarize the reports here and add my comments.

### CHIT'AM-NI SITE

During the excavation of this site in 1957, two areas were examined. In the first area, about 50 to 60 centimeters below the surface, there was an "Ancient Culture Layer" which was 50 to 70 centimeters thick. Below this was a "Primitive Culture Layer" of about 40 centimeters. In the second area, the "Ancient Culture Layer" began about 60 centimeters from the surface and its thickness was 50 to 70 centimeters. The "Primitive Culture Layer" was 20 to 40 centimeters thick. The main artifacts found in the Ancient Culture Layer of the first area were iron arrowheads, iron fishhooks, iron pieces, bronze discs, pottery, bricks, and pieces of roof tiles. From the Ancient Culture Layer in the second area, the following artifacts were found: iron arrowheads, iron refuse, bronze discs, Chinese Wu Shu coins, pipe-shaped jades, and ceramics. Among the ceramics a greyish cord-marked type was included. The Ancient Culture Layer, from its artifactual content, appears to belong to the period of the introduction of iron to Korea. The characteristic grey pottery seems to have been surface treated with a cord-wrapped paddle.

The ceramics in the Primitive Culture Layer were decorated with comb pattern or wavy lines of dots; a predominant form for the pottery was "Top-Shape." It appears that artifacts from two different cultures were mixed. The wave-dot motif consists of a double or consecutive pattern of tiny punctates or dentates (Fig. 7:17), and it falls within the Geometric Pottery; however, the Top-Shape Pottery belongs to a different period. In Area 2 there was an intermediary layer about 20 centimeters thick between the Primitive

Culture Layer and the Ancient Culture Layer. To the east of the intermediary layer, at about the same depth, was a Top-Shape Pottery layer, containing stone dagger fragments, a stemmed and barbed arrowhead (apparently a copy of a bronze prototype), fragments of a spoked stone mace head, and fragments of stone disk. Two sherds of Plain Pottery, with a bulging body and small flat base, were also found.

Thus at Chit'am-ni there were three strata of different periods, ranging from Geometric Pottery (Neolithic) to Top-Shape Pottery (Early Bronze Age) to Cord-Wrapped Paddle Pottery (Late Bronze Age). Another site which contained these three layers was the Sejung-ni site. By combining information from these two sites (Chit'am-ni and Sejung-ni) we can construct a chronology of Neolithic, Bronze Age, and Late Bronze Age for the northwest.

From the oldest layer of Chit'am-ni, three base forms were recovered—pointed, rounded, and a round-to-flat transition (Fig. 12). The pointed bottom is always associated with an ovate-shaped body, while the other two base forms have a more rounded body. Decoration was applied to the total surface; however, on some of the bowl-shaped vessels, the lower half was left undecorated (Fig. 12:6). The rim and body were often decorated with different designs, the herringbone patterns for the body being dominant. The wave-dot design which was reported (Fig. 12:1) is the same as the double or connected arc motif created by comb teeth, which was divided from the comb marking. I think, however, that they both fall within the Geometric Pottery category. The latter form can be seen from Amsa-ri (Fig. 7:17).

From the Primitive Culture Layer in Area 2, stone artifacts such as arrowheads, spears, grinders, plows, sickles, and hammers were unearthed. The stone sickles appeared in the Plain Pottery Culture for the first time; this layer thus appears to belong to the end of the Geometric Pottery Culture and shows contact with the Plain Pottery Culture.

The most notable remains from the Primitive Culture Layer of Chit'am-ni were 0.18 liters of carbonized grain found in the round bottom of a Geometric vessel from House Site No. 2, Area 2. Although they were not examined microscopically, they look like grains of *Setaria italica* or *Panicum crus-galli*. Since stone sickles and Top-Shape Pot-

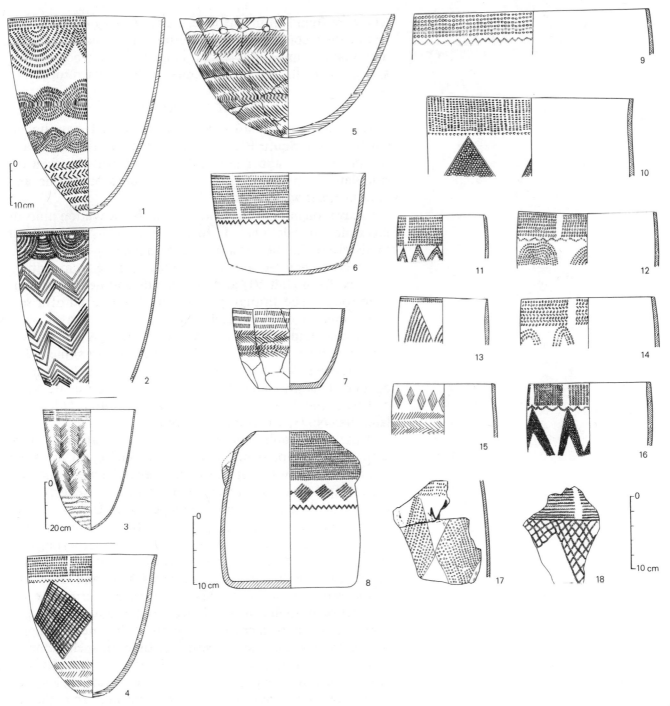

Figure 12. Pottery from the Chit'am-ni site

tery were found from this layer, it appears to represent the end of the Geometric Pottery Culture. The finding of grain in this layer is important since it indicates the introduction of agriculture by the end of the Geometric Pottery Culture.

## KUNGSAN SITE

This site is on a hill called Sokungsan, in Haeun-myon, Onch'ŏn-gun, South P'yŏngan Province. On the southeastern slope of the upper portion of the hill was the shell accumulation. In the shell deposit, ceramics and lithic and bone artifacts were found.

Excavation in 1950 concentrated on six excavation units or pits which were designated I to VI. Stratigraphy was difficult to discern in the shell accumulation on the slope. Five dwellings were recognized, one from Unit III, three from Unit V, and one from Unit VI, and post molds and hearth remains were found. The stratigraphy of Unit V consisted of a surface humus layer of about 10 centimeters; an A layer of 50 centimeters and a B layer of 60 centimeters. A and B were separated by a clay layer less than 50 centimeters thick. The layer designated A contained primarily oyster shells, while B contained mainly clams. From the B layer, House Site No. 2 and from the A layer, House Site 3 were found. No. 2 was later than No. 3, according to the report.

If the stratigraphic relation is certain, the artifacts from each dwelling would be important chronological markers; however, there was not much difference between the two assemblages. We have often found that, as a general rule, two layers divided by a thin clay layer, as in Unit V, do not always constitute chronologically distinct strata. In the Ungch'ŏn shell mound, Ch'angwŏn-gun, South Kyŏngsang Province, the upper and lower layers were divided by a clay layer 5 to 20 centimeters thick in Areas A, F, and G; yet the strata were not culturally distinct. Perhaps during the accumulation of shell layers, soil occasionally covered the shell heap and was in turn covered by more shells, the whole process taking place in a short period of time. In shell mounds, there are problems not only of geological stratigraphy, but also of reuse of dwelling areas at intervals of varying length.

The dwellings were all semisubterranean. From the arrangement of post molds, it appears that four of them were originally round, while the fifth was a square pit with rounded corners.

The post molds of House Site No. 1 indicated that the posts leaned in toward the center, while the rest of the posts seem to have been vertical. Thus, there appear to have been two kinds of roof superstructures. An important contribution has been made by the study of the post molds.

Shortly after the commencement of the Kungsan excavations in 1950 the Korean War began, and only 30 percent of the artifacts could be saved. It should be kept in mind that the report was written under this kind of disadvantage.

Ceramics constitute the largest category of artifacts, decorated sherds being particularly abundant. As mentioned earlier, only 30 percent of the ceramics remain, and none can be restored. However, the original form can be guessed at by the base, body, or rim sherds. Of the 36 bases recovered (Fig. 13), 24 were round, 1 was flat, and 1 was pointed. The flat bottom has a gentle curve toward the body. This kind of base was seen in the Chit'am-ni site, where it was usually part of a bowl-shaped body.

Decoration on the rim differed from those on the body (Fig. 14), the latter being mostly herringbone. On the rims there were many tiny circles or comb-tooth patterns, and among these was the so-called wave-dot pattern (Fig. 14:5). Of the bowl-shaped vessels, a substantial number had no decoration on the lower half of the body, a characteristic seen in the later period of the Geometric Pottery.

Mention is made of undecorated pottery recovered from the site. The shape of the vessels is not clear; however, it can be taken as an indication of contact with the Plain Pottery Culture at the end of the Geometric Pottery Culture, as seen in the Chit'am-ni site.

The stone artifacts include 40 arrowheads, 10 spearheads, more than 13 sinkers, more than 430 grinders, 1 stone hoe, 14 stone adzes, 2 flat planoconvex adzes, 1 chisel, whetstones, and stone saws (Fig. 15).

The arrowheads (Fig. 15:18–35) comprised the following types: unstemmed with barbs on both sides, stemmed triangles, and willowleaf-shaped. The unstemmed form with side barbs on both sides was dominant. Sections of the heads were mostly flattened hexagonal, and among these there

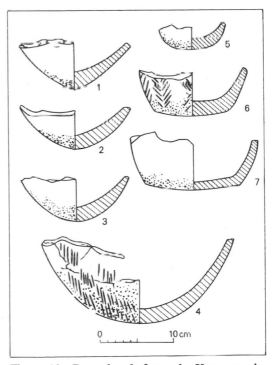

Figure 13. Base sherds from the Kungsan site

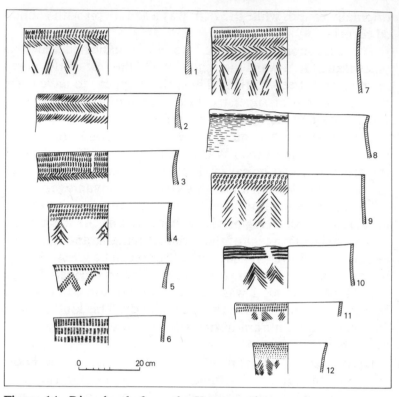

Figure 14. Rim sherds from the Kungsan site

were some in which the central portion of the hexagon was concave. This style was influenced by that of the bronze arrowheads and is characteristic of the arrowheads which accompany the Top-Shape Pottery. It is important to note that this type of stone arrowhead was unearthed from the Kungsan site, and it proves that the final period of the Geometric Pottery Culture had contact with the Plain Pottery Culture. There were also harpoons which had the same forms as the arrowheads but were larger in size. Some of the spearheads had cross sections of diamond shape. Stone mortars were of saddle shape, slightly concave in the middle. More than 30 saddle querns were unearthed from this site.

The width of the blade of the stone hoe was 11.0 centimeters, and the width of the bit was 8.5 centimeters; thus the blade was broader than the bit. Probably it was used for primitive agriculture.

As for the stone adzes (Fig. 15:10–17), there were a variety

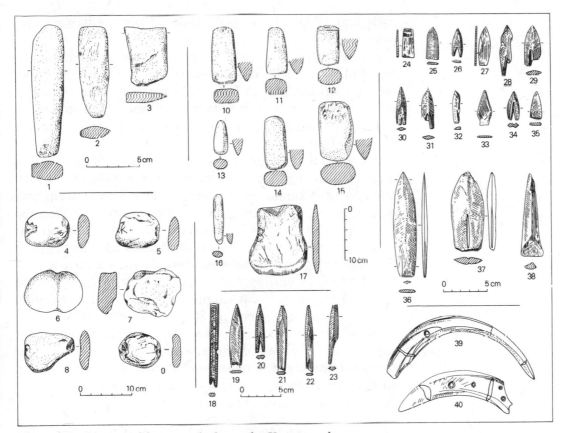

Figure 15. Stone and bone tools from the Kungsan site

of cross sections, such as square, lenticular, and small flat; however, the square cross section was predominant. All of the adzes had blades polished on both sides. In addition, the small, flat planilateral adze, characteristic of the stone tools of the Plain Pottery Culture, was present.

Only one stone chisel, with oval cross section and single-faced bit, was found. This type is typical of the Plain Pottery Culture.

Abundant bone and antler artifacts were found in the Kungsan site (Fig. 15:39, 40). There were 110 perforators, 70 spatulas, 25 hoes (?) made of antler, more than 60 antler digging sticks, 6 sickles made of boar tusk, 26 cutting tools made of boar tusk, 4 bone needlelike objects, more than 10 knitting needlelike objects, and others. The exact function of the antler "hoes" is not clear. The decorative artifacts include jade pipe-shaped objects and jade axes. Unbaked clay balls and 18 spindle whorls made of potsherds were also recovered.

Faunal remains from Kungsan include more than 100 mandible fragments of antelope *(Capreolus)* and the bones of two individuals of *Bubalus.* The water buffalo *(Bubalus)* would appear to be subtropical and may be an important climatic indicator. Clams, oysters, and cowries *(Cypraea)* were also found.

A temporal difference between the ceramic decorations of dots and herringbone is suggested in the Kungsan report; however, this cannot at present be related to stratigraphic separation or differences in ceramic forms. Differential distribution of these forms of decoration within each pit was noted; I think, however, that both the dot and herringbone decorations belong to the same period—the Geometric Pottery Period. In northern Europe, comb impression and pit impression had different origins and there was a temporal separation between them; in Korea, however, even in the Amsa-ri site, for example, these forms were found in the same layer. The wave-dot design developed later than the straight-line designs, such as herringbone; at a certain period within the Geometric Pottery Culture, however, both types of decoration coexisted in Korea.

### SEJUNG-NI SITE (LAYER I)

The Sejung-ni site is in Yŏngbyŏn-gun, North P'yŏngan Province, situated on the alluvial bank of the Ch'ongch'ŏn River. During two excavations in 1962 and 1963, four areas, constituting a relatively wide area, were excavated. Numerous dwelling sites were excavated from the various strata, and three major layers, from the "Primitive Culture" to the "Ancient Culture," were recognized. The bottom layer contained Geometric Pottery; the second, Top-Shape Pottery and Karak-ni type pottery, in association with black pottery; and the third, greyish pottery marked with a corded paddle, in association with iron artifacts. For our present discussion, the bottom layer is most important; it yielded only pottery and lithic artifacts. Dotted and linear designs occurred on the pottery (Fig. 16), herringbone being the most abundant. One sherd decorated with the thunder pattern was also found. The bases were pointed, round, and flat. It is difficult to distinguish the flat bottom from the rounded body of the

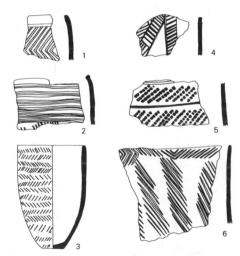

Figure 16.  Pottery from the Sejung-ni site

vessel. From the "general culture layer" (not the dwelling sites) of Area 4, a complete vessel with geometric decoration (Fig. 16:3) was recovered. Fine sand and mica were mixed into the paste, and the surface of the vessel, from mouth to base, was covered with incised herringbone design. The base is flat and is not clearly demarcated from the body.

Stone artifacts were rare, with only one pestle and a fire-making stone from House Site No. 7. The pestle was an oblong river cobble, utilized in its natural form: one side showed wearing down, and the length was 37 centimeters. The fire-making stone (used with a drill?) was also a natural cobble with rounded hollows created on its surface. Besides these stone artifacts, there was an oval stone ornament with two central perforations, recovered from House Site No. 7. Stone artifacts were generally rare from this layer.

House Site No. 7, partly eroded by the river, extended 4.5 meters from east to west and 4.5 meters from north to south. It is thought originally to have been rectangular. The subterranean portion was 2.7 meters deep, the floor consisting of hardened clay. In the middle of the floor were the remains of a hearth delineated by two oblong river stones on either side of a square pit. Reddish burnt clay from 20 to 30 centimeters thick was found inside it. This follows completely the form mentioned from Amsa-ri. From this dwelling, Geometric Pottery sherds and three stone artifacts were found. The smallness of the artifact sample from the bottom layer of Sejung-ni is a problem; however, the dwellings in the second layer contained abundant artifacts right up to the surface of the third (uppermost) layer.

The thunder pattern on the pottery proves that the site belongs to a slightly later period of the Geometric Pottery Culture. The complete vessel previously mentioned had a flat bottom which conveyed the feeling of a later period; this would also suggest a late temporal position for the site. However, the structure of the fire pit and the form of the grinding stones fall within the tradition of the Geometric Pottery Culture.

## SINAM-NI SITE (LAYER I)

The lowest layer of the stratified Sinam-ni site (Yongch'ŏn gun, North P'yŏngan Province) also appears to date to the end of the Geometric Pottery Culture. The first excavation

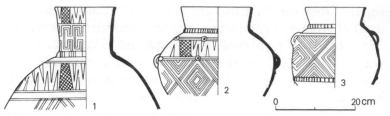

Figure 17. Ceramics from the Sinam-ni site (1)

concentrated on the hill to the west of the village (Area 1) and the hill to the north (Area 2). The second excavation continued in Area 2; on the third occasion, the southwestern portion (Location 3) of Area 1 was excavated. The elevation of these hills is about 35 meters.

In the first excavation, ceramics decorated mainly with herringbone and thunder patterns (Fig. 17) were found in Location 1, and pottery of the type found in the upper layer of Misong-ni was found in Location 2. However, in the second excavation, the excavators found House Site No. 5 situated over House Site No. 6 in sections Nos. 6 to 9 of Location 2; from this stratigraphic position, we can determine that the decorated ceramics and Misong-ni upper-layer pottery were in the correct stratigraphic order. From House Site No. 6, which was in the lower layer, decorated ceramics such as those found in Location 1 were excavated; and House Site No. 5, from the upper level, yielded the same kind of Misong-ni upper-layer ceramics as were previously found in Location 2. In Area No. 3 of Location 2, a layer of Koguryo remains occurred over the two older cultural layers. These layers were termed Layers I and II, and the Koguryo Layer. In the first excavation, another culture layer between Layer II and the Koguryo Layer was recognized; however, it may have been included in the Koguryo Layer.

Most of the vessel bases were completely flat, while a few had rounded bottoms. The dominant vessel shape was a jar with curving sides and broad shoulders (Fig. 18:1–10). A few had flaring sides (Fig. 18: 13–15). Sherds of the foot portion of mounted cups were noted (Fig. 18:12).

Some vessels had long necks and symmetrically placed handles either on the neck or the shoulder (Fig. 18:1–4, 6), while others had short necks with flaring mouths (Fig. 18:5, 7–10). Most of the vessels were decorated. The designs were composed of the thunder, herringbone, and triangle pat-

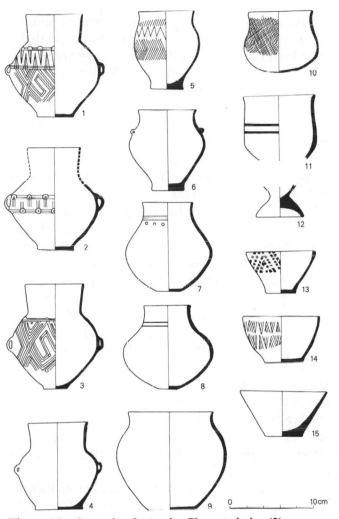

Figure 18. Ceramics from the Sinam-ni site (2)

terns. Especially well-developed beautiful thunder patterns were evident (Fig. 17). Undecorated ceramics were mostly polished black, with similar shapes to the red-painted, polished pottery.

Ceramics from Layer I had shapes completely distinct from the Geometric Pottery, with a long neck, flaring mouth, and beautiful curving lines from the shoulder to the body. Their flat bottoms resemble those of the Plain Pottery. Despite these changes, the traditional decoration patterns of herringbone, thunder, and triangle pattern still remained.

The long neck, full body, and crescent-shaped handles are

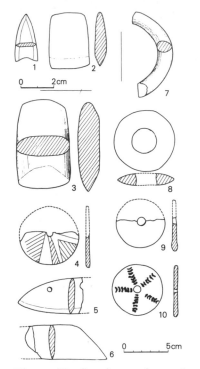

Figure 19. Specimens from the Sinam-ni site

very close to the forms of northern Chinese painted pottery. In addition, the thunder motif on the shoulder is also a feature of northern Chinese ceramics. There seem to be clear indications of north Chinese influences on Sinam-ni Layer I. Also, the presence of black pottery and footed pottery in Layer I would seem to give further proof, since they are characteristic of both the painted and black pottery cultures of northern China.

Plain reddish-brown pottery was also found in this layer. Sherds indicating a full body and constricted neck were found from House Site No. 6 in the second excavation.

Stone artifacts from Sinam-ni Layer I included the following categories: arrowheads, axes-adzes, crescent-shaped knives, circular axes, sickles, spindle whorls, net sinkers, and ornaments. A ceramic spindle whorl was also recovered (Fig. 19). The arrowheads were slate, with a flattened hexagonal cross section (Fig. 19:1), while the axe had an oval cross section and a bifacial cutting edge (Fig. 19:2, 3). Six crescent-shaped knives were found; they had curving backs and blades, creating a fishlike silhouette, and a hole was pierced close to the back side (Fig. 19:5). The spindle whorls were all flat and circular, the earthenware examples being decorated with curvilinear designs (Fig. 19:9–10). The particular forms of the arrowheads, with flattened hexagonal section—and the crescent-shaped knives and stone sickles—are typical of the Plain Pottery Culture, and offer important clues for estimating the date of Sinam-ni.

From the stone artifacts and ceramics, Sinam-ni Layer I appears to constitute a transitional step from the Geometric Pottery Culture to the Plain Pottery Culture. Only in the area of ceramic decoration (herringbone, thunder, and triangle patterns) did the tradition of the Geometric Pottery persist; however, even these patterns belong to the end of the period. In particular, the thunder pattern, which shows influence from China, appears to be quite late in the Geometric Pottery sequence.

## NORTHEAST AREA
### NONGP'O-DONG SITE

Before the war, some sites yielding geometric-decorated pottery were known from the northeast of the peninsula;

most of the data, however, were derived from surface collections. The only formal site report was written by Shozaburo Yokoyama on the Nongp'o-dong shell mound at Yup'an, Kyŏngsŏng-gun. In the postwar years, as far as we know, only two or three excavations have been carried out, one of these being a reexcavation of Nongp'o-dong. The site is near Yup'an, and falls within the present administrative division of Ch'ŏngjin City. This site was excavated in 1956 for about 40 days, and a great quantity of remains was recovered: however, no official report has been published other than an interim resumé. I will use the materials excavated by Yokoyama for purposes of illustration.

The Nongp'o-dong site is a shell mound on the north and south sides of a hill about 30 meters in height. Two places, Locations A and B, were designated on the north side, while two more, C and D, were laid out on the south side. The shell deposits of A, B, and C were derived from eroded material which accumulated at the bottom of the hill; however, Location D appears to be the original uneroded deposit. Ceramics and stone and bone artifacts totalled 3,632 items. It is noteworthy that flaked obsidian artifacts constituted 2,546 items. Ninety-one ceramic spindle whorls and 72 net sinkers are very large quantities for Korean sites. Other artifacts were 124 harpoons, fishhooks, and needles, and 13 clay zoomorphic and anthropomorphic figurines and ornaments.

Most of the ceramics were decorated, some with painted designs. There were, however, some undecorated flat plates. The bases of the vessels were flat, as reported by Yokoyama. The fact that no pointed or round bottoms were recorded suggests clearly that the chronological position is different from the Geometric Pottery. Vessel forms included jars, deep pots, cylinder-shaped vessels, and a few bowls and plates.

One of the features of these ceramics is that the decoration starts on the shoulder or the body, leaving the mouth area undecorated. Herringbone is the most abundant motif, and there are slanting lines, punctates, and the thunder pattern (Fig. 20). The thunder pattern, made with two parallel lines bent at right angles, or comprising a zigzag lightning pattern (Fig. 20:1–4), is the same motif as seen at the site of Sinamni. A characteristic of the thunder pattern of Nongp'o-dong

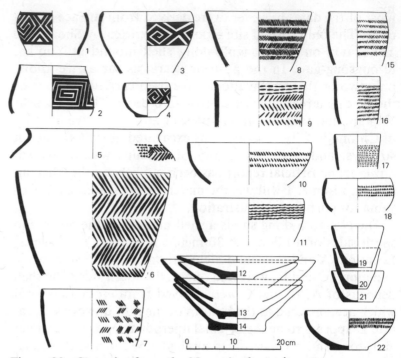

Figure 20. Ceramics from the Nongp'o-dong site

is the filling up of the space between the two lines with short slanted lines or dots, and this is also seen in the sites of Wŏnsudae shell mound, Unggi shell mound, and Pongŭi, Hoeryŏng, showing a common areal similarity. A similar thunder pattern was found in the site of Zaisanovka I of the Soviet Maritime Province, and we can postulate some diffusion between these sites considering their geographical proximity.

The decorative patterns, such as herringbone, parallel short slanting lines, and punctates, appear to be very coarse, suggesting a deterioration of the decoration motifs.

The very large number of flaked obsidian tools suggests that Nongp'o-dong may have been a factory.

Most of the stone arrowheads have concave bases (Fig. 21:1–9). Among the obsidian tools from the prewar excavations were special artifacts called stone saws. The same stone saw form has been found at Unggi, at Musan, and also at the Tongsam-dong site in Pusan to the south. It has been tentatively regarded as a harpoon. Polished stone artifacts were

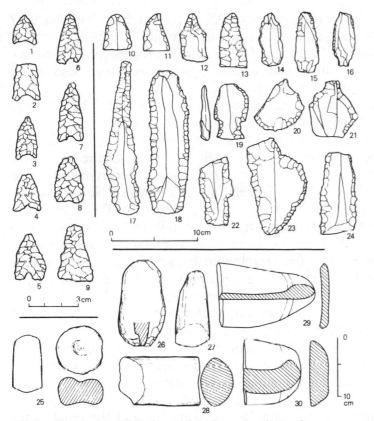

Figure 21. Stone tools from the Nongp'o-dong site

very few, consisting of axes and arrowheads. The stone axes had oval cross sections with bifacial symmetrical blades, and the arrowheads were triangular and stemless. Stone mortars and pestles (Fig. 21:29–30) were recovered; all appear to be fragmentary, although one with a raised side may be complete. A similar grinding stone was excavated from the Amsa-ri site.

Numerous bone awls, needles, and fishhooks were found. The most noteworthy object excavated from Nongp'o-dong was a clay figurine. Unfortunately, it had lost its head; however, it was the first recovery of a clay figurine from a Neolithic site on the Korean peninsula. Also recovered were a dog's head of clay and a bird's head carved of stone.

No cultural stratigraphy has been recognized in the excavation of Nongp'o-dong; only one cultural period appears to have been represented. All of the ceramics had flat bottoms and some were painted, showing influence from the ceramics of northern China. Black polished pottery recovered from the site of Sinam-ni, mentioned above, also seems to indicate Chinese influence.

Herringbone and thunder patterns are shared by ceramics from Nongp'o-dong and Sinam-ni. From the flat bases and evidence of northern Chinese influences, Nongp'o-dong can be placed chronologically in the later stages of the Geometric Pottery Culture. However, the stone artifacts represent quite a different picture of relationships between Nongp'o-dong and Sinam-ni. At Nongp'o-dong, numerous flaked obsidian artifacts can be seen, whereas only polished artifacts occur at Sinam-ni. Since obsidian was available, it appears that Nongp'o-dong was influenced by Siberian traditions which were in relatively close proximity. On the other hand, at Sinam-ni in the northwest, the tradition of polished stone artifacts of the Plain Pottery Culture predominated. Polished axes and arrowheads were unearthed from the Nongp'o-dong site as well as from the Sinam-ni site; however, it is remarkable that crescent-shaped stone knives that were quite abundant in Sinam-ni were completely absent from Nongp'o-dong. A possible reason for this could be that Nongp'o-dong is close to the seacoast, and the inhabitants were engaged more in fishing, while the Sinam-ni site is on a hill and its inhabitants may have been engaged in cultivation. Saddle querns were recovered from the Nongp'o-dong site; however, they could have been used for grinding horse chestnuts rather than grain.

## SOUTHERN AREA

From the south, there are relatively few sites of the Geometric Pottery Culture. Before the war the Pusan area was surveyed thoroughly, and on the east coast the Sinam-ni site of Tongnae (former Ulsan) was well known. Geometric ceramics have been recovered in both North and South Chŏlla. However, very few new finds were made after the war. Recently, the shell mound of Kup'yŏng-ni, Sop'o-myŏn, Sach'ŏn-gun in South Kyŏngsang Province has been discovered, and there has been a reexcavation of the Tongsam-dong shell mound in Pusan, which was first studied before the war. However, no official reports have been published yet. The Kup'yŏng-ni site was excavated in 1967 and a simple introduction was published. Most of the ceramics were decorated, and undecorated ceramics were said to be found in a shallow layer beneath the surface of D and S trenches, but the stratigraphic relationship of the two layers is not clear. Decoration included herringbone and slanting checker patterns, punctate decoration being particularly rare. Pointed or rounded bottoms were rare. Stone tools particularly were absent; only one perforated sinker was recovered. Needles and fishhooks were made of bone, and shell was used for ornaments, with a few bracelets recovered. These are all the details available on the Kup'yŏng-ni site for the moment. Undecorated pottery has been recovered from the site, but we do not know its exact nature nor its relative stratigraphic location.

## TONGSAM-DONG SHELL MOUND

Tongsam-dong, near Pusan, was excavated by Shozaburo Yokoyama, Tamijiro Oikawa, and others before the war, and the reports were published by each of them. In 1963–1964, A. Mohr and L. Sample of the University of Wisconsin conducted excavations; before publishing detailed reports, they published an article concerning the chronology of the ceramics of Tongsam-dong and the immediate vicinity. From 1969, three excavations were carried out by the National Museum, but no report has yet been published.

Some new materials from surface collections including undecorated, decorated, and red-painted polished pottery, as well as stone, bone, and shell artifacts, are available (Plate 11). The Tongsam-dong site occupies a large area, and it seems that it was occupied for quite a long time. The materials which we have now and the excavated materials from before the war prove that artifacts such as decorated ceramics and red-painted polished pottery are from different time periods, although the exact stratigraphic relationships have not been clarified. At Location A, which was excavated by Yokoyama, a few decorated pottery sherds and plain sherds were found in the clay layer (A4) beneath the shell layer.

In the humus layer (A2) and the shell layer (A3), vermillion-painted body and handle sherds, as well as those of decorated and undecorated pottery, were recovered. Four complete vessels were found, one small bowl from the humus layer (A2) and two of ovate shape, plus another small bowl, from the shell layer (A3).

From Layers A2 to A4, both decorated and undecorated ceramics were found together. Therefore, there would seem to be no stratigraphic distinction between these two groups. Yet from Location C, dug by Oikawa and others, no decorated ceramics were found. Only thick, undecorated pottery was found in the bottom of the shell layer (C3).

From the layer immediately above C3, a band of black soil and shells, "comb-pattern" sherds were abundant. In addition, from C1, both "comb-pattern" and undecorated sherds were found, in an approximate ratio of 1:2.

Since undecorated pottery was found without other types in the bottom of Location C, one might conclude that it is older than the decorated pottery. But C2, above C3, yielded both kinds together, while C1, above C2, yielded more undecorated sherds than decorated. Thus there is no clear evidence that one is earlier than the other.

In the absence of firm data to support the relative chronology of stone or bone artifacts or ceramics from Tongsamdong, it would appear that the stratigraphy is disturbed.

Complete vessels from the site are important for discussing the form and function of the ceramics. From Location A, one small bowl, two ovate-shaped pots, and one larger bowl were recovered. From Location C, one undecorated jar with a long neck, one bowl-shaped vessel with herringbone design around the mouth, and two undecorated bowl-shaped vessels were recovered. In total, two semihemispherical pots, one long-necked jar, and five bowls were recovered.

The bowls have a flattened portion on the rounded bottom, and in most cases the whole surface, or at least the lower half of the body, is left undecorated. The particular bowl form is often seen in the later period of the Geometric Pottery Culture. In this case, only the long-necked jar shows the distinctive characteristics of Plain Pottery; however, it retains the characteristics of Geometric Pottery in the round bottom and the presence of decoration.

From the collection of sherds, it seems that the pointed and round bottoms were the most numerous; while some flat bottoms were present, there were no elevated bases or pedestals. Mouth rims were mostly straight, although a few curved outward. From the base forms and the rims, it seems that Geometric Pottery was the most common, and there were some vessels which were influenced by the undecorated pottery. The decoration consisted of slanting parallel lines (Fig. 22:1, 9), herringbone design (Fig. 22:18, 19, 24), slanting checkered design, sawtooth design (the triangle space being filled with slanting parallel designs), appliqué design (relief technique; Fig. 22:4, 8, 12). These decorations are typical of the Geometric Pottery of Korea. Although relief decoration is rare, it can be found in the Geometric Pottery Period. Notable by their absence are double arcs of tiny circles or dots, or the straight-line thunder pattern. Some vessels were decorated even to the bottom of the base (Fig. 23).

Some fragments of red-painted polished pottery exist in the collection of prewar and surface-collected materials. This kind of pottery was made of a finer clay with a very thin body. Iron oxide was applied after firing, then the red surface was polished so that the luster remains until today. It is well known that this red-painted and polished pottery was influenced by the painted pottery of northern China, distributed from northeastern China to the Korean peninsula. Often these ceramics accompany Plain Pottery in other Korean sites. The existence of red-painted polished pottery in the Tongsam-dong shell mound offers confirmation that the undecorated sherds are truly the post-Geometric Plain Pottery. Their later chronological position is borne out by the presence of flat bases and out-curving rims.

One of the most notable features of the ceramics from Tongsam-dong is the doubled-over rim. In the surface-collected materials there was a type with a broad clay belt around the rim, impressed with slanting finger impressions along the lower edge; and another type with a double, undecorated broad clay encircling band. There was also a type with short slanting lines around the lower edge of the place of attachment of the clay band. It appears that the clay band was attached to strengthen the rim; the fingerprint impressions were left when the band was pressed firmly to the vessel. Later examples appear to have substituted short slant-

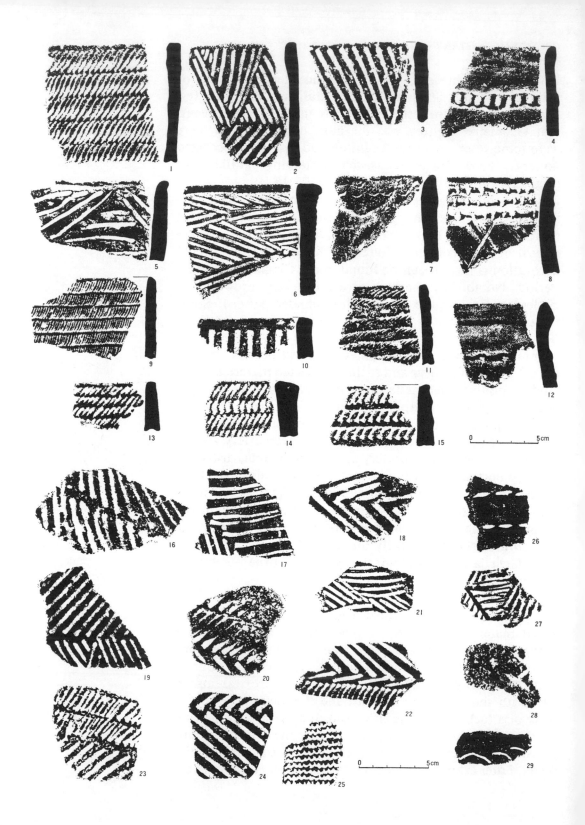

ing incisions for finger impressions. Finally, the clay belt was abandoned and only slanting short lines were used. This is a suggestion of the process of change of the doubled-over rim.

The technique of thickening the rim by attaching a broad clay band can be seen in the Neolithic ceramics of Siberia. This technique was used in Middle Neolithic ceramics in the Lena Basin, in combination with net decoration, incised horizontal straight lines, slanted lines, and triangle patterns. The characteristic base form was pointed. Predominant stone artifacts were microblades. Appliqué designs appeared at the end of the period. The Middle Neolithic of the Lena River is estimated to be equivalent to the Serovo Period of Baikal, about 3000 B.C., and the end of the Neolithic seems to be equivalent to the Glazkovo Period of Baikal—about 1700 to 1300 B.C.

If the double rim of Tongsam-dong is the product of Siberian influences, its chronological position must be quite late. Yet the Tongsam-dong rims are the oldest of their type in Korea. The double rim of the Top-Shape Pottery and Karak-ni Pottery apparently developed from the Tongsam-dong type. We have already pointed out that the obsidian stone saws and blades were culturally related to Siberia, through North Hamgyŏng Province. It also seems that there may have been some influence from Siberian ceramics on the ceramics of Tongsam-dong at different time periods, resulting in pointed bottoms, incised designs, appliqué designs, and double rims. The double rim may also be seen in the ceramics from the Annam-dong site, Pusan, and seems to fall within the later period of Geometric Pottery.

Relatively few stone artifacts were unearthed from the Tongsam-dong site. They included adzes, arrowheads, scrapers, spears, saws, blades, sinkers, saddle querns, grindstones (Fig. 24), and whetstones. Adzes were made by polishing and chipping, and the cross section was either rectangular or oval. All of them were made of slate. The arrowheads were made of either polished slate or chipped obsidian. A chipped obsidian saw was also noted (Plate 12). The form was found in Nongp'o-dong, Unggi, and Musan in North

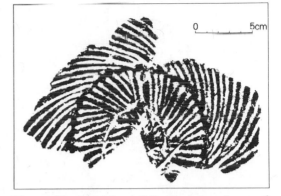

Figure 23. Rubbing of fragmentary base of vessel from the Tongsam-dong shell mound

Figure 24. Stone pestle from the Tongsam-dong shell mound

Figure 22. Rubbings of rim (1–15) and body (16–29) sherds from the Tongsam-dong shell mound

Hamgyŏng Province as well as from some sites in the Soviet Maritime Province. Since obsidian occurs in Siberia and North Hamgyŏng Province, it has been used for chipped artifacts in these areas; since it is very rare in other areas of Korea, very few chipped objects can be found. In the south of Korea, obsidian has been found in the area of Changki in Yongil-gun, North Kyŏngsang Province. We still do not know the provenience of the Tongsam-dong obsidian. The same kind of stone saw is abundant in Jōmon sites from northern Kyushu, such as those in the Goto Islands, and this connection deserves further attention.

In Yokoyama's report, two scrapers were described as crescent-shaped knives, and both were manufactured by chipping. One was broken, but the other was complete. Both were crescent shaped and unperforated; in form they are similar to the semilunar knives which are characteristic of the Plain Pottery Culture; however, they were not used for harvesting but for scraping. The chipping technique seems to be the same tradition as that of the Geometric Pottery. Among five artifacts termed whetstones by Yokoyama, three appear to be saddle querns. The whetstones which Yokoyama described as being numerous in North Hamgyŏng Province are probably grinding stones or querns. However, two other specimens from Tongsam-dong are true whetstones.

Bone and antler artifacts were relatively numerous from the Tongsam-dong site (Plate 11). Among those, pointed tools were most frequent, and fishhooks were relatively abundant. Certain shell artifacts suggest early trade routes. Perforated canine teeth appear to have been used as pendants.

Although artifacts were relatively abundant in Tongsam-dong, the stratigraphy was disturbed and an internal sequence is impossible. A relative chronology can be achieved by crossdating with other sites and by typological comparison.

## YŎNGSŎN-DONG SHELL MOUND

From the shell mound of Yŏngsŏn-dong in Pusan, Arimitsu was able to restore the shapes of at least 25 vessels. Among them, only two had a necked jar form while all the rest were bowls (Fig. 25:1) with straight, uncurving rims and

Figure 25. Pottery from the Yŏngsŏn-dong shell mound

pointed or round bottoms. These vessels are characteristic of
Geometric Pottery. This site yielded pottery with a pouring
lip (Fig. 25:1). From the technique it looks like a late type,
although it is absent from other sites. The ceramics had
decoration mostly on the rim or the upper half of the body.
Decoration over the entire body was rare and the repertory
of design was limited. The horizontal herringbone design was
the most frequent, and slanting checker, short slanting lines,
and punctation—all typical of Geometric Pottery—also occurred. These designs were roughly applied and seem to show
degeneration. The appliqué technique was also evident. The
vessel with the pouring lip had an appliqué decoration in the

shape of a zigzag V line with finger impressions on the upper half of the body. The double-rim technique was also found at this site. The rim was turned outward, and the lower edge was decorated with slanting incisions while the upper edge also had slanting incisions on it. Among the ceramics from this site, some were undecorated and some had incised decoration on the upper edge of the rim. This double-rim technique seems to be related to the Top-Shape Pottery of Karak-ni and later periods. The technique of lip incisions can be seen in the Karak-ni ceramics from Yŏksam-dong. The double-rim techniques of Tongsam-dong and Yŏngsŏn-dong appear at the end of the Geometric Period yet precede the Top-Shape or Karak-ni ceramics.

The necked jar vessels from the Yŏngsŏn-dong site had round bodies and were influenced by Plain Pottery, as far as shape is concerned. Both had round bottoms and angular motifs, such as herringbone, around the rim in the tradition of the Geometric Pottery Culture. Jar-shaped vessels and the pouring lip were features of ceramics at the end of the Neolithic Age in Korea. Restriction of design to the upper part of the body or the rim appeared in the Late Period of Geometric Pottery. Lip incision seems to indicate the transition from Geometric to Plain Pottery. The Yŏngsŏn-dong site also yielded dark brown pottery, thin, beaten pottery, red unglazed pottery, and horn-shaped handles, suggesting that a number of time periods are represented.

## CHRONOLOGY AND CHARACTERISTICS OF GEOMETRIC POTTERY CULTURE

Geometric Pottery in the Korean peninsula shows continuity in decoration, shape, and association with other kinds of artifacts, while at the same time displaying areal and chronological discontinuities. There are virtually no sites which contain strata of all chronological divisions or artifact categories; therefore, the construction of a chronology is difficult.

A disturbed area of the Amsa-ri site produced both Geometric and Plain Pottery together. However, the two kinds of ceramics are made of entirely different clays and are therefore easy to distinguish. Geometric Pottery was always made of sandy clay mixed with asbestos or mica, while the temper in Plain Pottery consisted of quartz grains. Although form may occasionally be confusing, such as round or pointed bottoms on Plain Pottery, the two wares can be distinguished on the basis of paste and temper.

Geometric Pottery from Amsa-ri had a predominance of pointed bottoms, while round forms were relatively rare. A few showed flattening at the base. Without exception, the rim on the Geometric Pottery is always straight and the vessel form is characteristically "half-egg" or ovate. From the few round bottoms which were found, a bowl form must have been present as well. The pointed shape is also characteristic of the early periods in Siberia. These forms can be found, for instance, in the Sub-Neolithic I, II, and III of Karelia and northern Russia and in the Isakovo Period of the Baikal area. As I mentioned earlier, the Geometric Pottery of Korea appears to be derived from the Neolithic ceramic traditions of northern Eurasia, the "half-egg" or ovate form being the basic one.

There appears to be a change from pointed to round bases, the round bases indicating a bowl shape; the same kind of change occurred in the ceramics of northern Eurasia. Examples can be found in the Serovo Period of the Baikal area and in the ceramics of the Early Gorbunovo Culture of the Middle Ural. The flat bottom, however, shows influence from another direction—from northern China. Here the introduction of the flat bottom and particular designs such as the meander or triangle pattern (Fig. 26) can be seen.

The transition from pointed bottom to rounded, to flattened, to flat seems to indicate a chronological change in Geometric Pottery. Because of the disturbance of stratigraphy in sites, we need to construct a typological chronology. (See Table 2.)

I wish to attempt a chronology by design motif and location of decoration on the vessel.

Decoration motifs of Geometric Pottery show temporal and spatial variation. However, there are a number of common elements. The most common of these are short slanting lines on the rim and herringbone and slanting checker design on the body. Comb decoration and pit marking were characteristic of northern Eurasian Neolithic ceramics; however, these techniques were rare in Korean Geometric Pottery.

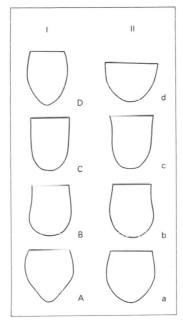

Figure 26. Development of pottery forms in the Middle Urals (column I forms are from east of the Urals; column II forms are from west of the Urals)

Table 2.   Vessel Forms in the Early, Middle, and Late Geometric Pottery Periods

| | Shape | | |
|---|---|---|---|
| Culture Period | Bottom | Rim, Neck | Typical Shape |
| Early Geometric Period | Pointed | Straight | Half-egg |
| Middle Geometric Period | Pointed | Straight | Half-egg, bowl |
| Late Geometric Period | Round, almost flat | Outward-curved neck, double-rim | Jar, bowl, cylinder |

Less common designs include double or consecutive arcs made by comb impression, the rectilinear thunder pattern, and appliqué decoration. Double or consecutive arcs, herringbone design, or comb impression show continuities with the ceramic traditions of northern Eurasia; however, the locating of the arc design on the lower edge of the rim was not in the tradition of northern Eurasian ceramics. This can be seen only in the sites of northwestern Korea and the central Korean peninsula. Perhaps this design reflects influence from the consecutive arc decoration which can be seen on the painted pottery of northern China. From the Unggi site, a painted jar with a consecutive arc motif in black seems to show a resemblance to Chinese examples. At any rate, the development of the arc or wavy motifs was a little later than the straight line geometric decorations and must have been created through foreign influence.

As mentioned earlier, the thunder pattern seems to show influence from northern Chinese painted pottery, since it appears only in the Geometric Pottery of the northeast and northwest in association with painted examples, as at Unggi.

Appliqué decoration is a special feature of the ceramics from the Pusan area, the method also appearing in the Late Neolithic ceramics of eastern Siberia. The appliqué decoration of the Korean peninsula must be later than the Siberian examples.

Location of decoration on the vessel surface also changes through time. I would consider northern Eurasian ceramics to be the sources of these changes. In the northern Eurasian

Table 3. Nature and Location of Decoration of Ceramics in the Early, Middle, and Late Geometric Pottery Periods

| Culture Period | Decoration | |
| --- | --- | --- |
| | Decoration Motifs | Location on Vessel |
| Early Geometric Period | Short slant lines, herringbone, slant-checkered, comb marking, pit marking | All over body; rim and body have same decoration |
| Middle Geometric Period | Double or consecutive arcs by comb marking in addition to Early Geometric motifs | Different decorations on rim, body; upper half of body decorated |
| Late Geometric Period | Thunder pattern, appliqué decoration, coloring, painting, in addition to Early, Middle Geometric motifs | Decoration only on upper body, or completely absent |

examples, comb decoration, pit impressions, and other decorations were applied all over the surface of the pottery. I would like to think that the application of decoration to the entire body was the basic method. Therefore, those which have the same decoration both on the rim and the body should be earlier than those which had different patterns on the rim and on the body. It also seems that the omission of design from the lower half of the body appears latest, reflecting the transition from Geometric to Plain Pottery. Table 3 summarizes the kinds of designs and the areas to which they were applied.

The chronology which has been constructed is based on shape, decoration, and location of decoration. This framework can only be regarded as temporary until a chronology can be built on stratigraphic relationships and scientific chronometry. One can find many complications in the stylistic typology, so that early and late forms are found mixed together.

Shapes and decorations from different time periods appear in the same layers of some sites. For instance, there was a typical ovate form in the ceramics from Chit'am-ni. I have said that this shape is characteristic of the Early Period.

Figure 27. Ceramic vessel from the Yŏndo-ri site

Decoration appears to indicate the Early Period as well, since it consisted of herringbone all over the surface. But the rim, body, and bottom also contained different motifs, suggesting the Middle Period. Other Middle Period characteristics include the double-arc motif located on the upper portion of the body.

Yet there were also ceramics with flattened bottoms and no design on the lower portion of the body, as well as Top-Shape Ceramics; these should be placed at the end of the Geometric Period. Judging from the framework just presented, there are very few Geometric sites which can be placed in the Early Period. One vessel (Fig. 27) from the Yŏndo-ri site of Yonggang-gun, South P'yŏngan Province displays the typical ovate shape, with herringbone decoration all over the surface, from the rim to the base; it seems, therefore, to fit into the Early Period. However, associated artifacts are not known, and the chronological position of the site cannot be determined from one vessel.

The Tongsam-dong site seems to contain a number of Early and Late elements; it is premature to assign a chronological position to the site. Some of the ceramics were decorated with a twisted cord impression. The dark brown color of the pottery seems to show a primitive method of firing suggesting a connection with the early ceramics of Siberia. We might hypothesize that these ceramics constitute an old culture layer, Tongsam-dong I; we could then call the layer with the degenerated geometric designs and doubled-over rims Tongsam-dong II, and the layer with the undecorated and red-painted polished pottery Tongsam-dong III. Tongsam-dong I would correspond to the Early or Middle Period of the chronology of Geometric Pottery, and Tongsam-dong II would fit into the Late Period. Tongsam-dong III would correspond to the Plain Pottery Culture, which is completely different from the Geometric Pottery Culture.

Ceramics from the Yŏngsŏn-dong shell mound show characteristics of the Late Period of Geometric Pottery, such as the bowl shape, appliqué decoration, and degenerated geometric motifs. The pouring lip seems particularly to be a feature of the Late Period.

The Amsa-ri site in the central part of the peninsula could be said to have a single cultural layer showing ceramics that represent the Middle Period of the central peninsula. The ovate vessel shape with pointed bottom, characteristic of the Early Period, was dominant, but at the same time there were bowl-shaped vessels with round bottoms. Some of the decoration consisted of the same motif over the entire body, while others had different decorations on the rim and the body. With these later forms, the double arc motif also appeared. Amsa-ri could be considered to be a single cultural unit which we could term the Amsa-ri Culture.

In the northwest, the first cultural layer of the Chit'am-ni site could be considered to be the Middle or Late Period, even though there are some problems in the stratigraphic relationship. The Kungsan site should be placed in almost the same period. The first cultural layer of Sinam-ni yielded necked jars with flat bottoms, and the decoration consisted of a beautifully executed thunder pattern; it could be placed in the Late Period of Geometric Pottery. This site also yielded black pottery.

In the Geometric sites from the northeast, Early ovate-shaped vessels with pointed bottoms are not found. Most of the ceramics had flat or elevated bottoms and the rims were straight or slightly everted. For instance, the ceramics from Nongp'o-dong had truly flat bottoms in most cases. Some also had elevated bases and there were bowl, jar, wide-mouth jar, and cylinder vessel forms—representing the Late Period. Ceramics from the Hŭkkubong site of Pongŭi, the Unggi site, and the Ssangp'o-dong site of Sŏngjin had a high frequency of flat bottoms with out-curving rims; wide-mouthed jars and cylindrical shapes were also numerous.

Although one would expect from its proximity to eastern Siberia that earlier influences would be visible, Geometric Pottery in the northeast shows characteristics of the Late Period such as the thunder pattern, which is influenced by north Chinese painted ceramics as seen at the Unggi, Hŭkkubong, and Nongp'o-dong sites.

From these site descriptions it can be seen that relatively few artifacts other than ceramics have been recovered from Geometric sites. It may be that not enough attention has been devoted to stone artifacts at the time of surface collection, since chipped artifacts may have been relatively abundant. However, even the Sejung-ni site in the northwest, which was excavated by an academic research team, yielded very few stone artifacts. The exception to the rule is the Sŏp'ohang site at Ch'ŏngjin, which yielded thousands of lithic artifacts.

Some of the stone and bone tools may indicate a general chronological position. Stone artifacts generally found in Geometric Culture sites include adzes, arrowheads, scrapers, points, and weights; however, crescent-shaped knives or sickles such as those found at Sinam-ni in the northwest should be considered to be diagnostic of a later period, since these are characteristic artifacts of the Plain Pottery Culture.

Adzes manufactured by chipping and polishing had rectangular trapezoidal sections; perhaps there are connections with the adzes of northern China. Chipped or polished arrowheads vary in form, those with hexagonal cross section being of a slightly later period. Flaked obsidian artifacts from Geometric sites in the northeast retained the Palaeolithic manufacturing technique of Siberia into the Late Neolithic.

Some radiocarbon dates are available for the Geometric Culture. From Tongsam-dong one determination of 2995 ± 125 B.C. (GX–0379) and two determinations of 1450 ± 150 B.C. (GX–0492 and GX–0493), from two different locations, were obtained by L. Sample and A. Mohr. Also, a determination of 3230 ± 125 B.C. was obtained on shell collected by Teruya Esaka of Keio University, Japan. The earlier dates are very close and would correspond to the Serovo Period of Siberia. About 3000 B.C. would be acceptable as the upper limit of the Korean Neolithic Age, although of course we should wait for the confirmation of this from new materials. The date from Amsa-ri, which is about a millennium later than the early Tongsam-dong dates, might be appropriate for the Geometric Culture Middle Period. There is no accurate way to guess the date of the end of the Geometric Culture and the beginning of the Plain Pottery Culture. I shall discuss this problem in the next chapter.

CHAPTER 3

# The Bronze Age—
# Plain Pottery Culture

## PREFACE

The term "undecorated" or "plain" pottery is used in contrast with "decorated" pottery, which now refers to Geometric Pottery. The characteristics, chronology, and periodization of Plain Pottery are not yet very clear. Plain Pottery is not entirely free of decoration; some vessels have short slanting lines on the lip or perforations (Plate 13), while others are polished. However, decoration is rare and restricted in its location on the vessel. The second major characteristic of Plain Pottery is its shape. The most noticeable feature is the flat bottom, which is in contrast to the pointed bottom of the Geometric Pottery. In the later periods of the Geometric Pottery Culture, the flat bottom had already appeared, apparently as the result of influence from the Plain Pottery Culture. I would like to outline the Plain Pottery Culture by giving examples from a number of different areas.

## NORTHWEST AREA—HWANGHAE PROVINCE

Very small bases of Plain Pottery vessels have been found in northwestern regions such as Hwanghae and South P'yŏngan provinces. Vessels with a wide mouth and slightly extended body and a small base have been called "top-shaped" or "*koma*-shaped" in Japanese. The other type of pottery found with the "Top-Shape" ceramics is a jar with a

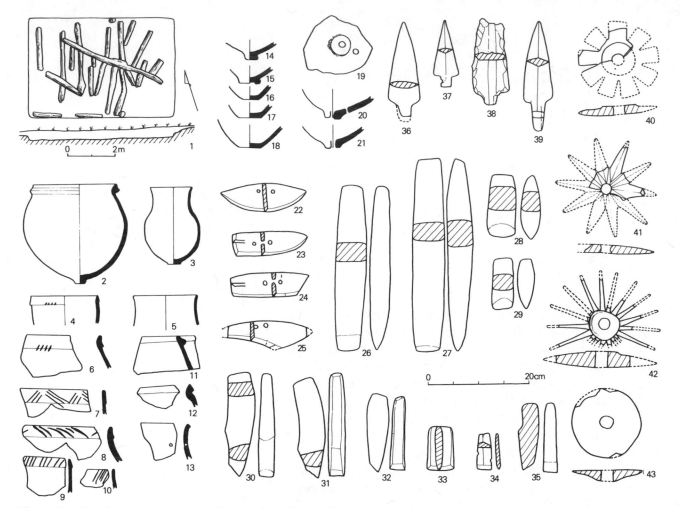

Figure 28. Specimens from the dwellings of the Sŏkt'al-li site

constricted neck and an extended round shoulder or body. Both types of jar appear to be very unstable, considering the size of the vessel in relation to the base.

### SŎKT'AL-LI SITE

The Sŏkt'al-li site of Songnim City, Hwanghae Province has yielded typical "Top-Shape" pottery (Fig. 28). From a large area of 100,000 square meters centering on Sŏkt'al-li, more than 100 dwelling sites and several stone cist coffins were discovered. Twelve house sites and two cist coffins have been examined in detail. House Site No. 2 is relatively well preserved, except for partial damage created in the later construction of rice paddies. It is a rectangle of 6.6 meters from east to west and 4 meters from north to south, and the depth of the pit dwelling is about 40 centimeters. Large post holes of about 20 centimeters in diameter and small holes of about 10 centimeters were found along the wall. It appears that the roof beam was placed on top of two large pillars, and the roof then sloped down on two sides. The fireplace consisted of a round hole dug into the floor surface; no stones were placed around the edge. Artifacts were most numerous from House Site No. 2. Stone artifacts were most frequent along the western wall, while ceramics were found mostly along the northern wall. Stone artifacts consisted of 1 polished bifacial stone adze, 1 spear point, 2 stepped adzes, 4 arrowheads, and 2 crescent-shaped stone knives. From the ceramics, 1 typical Top-Shape vessel with wide mouth and extremely narrow base could be restored.

House Site No. 3 was also relatively well preserved. It was a rectangular pit dwelling 6.3 meters from east to west and 4.4 meters from north to south. The house posts and the roof were found fallen down, showing that the roof was of the slanting or gable type, as in House Site No. 2. Post holes were found only in the midsection along the northern and southern walls; therefore the other house posts must have been set on the floor without holes having been excavated.

As encountered in other sites, stone artifacts were placed along the western wall, and ceramics along the northern wall. Sherds from about five vessels were recovered. The greyish black vessels had long, constricted necks, and some had two holes pierced at the bottom.

House Site No. 4 was an almost square-shaped dwelling 4.2 meters from east to west and 5 meters from north to south. Post holes were placed irregularly along the four walls, and the holes were about 10 centimeters in diameter. Sherds from about 3 vessels, including 1 with a constricted neck; 1 polished axe; 1 crescent-shaped knife; 1 tanged adze; and 1 stone spindle whorl were found.

These dwelling sites from Sŏkt'al-li are representative both in terms of house form and associated artifacts. Generally, the dwellings of Sŏkt'al-li were rectangular in shape except for a few square examples, and the pit excavations were usually 40 centimeters deep. Floor treatment involved the application of a layer of clay which was fired for hardening; this could be seen even in those sites which were not burned.

Two forms of roof support can be seen: in one case, a large hole was dug into the center of the house; in the other, only small holes were located close to the wall. In some cases, post holes seem to be absent, indicating that pillars might have been set up without holes having been dug. In House Sites No. 5 and No. 9, one portion of the floor was concave, in the form of a semicircle about 2 meters wide; a large stone was placed in this area, and hammers, crescent-shaped knives, and spears were found around it. Near this area, a partially completed stone axe, a broken fragment of a crescent-shaped knife, and a side-bladed axe were found. In House Site No. 9, an oval depression 15 centimeters deep, 2.6 meters long, and 1.7 meters wide was excavated, and in the center was a firepit of about 70 centimeters in diameter. These depressions constitute notable examples of the modification of the house plan for particular purposes.

About 35 meters southeast of House Site No. 9, Cist Coffin No. 1 was found. Cist Coffin No. 2 was found about 65 centimeters from No. 1. Both were damaged when rice paddies were constructed in the area. Cist Coffin No. 1 was constructed of four slabs of bluish-grey schist set upright for the four sides, while the floor was constructed with two slabs and small fragments. The cover stone was lost. No artifacts were found in these stone coffins. The relationship of the stone cist coffins to the dwelling site at Sŏkt'al-li is not clear; grave goods might have aided in determining the relationships. House sites from Sŏkt'al-li yielded ceramics and stone artifacts; no metal objects were found. Artifacts from House Sites No. 1 to No. 12 are shown in Table 4.

The mouth rim of Top-Shape vessels had a rim which is often doubled over toward the outside; often the rim was decorated with incised lines. The short lines slant to the same direction or, in some cases, three lines slanting in one direction were alternated with three lines in the opposite direction, with a triangular space between the groups.

The extremely small base, typical of this kind of Top-Shape Pottery, was made by attaching a circular piece of clay 3 to 4 centimeters in diameter to the pointed bottom. The

Table 4. Distribution of Artifacts in the Dwellings of the Sŏkt'al-li Site

| Dwelling Sites | Pottery Vessels | Stone Adze | Stone Hammer | Stepped Adze | Stone Chisel | Flat Side-Bladed Stone Adze | Spoked Mace Head | Crescent-Shaped Stone Knife | Short Dagger (Polished Stone Dagger) | Stone Adze | Stone Spear Head | Spindle Whorl | Whetstone | Stone Disc | Saddle Quern Upper Stone | Saddle Quern Lower Stone |
|---|---|---|---|---|---|---|---|---|---|---|---|---|---|---|---|---|
| No. 1 | 2 | 1 | | | | | | | 1 | | | | 1 | | | |
| No. 2 | 14 | 2 | | 3 | 2 | 2 | 1 | 3 | 2 | 4 | | | | 5 | | |
| No. 3 | 9 | | 1 | 2 | | | | 4 | | | 2 | | | few | | 1 |
| No. 4 | 11 | 2 | | | | | | 3 | | 2 | | 1 | 1 | few | | |
| No. 5 | 8 | 1 | 1 | | | 1 | | 1 | 1 | | | | | few | | |
| No. 6 | 5 | | | 1 | | | | 3 | 1 | | | | | 5 | | |
| No. 7 | 15 | 1 | | | | | 1 | 4 | | | | 2 | | 4 | 1 | 1 |
| No. 8 | 1 | | | | | | | 1 | | | | | | | | |
| No. 9 | 4 | | | 2 | 2 | 1 | | 2 | | | | | 1 | few | | |
| No. 10 | few | | | | | | | | | | | | | | | |
| No. 11 | few | | | | | | | | 1 | | | | | | | |
| No. 12 | few | 1 | | | | | | | | 1 | | 1 | | | | |
| Total | 7 | 7 | 2 | 5 | 5 | 4 | 2 | 21 | 6 | 7 | 2 | 4 | 3 | 3 | 1 | 2 |

typical size for these vessels was 22 centimeters in height, 18 centimeters in mouth diameter, and 2.5 centimeters in base diameter (Fig. 28:2). The paste of these ceramics contains steatite, is reddish-brown in color, and is relatively soft. Another form, that of a jar with constricted neck, usually has a slightly flaring mouth with a rounded body and very small bottom. A complete example, from House Site No. 7, has a height of 16.5 centimeters, a mouth diameter of 8.7 centimeters, and a base diameter of 3.5 centimeters (Fig. 28:3). While the thickness of the large-mouthed jar form mentioned above is 0.4 to 0.5 centimeter, the thickness of the latter type is 0.2 to 0.3 centimeter. Steatite was mixed with the paste, and the color was brown rather than reddish brown. This type of jar has a plain mouth form, usually without decoration; however, some examples had slanting incisions on the rims, some of which were doubled over (Fig. 28:7). Four kinds of base shapes were excavated from Sŏkt'al-li. The first form, with a small circular flat base, is the diagnostic form with Top-Shape Pottery (Fig. 28:14). The second type has one or two holes pierced into the bottom of the small circular portion. In some cases, one hole was pierced into the middle of the base, while in others, a second hole was pierced nearby (Fig. 28:19–21). The average diameter of the holes was 0.8 to 1 centimeter, and the holes were pierced before the pottery was fired. Such forms were found in Simch'ol-li of Hwangju-gun, and Sinhŭng-dong, Pongsan-gun, Hwanghae Province. What is the purpose of piercing a round hole into such a small base? Usually vessels with perforations in the bottom are used for steaming cereals; however, in the case of the Top-Shape Pottery, the bottom is extremely narrow and the number of holes is very small, and this feature raises many questions. One might suggest that this vessel may be proof of the consumption of steamed rice at this time period. The third type, which is quite rare, had a raised bottom. A clay base was added to the bottom of the pot. Only one example was found in House Site No. 2 (Fig. 28:15). The fourth type has a very round bottom, with no clear distinction between the body and the base. Four examples were recovered from Sŏkt'al-li (Fig. 28:16–18). However, only the bases were recovered. The upper portion was probably the typical jar with the constricted neck form.

Pottery vessels from Sŏkt'al-li can be divided into two categories. One form is a deep jar with wide mouth, while the other has a constricted neck. The deep, wide jar form generally has a "double rim" which in some cases has short slanting lines, which were applied in a number of patterns—either with continuous short lines in the same direction or in groups in alternating directions, with intervening open spaces.

The narrow-necked vessels from Sŏkt'al-li usually do not possess the doubled rim on the mouth; however, there are doubled examples from other sites. A few rim sherds have a horizontal line incised about 2.5 centimeters below the lip, giving the same effect as the double rim; below the line, a slanting incision decoration was used (Fig. 28:7). The paste of ceramics from Sŏkt'al-li usually contains steatite, sand, or mica, and the color is brown or reddish brown. House Site No. 4 yielded pottery in which no materials were added to the paste, the color being dark grey. Similar ceramics were found in other sites which produce Top-Shape Pottery; there is a suggestion of influences from Chinese black pottery in the color and the paste.

Table 4 shows a good range of representative artifacts from Plain Pottery sites: 21 crescent-shaped knives, 10 stepped adzes, 9 arrowheads, 4 swords, 4 thin, planoconvex adzes, 4 spindle whorls, 3 whetstones, and 2 spoked mace heads. The most predominant form of the stone knife had one convex cutting edge and a straight or slightly curved back. I have termed these "crescent-shaped" stone knives. An exceptional example from Sŏkt'al-li House Site No. 7 had a slightly convex blade, which was produced by extensive wear (Fig. 28:22–25). Some adzes had two "steps" on the same side (Fig. 28:30, 31); sometimes these bevels were not very clearly demarcated (Fig. 28:32). The largest one was 21 centimeters long and the smallest (termed a chisel), 9.5 centimeters long, 2.3 centimeters wide, and 1.5 centimeters thick. Grooved adzes are also known from surface collections. Actually, these forms appear to have been close to stepped adzes (see Fig. 28:35). The arrowheads had a typical diamond cross section; only one exception had a biconvex section. All of the arrowheads, including those with willow-leaf shape, had stems. One large example, 9.5 centimeters long, may be considered to have been a stone spear (Fig.

28:36–39). No examples of the stemless, hexagonal form were recovered from Sŏkt'al-li.

Of the polished adzes, oval-sectioned and rectangular-sectioned symmetrical axes were common. One from House Site No. 4 was unusually long (37.5 cm) and was 4.5 centimeters wide (Fig. 28:27). It could be called a pillar-shaped symmetrical stone axe. In the report, the term "polished stone short dagger" is used; it might be better to call this form a stone spear (Fig. 28:36–39). I think that these are the prototypes of the polished stone dagger and are seen in the late Plain Pottery sites; at present, the most frequently used name for these artifacts is "polished stone dagger." Important characteristics are the short stem and the diamond or biconvex cross section. Notches found on one or both sides seem to have been used for hafting the handles. The same type of stone dagger (Fig. 28:28, 29) was unearthed from the site of Simch'ŏl-li, Hwangju-gun, which I will describe later.

The polished stone daggers shared with the stone arrowheads such features as diamond or biconvex cross section, and they were not grooved, which means that they were not copies of metal weapons. Their length was 10 to 20 centimeters, and they were probably used as stone spears rather than as actual stone daggers. They could be called adze-shaped or spear-shaped stone daggers.

Planoconvex adzes have often been found in Plain Pottery sites in association with polished bifacial axes. About one in four was completely polished, while the remainder had polished blades (Fig. 28:33, 34). An unusual notched, triangular-sectioned axe was found from House Site No. 6 (Fig. 28:34). The spindle whorls all appear to be flat discs of schist, with a diameter of about 7.3 centimeters and a thickness of 0.6 centimeter. One of the mace heads was the so-called moon-shaped axe (Fig. 28:43); the other had a star shape (Fig. 28:42).

This axe was flat on one side, rounded on the other. Its thickness was 2.2 centimeters, while the total diameter was 14 centimeters and the diameter of the perforation was 2.5 to 3 centimeters. The star-shaped, spoked mace-head form looks like a toothed wheel. An example from House Site No. 7 had 18 teeth, a thickness of 3.3 centimeters, a central hole of 2.3 centimeters, and a total diameter of 22.2 centimeters. Two spoked mace heads were found from Sŏkt'al-li by surface collecting. One had 10 teeth, most of which were broken (Fig. 28:40). The upper and lower portions of a saddle quern were excavated from House Site No. 7, while the lower stone was found in House Site No. 3. The saddle querns usually came from both Geometric and Plain Pottery sites.

Stone discs, sometimes called "stone money," were also found. A small hole was pierced in the center of a disc of schist. The shape is reminiscent of a spindle whorl, but it is much larger. Their function is unknown; I am therefore calling them simply stone discs. They are abundant from other Plain Pottery sites in the northwest area.

In addition to the remains of the Plain Pottery Culture discussed previously, surface collections from Sŏkt'al-li include remains of the Geometric Culture, including a small quantity of sherds and stone arrowheads. The location of these finds is different from that of the Plain Pottery house sites. The clay was mixed either with steatite or sand, and the decoration consisted of crude incisions of short parallel lines. The design looks like the deteriorated form of the geometric design, at first glance. The arrowheads were stemless, with a concave base and a hexagonal cross section. These arrowheads are different in form from the Sŏkt'al-li Plain Pottery Culture arrowheads, which had diamond-shaped cross sections and stems. The Geometric Culture occupation may have been toward the end of the total Geometric Period, judging from the deteriorated nature of the decoration, or it may have overlapped with the Plain Pottery; the difference in arrowhead cross sections must be significant in this respect. Sŏkt'al-li is the largest village of the Plain Pottery Period which has been found thus far. Producing a wide range of everyday tools, it can be considered representative of the Plain Pottery Culture.

### SIMCH'OL-LI SITE

The Simch'ol-li site of Hwang-ju gun, Hwanghae Province shows many similarities with Sŏkt'al-li. To the northwest of Chŏngbangsan in Simch'ol-li, dolmens have been found spread over the slopes and valley bottom, and many dwelling sites have been found near the dolmens. Survey of the dolmens and dwelling sites was carried out in the fall of 1958 and the spring of 1959. I will discuss only a portion of the available materials—three dwellings found on the eastern side of Simch'ol-li Middle School and one dwelling site in Ch'unjin-dong—because these are the most easily available. Besides these, I will refer to remains from nearby dolmens to explore the relationships between the dwelling sites. I am numbering the sites near the Middle School Simch'ol-li House Site No. 1, No. 2, and No. 3 in the order of excavation.

The long axis of House Site No. 1 runs from east to west. The site is well preserved, except for partial damage on the southwest side. Total length from east to west was 6.2 meters, from north to south, 3.75 meters, and the depth was about 10 centimeters, measured to a concavity in the floor in which a piece of charred pillar was found. From the floor surface, axes, stepped adzes, crescent-shaped knives, and spindle whorls were found together with sherds.

House Site No. 2 was about 27 meters east of House Site No. 1. This example was the best preserved. Length from north to south was 5.8 centimeters, from east to west, 3.55 meters, and the depth was 10 centimeters. A considerable ash layer was accumulated on the floor surface, suggesting that House Site No. 1 may have caught fire. No fireplace was found, and the absence of post holes suggests that the pillars must have been set directly on the hard floor surface. Scattered over the floor surface were chips of slate, artifacts, and potsherds. From the sherds two vessels were restorable. Along the east-west wall, many stone daggers, arrowheads, axes, stepped adzes, planoconvex adzes, chisels, and crescent-shaped knives were unearthed.

House Site No. 3, about 15 meters from House Site No. 1, was largely destroyed; thus the original shape cannot be determined. The rim of the house pit appeared about 30 centimeters below the ground surface, and the depth of the pit was about 10 centimeters. A fireplace, with clay piled around the rim, was about 80 centimeters in diameter. No other furnishings were found. Artifacts included axes, stepped adzes, crescent-shaped knives, spindle whorls, arrowheads and whetstones. The four dwelling sites of Ch'unjin-dong yielded remains almost identical with those from Sŏkt'al-li, in terms of both form and function. The two sites are both within Hwangju-gun and are close to each other in many respects.

Not all the tool categories are found in each house (Table

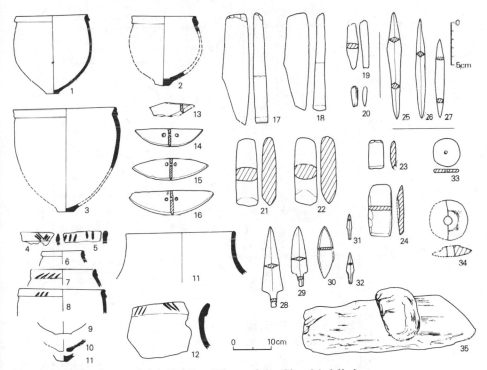

Figure 29. Specimens from the dwellings of the Simch'ol-li site

5). From Simch'ol-li one particular knife form, which has never been found in other Plain Pottery sites, was recovered (Fig. 29:13). Its shape differs from that of the crescent-shaped knives; the blade was made by polishing a flat, chipped piece of schist. It appears to have been held in the hand and used as a knife, since there was no preparation for hafting. The length was 12 centimeters, the width 3.3 centimeters, and the thickness 0.8 centimeter.

The ceramics from Simch'ol-li seem to be divided into two types; one is a deep jar with a wide mouth (Fig. 29:1–3) and a "folded-over" rim, while the other has a constricted long neck and expanded body (Fig. 29:11). The deep jar has a narrow base about 3 to 4 centimeters in diameter, and the example from House Site No. 1 had a hole in the bottom. The same form was found at Sŏkt'al-li; they probably served as steamers. The flat-bottomed jar with an almost round form was found in house sites from Ch'unjin-dong. The alternating slanting incisions, or slanting lines in groups (Fig. 29:4,

**Table 5. Distribution of Artifacts in the Dwellings of the Simch'ŏl-li Site**

Artifacts

| Dwelling Sites | Pottery Vessels | Stone Adze | Stepped Adze | Stone Adze Only | Plano-convex Stone Adze | Ring Shape Tool | Cres-cent-Shaped Stone Knife | Short Dagger (Polished Stone Dagger) | Stone Arrow-head | Stone Spear-head | Spin-dle Whorl | Whet-stone | Saddle Quern Upper Stone | Saddle Quern Lower Stone | Small Stone Knife |
|---|---|---|---|---|---|---|---|---|---|---|---|---|---|---|---|
| House Site No. 1 | 4 | | 1 | | | | 1 | | | | 2 | | | | 1 |
| House Site No. 2 | 15 | 2 | 1 | 2 | 2 | 1 | 3 | 2 | 3 | | | | | | |
| House Site No. 3 | 5 ⑴ | ⑴ | ⑴ | | 1 | | 1 ⑵ | | ⑵ | | 1 ⑴ | 1 ⑴ | 2 | 1 | |
| Ch'unjin-dong | 10 | 1 | | | 2 | | 1 | | | 1 | 1 | | | | |
| Total | 34 ⑴ | 3 ⑴ | 2 ⑴ | 2 | 5 | 1 | 6 ⑵ | 2 | 3 ⑵ | 1 | 4 ⑴ | 1 ⑴ | 2 | 1 | 1 |

Note: The circle ◯ indicates artifacts found before the excavation. The number of pottery vessels was determined by a count of the bottom parts.

5, 7, 8, 12), were identical to the decoration motifs from Sŏkt'al-li. A form with no decoration and a slightly con stricted neck was found in House Site No. 2.

The body of the ceramics had inclusions of sand and steatite. Although there were a few dark brown or polished black sherds which seemed to show the influence of the black pottery of China, brown was the predominant color. The height of the vessels seems to have been about 20 centimeters to 30 centimeters, while the mouth diameter ranged around 10 centimeters. Thickness was about 6 millimeters. Most numerous among the artifacts from Simch'ol-li were stone knives (Fig. 29:14–16). As in Sŏkt'al-li, the general form was once more the crescent shape. The largest example was 21.5 centimeters long, 6 centimeters wide, and 0.8 centimeter thick, while the small one was 14.5 centimeters long, 4.7 centimeters wide, and 0.8 centimeter thick. The second most numerous category was stone arrowheads. These were stemmed and had a diamond-shaped cross section (Fig. 29:31, 32). One extremely weathered example may have had a willow-leaf shape. Five flat, planoconvex adzes were of the same type as in Sŏkt'al-li. The largest was 13.5 centimeters long, 6 centimeters wide, and 1.3 centimeters thick (Fig. 29:23, 24). Four large axes, about 17 to 18 centimeters in length, were found. The cross section was close to oval, and they were bifacial and symmetrical (Fig. 29:21, 22). The stepped adzes were of the same form as Sŏkt'al-li; some of them had multiple indentations. The largest was 28.5 centimeters long and 6.8 centimeters thick; while a second example was 26.2 centimeters long and 6.1 centimeters thick (Fig. 29:17, 18). Very small stepped adzes were classified by the reporter as chisels. They were different from the largest stepped adzes in that they possessed only one step, and the blade was on the opposite side from it (Fig. 29:19, 20). Only two polished stone daggers were found. Both had a diamond-shaped cross section, a short stem, and notches on both sides, in the same manner as in Sŏkt'al-li. One was 22.5 centimeters long and the other 15.3 centimeters (Fig. 29:28, 29). A fragment of a ring-shaped axe of schist with an elevation around the perforated center had a serrated edge and was 10.4 centimeters in diameter, 2.5 centimeters thick, with a central hole of 2.3 centimeters (Fig. 29:34). The upper and lower parts of a saddle quern were found in House Site No. 3. The lower stone was 53 centimeters long, 27 centimeters wide, 7 centimeters thick, and had a rectangular shape, while the upper stone was 36 centimeters long, 12 centimeters wide, and 3.5 centimeters thick. Both showed wear on one side (Fig. 29:35). The spindle whorls had the usual disc shape; a typical example was 7 centimeters in diameter, 0.8 centimeter thick, and the diameter of the perforation was 0.7 centimeter (Fig. 29:33). In addition there were stone discs, which were regarded as stone money in the report; these were larger than spindle whorls, and were of the same form as discs found in Sŏkt'al-li.

### SIMCH'OL-LI SITE—DOLMENS

Groups of dolmens were found around the dwelling sites mentioned above, and appear to be related to them. There are more than 200 dolmens in the Simch'ol-li area, but they have not all been surveyed. For discussion I have selected a few typical instances. Dolmens in the Simch'ol-li area can be divided into two kinds: one (the so-called northern style) has supporting stones which make a table shape while the other (the so-called southern style) has lower supporting stones, and under the cover stone there is a cist coffin. The southern style is dominant in the Simch'ol-li area.

Dolmen No. 2 found near the Middle School has a half-broken cover stone. The present length is 2 meters, the width 1 meter, and the thickness is 50 centimeters. The stone coffin was constructed by the combination of relatively thin slabs about 3 centimeters thick to make a rectangular shape. The coffin was oriented approximately north-south and was surrounded by cobbles about 30 centimeters in diameter. In the well-preserved portions, the length of the coffin was 1.35 meters, the width 40 centimeters, and the depth 50 centimeters.

The cover stone of Dolmen No. 2 of Sindae-dong (Fig. 30) was a granite slab 2.7 meters long, 2 meters wide, and 50 to 60 centimeters thick. Two slabs to the right and left of the four supporting stones had fallen down. One of these, a granite slab, was 1.8 meters long, 1.2 meters wide, and 20 to 30 centimeters thick. Between these two slabs, thinner slabs were placed on the north and south sides to make a rectangular outer frame for the coffin. On the floor surface of

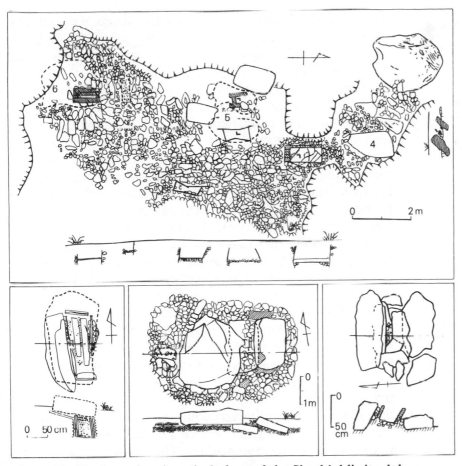

Figure 30. Horizontal and vertical plans of the Simch'ol-li site dolmens: top, Ch'unjin-dong, Dolmens Nos. 4, 5, and 6; lower left, dolmens from the area near the Middle School; middle, Sindae-dong No. 2 Dolmen; right, Dolmen No. 6 from Kŭksŏng-dong

the stone outer frame for the coffin, pebbles were spread. Around the dolmen, rocks were accumulated in a pile which extended to Dolmens No. 3 and No. 4 to create a kind of grave area. A restoration of the stone outer frame suggests that the length was 1.6 meters, the width 0.8 meter, and the height almost 1 meter. This frame was apparently intended to be completely buried.

The cover stone of Dolmen No. 6 at Ch'unjin-dong (Fig. 30) was 2.3 meters long, 1.6 meters wide, and 40 centimeters thick, and it originally covered two cist coffins. In its present

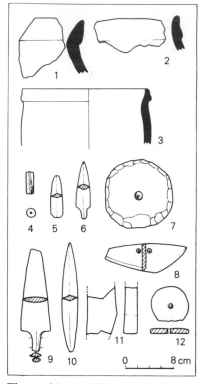

Figure 31. Artifacts from the dolmens of the Simch'ol-li site

state, it has been moved over and only covers the southern coffin. The orientation of these coffins varies, the northern one being placed in an east-west direction, the southern one in a north-south direction. The coffin on the north side was 90 centimeters long, 45 centimeters wide, and 20 to 40 centimeters high, while the coffin on the south side was 75 centimeters long, 30 centimeters wide, and 25 centimeters high. On the floor of the northern coffin, pebbles were spread, and sherds of Top-Shape vessels and jars with constricted necks were found in these pebbles. On the floor of the southern coffin a stone slab was placed. One stone arrowhead was found in the pile of stones on the eastern side of the coffin. The grave goods are illustrated in Figure 31.

In the vicinity of Kŭksŏng-dong, which is at the foot of Chŏngbangsan Mountain, about 100 dolmens are crowded into an area of about 300 meters on the southwestern slope of the valley. Dolmen No. 6 contained a rectangular stone cist coffin constructed of four thin stone slabs with two thicker granite slabs as supporting stones, plus a third granite stone lying in an east-west direction. Over these a large cover stone was placed. One of the supporting stones was 1.1 meters long, 40 centimeters wide, and 20 to 25 centimeters thick. The interior stone coffin was 50 to 60 centimeters long, 25 centimeters wide, and about 25 centimeters high. This is a very small example. On the floor surface there was a mixture of soil and pebbles. The interior coffin and the associated accumulation of cobbles show the same configuration as Dolmen No. 7.

These examples from the Simch'ol-li area give an impression of the structure of the dolmens. Let us now look at the associated artifacts.

Dolmens No. 1 and No. 4 each yielded a stone dagger. There were no ridges on the blade, the cross section was lens shaped, and notches were cut into both sides of the stem. The same kind of notching was seen in the dagger from House Site No. 2. The specimen of Dolmen No. 1 had a broken tip; the present length is 22.4 centimeters, the width, 6 centimeters, and the thickness, 1 centimeter. The example from Dolmen No. 4 was also incomplete; however, the restored length is estimated to be about 22 centimeters (Fig. 31:9). One stepped adze was found in Dolmen No. 1 of Simch'ol-li.

Although only the middle portion was found, the method of making the steps seems to be similar to the examples from Dolmens No. 1 and No. 2 (Fig. 31:11). Dolmens No. 5 and No. 6 each produced one stone arrowhead; in addition, five were found from the dolmens at Ch'unjin-dong and five were found from Kŭksŏng-dong. All of the examples were stemmed and had a diamond-shaped cross section. One example had a willowleaf shape (Fig. 31:5, 6, 10). A stone knife with a triangular cutting edge and two perforations near the back was also found (Fig. 31:8). A spindle whorl was found in the dolmen at Kŭksŏng-dong (Fig. 31:12). It had a disc shape, was 6.5 centimeters in diameter and 0.8 centimeter thick. The central perforation was 0.6 centimeter in diameter.

One specimen was found in Dolmen No. 2 from the Sindae-dong site. It had a diameter of 75 centimeters and was about 5 centimeters thick. The central perforation was biconical (Fig. 31:7). Although the shape was the same as that of a spindle whorl, it is far too large to serve this function. A "pipe-shaped" object was recovered from a stone cist coffin in one of the dolmens from Ch'unjin-dong. The material was amazonite (Fig. 31:4).

Potsherds were found from the cist coffins of Dolmens No. 3 and No. 4 of Simch'ol-li. Two of the rim sherds had the "double" or "folded-over" form, and one of them had short slanting incised decoration. It is important to note that the sherds were of the Top-Shape type. Some sherds showed the constricted neck form that is also characteristic of other sites (Fig. 31:1–3). From these examples, it seems clear that the artifacts found in the dolmens of Simch'ol-li are quite similar to those from dwellings in the same area. In particular, the forms of daggers, axes, and adzes were the same, indicating that the remains of dwelling sites and dolmens belong to the same period and the same culture.

## SINHŬNG-DONG SITE

The Sinhŭng-dong site of Pongsan-gun, Hwanghae Province has been considered for some time to be one of the representative sites yielding Top-Shape Pottery. During the excavation in 1958, seven house sites were examined. Two of them were constructed directly on the ground surface, while

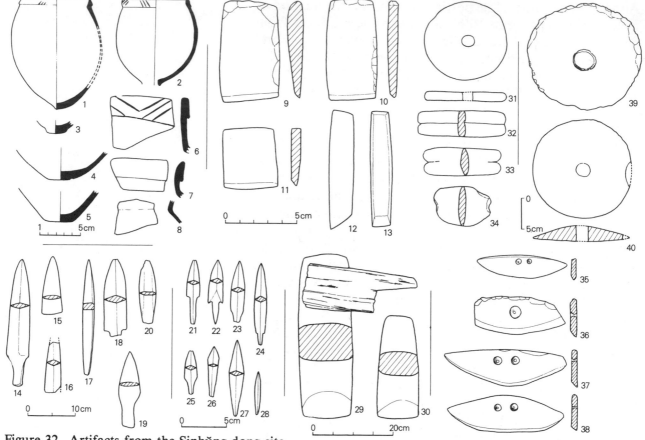

Figure 32. Artifacts from the Sinhŭng-dong site

the rest appeared to be pit houses. The same two vessel forms as were found in other sites—Top-Shape and jars with constricted necks—were found. The rim of the Top-Shape Pottery had groups of three to four short slanting incisions, in some cases in alternating directions, and the base was constructed by the attachment of a small disc-shaped clay foot to the bottom point. In the same manner as in the Sŏkt'al-li site, a hole about 2.5 centimeters in diameter was pierced in the center of the small bottom portion, which was only 4 centimeters in diameter (Fig. 32:2). In addition to this base form, the flattened round-bottom form, similar to those from other sites yielding Top-Shape Pottery, was recorded. Stone artifacts were of the same types as those from other Plain Pottery sites in the northwest.

Five stone daggers, with diamond cross section and notches on both sides of the stem (the same as in the sites mentioned previously), were recovered. The length was about 20 centimeters. One example from House Site No. 7 had a convex cross section (Fig. 32:15).

Three stone spears—larger than arrowheads and smaller than stone daggers—were recovered. One of them had a diamond cross section and a partially broken stem. The present length is 8 centimeters. Another example had a willowleaf form with grooves on both sides and a length of 7 centimeters (Fig. 32:17–20). Eleven stone arrowheads were also found. All of them were diamond shaped in cross section, and some of them had a pronounced tang. Another example had a narrow, penlike shape, and was 5.5 centimeters in length (Fig. 32:17–20).

Four stone adzes were also recovered. In section they were rectangular or oval. All of them were biconvex. One example, with an almost oval cross section, had a burnt wooden handle attached. This affords an excellent chance to study the hafting (Fig. 32:29).

One round stone adze or weeding tool was also recovered. It was of the same style as other examples from Plain Pottery sites; one side was flat, while the other side was elevated (Fig. 32:40). A hole was pierced in the center, and the edge was polished to make a sharp blade. The diameter was 13 centimeters, and the diameter of the central hole was 2 centimeters.

Four flat planoconvex adzes (Fig. 32:9, 10, 11), similar in style to those from other Plain Pottery sites, appear to have been used as knives since they are so small (some were 8 centimeters long, 4 centimeters wide, while others were 4 centimeters long and 4 centimeters wide). One polished diorite chisel, trapezoidal in section with a length of 8.3 centimeters, was also recovered (Fig. 32:12).

Eight crescent-shaped stone knives, with a flat or curved back section and a convex blade, were also recovered (Fig. 32:35–38). Depending on the shape of the back, they can be divided into crescent shape and fish shape. Two holes were pierced near the back in most cases, although in one instance there was a single perforation. The largest example was 17 centimeters in length, while the smallest was 13 centimeters.

Two complete lower stones, two upper stones, and two fragments of upper stones of saddle querns were also recovered. One of the lower stones was 54 centimeters long, 26 centimeters wide, and 8 centimeters thick. A single spindle whorl was also recovered from House Site No. 3. It had a flat disc shape, and the diameter was 6 centimeters (Fig. 32:31). More than twenty net sinkers, created by chipping two concavities on schist pebbles, were also recovered from House Site No. 2. The largest sinker was 6 centimeters long; and the smallest, 4 centimeters long (Fig. 32:32–34). More than ten hammer-stones were also recovered; these were round stones about the size of one's fist; one of them was oblong in shape.

Disc-shaped stone artifacts were found in almost all of the dwelling sites. Five of them were found side by side in House Site No. 2; they were also lined up on the surface of the floor of House Site No. 5. A complete specimen had a diameter of 62 centimeters and was about 3 centimeters thick. The diameter of the central perforation was about 12 centimeters (Fig. 32:39). Among the disc-shaped stones, some had a diameter of 8 to 10 centimeters. Of the specimens in this range, some had a hole in the center, while others were unperforated. We still do not know how they were used.

A single sandstone whetstone (8.5 centimeters long, 5.5 centimeters wide and 1 centimeter thick) and a single stone knife with a blade made by polishing the edge of a triangular flake (15 centimeters long and 1.5 centimeters thick) were also recovered. One bronze button, with a diameter of about 2.5 centimeters, was found on the floor of House Site No. 7. It disintegrated on exposure to the air. This style of bronze button is rarely found in Top-Shape Pottery sites. From Layer II of Location No. 3 of Sinam-ni, Yongch'on-gun, a bronze button was recovered along with a bronze knife with ring handle. A button was also found in the stone cist coffin of Orŏe-myŏn, Kanggye-gun, North P'yŏngan Province. However, the ceramics accompanying these buttons appeared to be different from Top-Shape Pottery.

Ceramics and stone artifacts from Sinhŭng-dong were of the same types as those found in other sites yielding the Top-Shape vessel form. Of the stone artifacts, the stone daggers and knives were typical. The crescent shape of the knives was the same form found in the Lungshan Culture. One important circumstance was the lack of stepped adzes which are common in other Top-Shape Pottery sites. The bronze buttons are the same style as in the Karasuk Culture (Fig. 92), and they are found in the Early Period of the Bronze Age in Korea.

## NORTHWEST AREA—SOUTH P'YŎNGAN PROVINCE

The major sites which yield the Top-Shape Pottery form are concentrated in Hwanghae Province. However, sites are also found in the basin of the Taedong River in South P'yŏngan Province, adjacent to Hwanghae Province. Earlier excavations took place at the Chinp'a-ri site, the Mirim-ni site, the Kŭmt'al-li site, the Ipsŏng-ni site, and the Wŏnam-ni site.

### CHINP'A-RI SITE

The Chinp'a-ri site of Chunghwa-gun was found by accident in 1941 in the excavations of the Koguryo mounds around the tomb of the legendary king Tongmyong. No report, however, has been made on that site. All that has been published is one scale drawing of a Plain Pottery Culture house site and an illustration of two restored pottery vessels.

The excavation uncovered a rectangular pit dwelling oriented north-south on a hill at Chinp'a-ri. The length was about 10 meters, the width 4.9 meters, and the depth 30 centimeters. The artifacts consisted of 5 potsherds, 1 stone dagger, 2 spindle whorls, and 3 disc-shaped stones. One of the restored ceramic vessels had an extremely small flat bottom with a slightly expanded body, and was a good example of a Top-Shape vessel (Fig. 33).

### MIRIM-NI SITE

The Mirim-ni site in P'yŏngyang City was surveyed by Ryuzo Torii in 1916. He recognized two cultural layers in this site. From the upper layer, the ceramics were an ashy grey-brown color and were marked with a straw mat or checker motif. These were found in association with iron artifacts. The lower layer yielded adzes, crescent-shaped stone knives, arrowheads, spoked mace heads, sinkers, whetstones, and bone arrowheads.

Ceramics from the lower layer of Mirim-ni included comb-

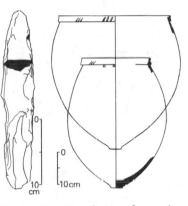

Figure 33. Specimens from the Chinp'a-ri site

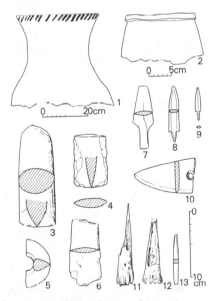

Figure 34. Specimens from the Mirim-ni Rock Shelter site

marked vessels with round bases, Top-Shape vessels, and stone artifacts including stone daggers, spears, axes, spindle whorls, crescent-shaped knives, stone arrowheads with flanges on both sides, and spoked mace heads, including four- and six-spoked forms. The Mirim Rock Shelter site yielded similar specimens, including Top-Shape Pottery (Fig. 34).

### KŬMT'AL-LI SITE

The Kŭmt'al-li site in P'yŏngyang City was excavated in 1955. It is a village site of considerable size, with many house sites. In the site report it is chronologically divided into a Neolithic Layer, a Top-Shape Pottery Layer, and an Ancient Culture Layer. In this section I will deal only with the dwelling sites from the Top-Shape Pottery Layer.

One of the house sites was about 6 meters in length and 3.5 centimeters in width, consisting of a rectangular pit dwelling with a depth of about 30 centimeters. As in the case of the Mirim-ni site, Top-Shape Pottery was found in association with comb-marked, round-bottomed pottery. From House Site No. 8, many cord-marked and round-bottomed vessels were found together with a few Top-Shape and polished red vessels. Two kinds of vessels—deep jars with constricted necks and doubled-over rims (Fig. 35)—were found. Stone artifacts included crescent-shaped stone knives, arrowheads, stone daggers, stepped adzes, thin, planoconvex adzes, and stone spindle whorls. The stone knives had straight backs with convex blades, and the stone arrowheads were stemmed. The stepped adzes had two steps, while the other plain adzes were oval in cross section (Fig. 36). In addition, disc-shaped stones were numerous.

### WŎNAM-NI SITE

The Wŏnam-ni site in Kangnam-gun was located on a hill about 500 meters to the south of the Taedong River, at Somae-dong, Wŏnam-ni. It was excavated in 1955, and two house sites were examined. House Site No. 1 was a rectangular pit house more than 6 meters in length, 5.53 meters wide, and 40 centimeters deep. Top-Shape Pottery sherds, adzes (including stepped forms), chisels, fragments of stone daggers, crescent-shaped stone knives, spindle whorls, ar-

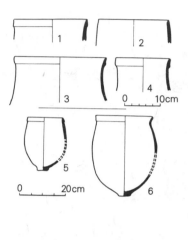

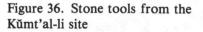

Figure 36. Stone tools from the Kŭmt'al-li site

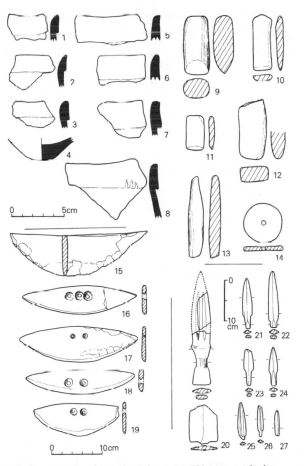

Figure 37. Specimens from the Wŏnam-ni site

rowheads, spoked mace heads, whetstones, and disc-shaped stone artifacts were found (Fig. 37).

Since House Site No. 2 was damaged, only the width, 3.18 meters, was recorded. Top-Shape potsherds and some fragments of stone daggers were found. Ceramics from House Site No. 1 had inclusions of sand or steatite, and the mouth rims were doubled over toward the outside. Decoration consisted of groups of three or four slanting incisions. Ceramics from House Site No. 2 did not contain sand or steatite but had the same rim forms. Two stone daggers were excavated. The example from House Site No. 2 was heavily damaged; through restoration, however, the original shape was recognizable. There were two steps in the area between the handle and the blade, and there were two grooves along the blade. The stone dagger found in House Site No. 1 was also fragmentary; it had sharp cutting edges with no grooves. Although it was broken, it seems that the handle was very short. The later forms (two-stepped and grooved) seem to be copies of the bronze dagger, and were inserted into a separate handle. The grooved form seems to be later in time period than the ungrooved.

One stone axe with rounded rectangular cross section and a biconvex symmetrical blade was found. The length was 11 centimeters, the width 5 centimeters, and the thickness 4 centimeters (Fig. 37:9). Two thin, planoconvex adzes were also recovered. One was 10 centimeters in length, 3.4 centimeters in width, and long and narrow in form, while the other was 7 centimeters long, 3.5 centimeters wide, and short and wide (Fig. 37:10, 11). One fragmentary stepped stone adze was also recovered. A chisel, similar in form to the stepped adze, was also recovered. It was small in size and must have functioned as a woodworking tool (Fig. 37:13). Crescent-shaped stone knives were the most numerous artifacts found in the Wŏnam-ni site. All of the blades were convex, and the backs were either straight or slightly convex. Generally, there were two holes perforated in them, but some had three holes. A number of incomplete specimens showed the process of shaping the blade before chipping and polishing (Fig. 37:15–19). Two spoked mace heads, one with long horn-shaped spokes in a radial arrangement and the other with six spokes, were found. Two spindle whorls, of the usual disc shape, were also recovered. Their diameter was from 6.8 to 7 centimeters (Fig. 37:14). As usual, many disc-shaped stones were also found; these had a hole either at the center of the disc or near the edge. The majority of the specimens were about 50 centimeters in diameter. In sites of the Plain Pottery Culture in the Taedong Basin, the ceramics show the same general characteristics as the Top-Shape Pottery. However, comb-marked ceramics with round bottoms were recovered from the lower layer of Mirim-ni and Kŭmt'al-li in association with Top-Shape ceramics. The Mirim-ri site was not excavated by a professional team; thus the description of the stratigraphy may not be very accurate. From the Kŭmt'al-li site, structures of various periods were found, and the stratigraphic relationships of dwelling sites with Top-Shape Pottery and comb-marked pottery with rounded bottoms were not clear. If the stratigraphic relationships were reliable, the association of the Top-Shape Pottery and the cord-marked pottery would be an important indication of an overlap between the two periods. Stepped adzes were rare; one was found in Kŭmt'al-li and one in Wŏnam-ni. The example from Kŭmt'al-li had two steps. Stone daggers were found in each of the previously mentioned sites in the Taedong River Basin. The reporting of styles of the daggers is not always clear but two distinct kinds can be identified from Wŏnam-ni. The example from House Site No. 1 had a diamond-shaped cross section with a short stem and was similar to the type excavated from the Plain Pottery sites in Hwanghae Province. However, the type found in House Site No. 2 had sharp grooves on both sides of the blade and appeared to be a later form.

## MAJOR CHARACTERISTICS OF THE PLAIN POTTERY CULTURE IN THE NORTHWEST

It is difficult to establish a chronology of ceramics and stone artifacts of Top-Shape Pottery sites in Hwanghae and Southern P'yŏngan Provinces. At this point, about all that can be said for certain is that sites in Hwanghae Province are abundant and the artifact range and variation is greater than in South P'yŏngan Province.

In most sites, the deep jar (Top-Shape vessel) and the jar with constricted neck were found. In particular, the base of the deep jar style of pottery was characterized by the attachment of a small disc of clay to the pointed bottom. It can be regarded as the result of adapting the flat bottom of a new pottery tradition to the pointed bottom of the Geometric Pottery. The doubled-over rim with short slanting incisions also constitutes a continuity from the Geometric Pottery. The method of doubling over the mouth and pressing the lower edge with the fingers or decorating with short slanting incisions can be seen in the later period of Geometric Pottery, in sites such as Annam-dong or Tongsam-dong in Pusan. The method of incising lines around the mouth to create the same effect as the decoration mentioned above can also be seen on Geometric Pottery from the same sites. The same flattened bottom form can be seen in Geometric and Plain Pottery. The form is most common in the later period of the Geometric Pottery Culture.

What is the source of the new pottery forms of the Plain Pottery Period? The new jar form with the narrow neck, the flat bottom, and the absence of decoration—where did these innovations come from?

Flat-bottomed jars are known from both Chinese Yang Shao and Lungshan Cultures, and also in the Plain Ceramics of northeastern China. These Chinese ceramics belong to a different time period; however, they all appear to be culturally related. Therefore, the direct or indirect influence of northern Chinese cultures on the Korean peninsula should be considered.

The Korean ceramics of this time period are reddish brown, while a few exceptions are ashy grey black. Lungshanoid ceramics are ashy grey and orange; a chief characteristic is the lack of decoration. There were also plain red ceramics in the northeast part of China. The various colors were produced by varying the content of the clay and the firing method; the red or black colors were often produced by using iron oxide or black lead. In the Plain Pottery Culture of Korea, red and black ceramics also occur and the technique of polishing the surface is also present. Influence can also be documented in the shape of the Korean Plain Pottery. One of the prominent features of the Plain Ceramics of South P'yŏngan and Hwanghae provinces is the constricted neck and the rather large mouth. It appears that in later periods the mouth became smaller and the neck more constricted; therefore, chronological divisions are evident in the pottery-making techniques.

The change of the vessel shape from the pointed bottom of the Geometric Pottery to the flat bottom of the Plain Pottery entailed a reduction in the total size of the vessel forms. Some of the ceramics from South P'yŏngan and Hwanghae provinces may be identifiable as early shapes. The deep jars or the jars with constricted necks may fall into this category.

The influence of black and red Chinese pottery appears in a few sherds. From later Plain Pottery sites, lustrous black pottery with a refined paste has been found.

Crescent-shaped stone knives were the most numerous ar-

tifacts. Absent from the Geometric Culture, they are diagnostic of the Plain Pottery Culture, along with other stone
artifacts. It is generally agreed that these were agricultural
tools for harvesting cereals, since they were found in large
numbers in the Plain Pottery sites in the Taedong Basin and
Hwanghae Province. It would seem that the people in these
regions depended heavily on agriculture. It is not yet known
whether this was paddy or dry-field cultivation.

In the northwest, paddy agriculture seems to have begun
quite late because of climatic conditions; according to the
*Wei Chih* in the *San Kuo Chih,* no rice paddies existed north
of the Han River at the time the record was written, which
was about the third century A.D. In the section called the
*Tung-i Ch'uan,* paddy and dry-field farming are clearly indicated for southern areas such as Mahan, Pyŏnhan, and
Chinhan. However, in the northern areas such as Puyŏ,
Koguryo, Okchŏ, and Wei, the descriptions mention only
field farming. Thus, the crescent-shaped knives found in the
Top-Shape Pottery sites in the Taedong Basin and Hwanghae Province were being used to harvest field-grown cereals.
From those sites stone arrowheads and spears were found in
considerable numbers, indicating that hunting was well
developed also. No fishing tools, such as net sinkers, have
been unearthed, indicating that very little fishing was done at
that time. It seems that there was a gradual increase in emphasis upon agriculture, although hunting and fishing continued to be important. The style of stone knife which was
used is the same as that of the Lungshanoid Culture of
China. In contrast, knives of the Yang Shao Culture are
usually square, sometimes with notches on both sides. This
rectangular form is rather abundant in certain areas such as
northern Hamgyŏng Province. It may have entered Korea
from a different source than the knives which relate to
Lungshan. Connections with the Lungshan may be a useful
way of dating the Plain Pottery Culture. Although there are
many stepped adzes from sites in Hwanghae Province, they
are rare from sites in the Taedong Basin. The step was used
as an aid in hafting; the bevel of the cutting edge is on the opposite side from the step. However, stepped adzes from sites
in Hwanghae Province and the Taedong River Basin are
generally "two stepped," with the blade on the same side as

the step. Some of the single-stepped adzes are small in size, and probably functioned as chisels. It is important to investigate temporal relations of these two forms.

In terms of form, the adze which had the blade on the same side as the step is the original shape. It appears that the central and southern Chinese forms which influenced the Korean adzes were of this form. The change from the single step to the double step seems to represent a change in function. The stepped adze seems to have been used as a hand adze by the attachment of the wooden handle with the curved neck on the opposite side of the step to gouge wooden material. In the case of the form with two steps, the bevelled bit is on the outside of the adze; thus the tool could not be used in a scraping motion. In the case of the stepped adze from Sŏkt'al-li (Fig. 28:30, 31), the opposite side of the step was curved slightly outward so that it would be difficult to attach the adzelike handle. I believe that the implement was grasped in the hand and used as an agricultural tool. The method of constructing the blade on the same side as the haft would make it convenient to dig and push earth outward, away from the person holding the tool. This type had a longer blade, about 21 centimeters on the larger examples and about 16 centimeters on the smaller ones. The examples from Simchol-li were even larger, ranging around 28.5 centimeters and 26.5 centimeters in length (Fig. 29:17, 18) while the smaller forms, with the same blade as the notched adzes, were 5 centimeters and 12.5 centimeters in length (Fig. 29:19, 20). These were probably used as woodcutting tools; the smaller one, however, was probably used as a scraper. Thus the Top-Shape Pottery sites in Hwanghae Province and the Taedong Basin had two types of stepped adzes with separate functions.

Stepped adzes are found widely distributed in Southeast Asia, Polynesia, and southeastern China. They are not found north of Shantung Province in northern China, or north of the Great Wall. The northern limit within China seems to be Kiangsu Province. Probably the stepped adzes were introduced into the Top-Shape Pottery sites of Hwanghae Province and the Taedong Basin from coastal China to the Yellow Sea coast. Dolmens, which are also related to the Plain Pottery Culture, are also found widely in southeastern

China, Southeast Asia, and Taiwan—an interesting distribution in the light of the distribution of the stepped adzes. The northern limit of dolmens seems to be Shantung Province; dolmens might have spread from that area to the northwest coast of the Korean peninsula along the coast of the Yellow Sea.

While most of the elements of the Plain Pottery Culture seem to show influence from the northern China—Siberia region, a few elements such as stepped adzes or dolmens appear to come from central or southern China. Thus the origins of the Plain Pottery Culture are not simple. There were two styles of stepped adzes, the two-step form being an indigenous development. The stepped adzes were found only in Early Plain Pottery sites, while the grooved adzes were later. The different styles of stone arrowheads seem to have chronological significance. Most of the stone arrowheads found in Top-Shape Pottery sites in the northwest had a diamond-shaped cross section and are stemmed; a few with a biconvex section can be included in the same style. Stemmed arrowheads with a diamond-shaped cross section and stemless arrowheads with a flattened hexagonal cross section appear to be part of a set in sites of the later Plain Pottery Period. The form with the flattened hexagonal shape, particularly with grooves on both sides, was obviously a copy of the bronze arrowhead. Top-Shape Pottery sites in Hwanghae and in the Taedong River Basin in which this form of arrowhead was found must belong to the early period of Plain Pottery Culture.

The stone daggers had the same type of cross section as the stone arrowheads—biconvex or diamond shaped—and are stemmed. One exceptional stone dagger, from House Site No. 2 of the Wŏnam-ni site (Taedong River Basin), had grooves on both sides of the central ridge and two steps in the handle. This form seems clearly to be a copy of a bronze dagger with a handle and was apparently of a later time period than the former type. Stone daggers with diamond-shaped cross sections and stems had the same general form as the arrowheads, except that they were bigger and there were notches on both sides of the stem for attaching the handles. These earliest forms of the stone daggers look like stone spears.

In relative terms, the early stages of the development of stone daggers can be dated. Daggers of the spear type found in the Top-Shape Pottery sites of the Taedong Basin and Hwanghae Province probably indicate that these sites are relatively early within this time period. The later polished stone daggers are not known from China, but seem to have developed in various ways in Korea. They are earlier than the bronze daggers, but were used for the same function—that of sticking and piercing. The prototypes of the stone daggers derived from stone arrowheads or spears, the first stage of the transition being from the stemmed, spearlike stone form to the type with the single-stepped handle. These forms were found in sites slightly later in time period than the earliest prototypes. However, the grooved stone examples with the two steps in the handles were obviously copies of bronze daggers and halberds and must surely have come from a later period.

The general explanation for the origin of the stone daggers has been that they were made as copies of bronze weapons; I believe, however, that the prototype was the stemmed stone spear which in turn developed from earlier stone artifacts, which were functional rather than strictly ceremonial.

A few other sites of the Plain Pottery Culture should also be mentioned.

### MISONG-NI CAVE (UPPER LAYER)

Misong-ni is an example of a variation from the Plain Pottery Culture of the Taedong Basin or Hwanghae Province. The site is a large limestone cave 10 kilometers northeast of Uiju in North P'yŏngan Province. Excavation carried out in 1959 revealed two separate cultural layers, the lower yielding Geometric Pottery and the upper yielding Plain Pottery. In addition to Plain Pottery, the upper layer contained stone artifacts such as arrowheads, chisels, jasper pipe-form beads, and spindle whorls, as well as bone needles and awls. Two bronze axes were also found. The Plain Pottery had two vessel forms, one with a constricted neck and the other a deep jar, but they differ from Top-Shape Pottery. Although incised decoration occurred on the rims of some of the deep jars, the folded-over rim was absent (Fig. 38:5–8). One of the unusual features of the jars was the high neck and wide

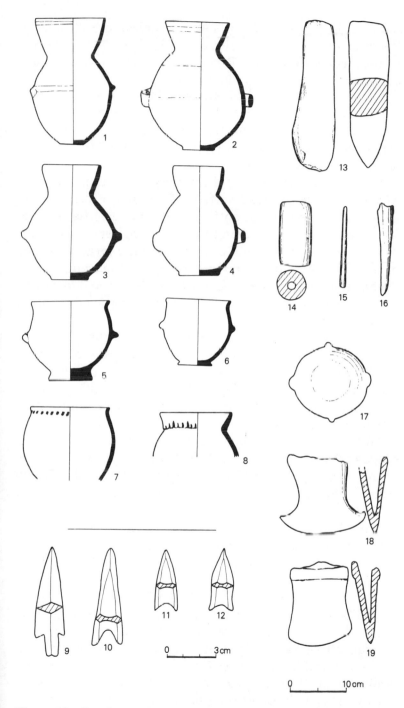

Figure 38. Specimens from the upper layer of the Misong-ni site

mouth (Fig. 38:1–4). Handles were attached to both sides of the body on both forms. These handles appeared at the end of the Geometric Pottery Period of the northwest, but there are no such precedents in Plain Pottery.

In the Middle Period of Karak-ni (to be discussed later) there were small nipplelike handles, which appear to represent a retrogression from more developed forms. Handles are conspicuously absent in Plain Pottery; the Misong-ni examples are thus exceptions.

Another characteristic of the pottery of the upper layer of Misong-ni is the polished surface. This kind of ceramic can be seen in the stone cist coffins of the Sungari Basin, near Kirin; the style must therefore show influence from the ceramics of northeastern China. Among the ceramics found in the dolmens of Mukpang-ni, Kaech'on gun, South P'yŏngan Province, there were some which looked like those of the upper layer of Misong-ni, suggesting a relationship between them.

Sixteen stone arrowheads were unearthed, three of which were the stemmed form with a diamond-shaped cross section (Fig. 38:9), while the remaining specimens were stemless with a hexagonal cross section (Fig. 38:10–12). In this group, a notable feature of some specimens was a depression in the center of both sides.

Two bronze axes were also found. One had a wide, fan-shaped blade at the top (Fig. 38:18), which is a characteristic of the Liaoning Bronze Culture. Again, a relationship is suggested with the Bronze Culture of northeastern China (Fig. 83, 84).

Considering the styles of ceramics as well as bronze and stone artifacts, as well as the absence of iron, it can be said that the upper layer of Misong-ni belongs to the Bronze Age.

## SEJUNG-NI SITE (LAYER II)

The Sejung-ni site, Yŏngbyŏn gun, North P'yŏngan Province, has almost the same characteristics as the southern Korean site of Karak-ni. Sejung-ni is composed of three different cultural layers. Layer I contained Geometric Pottery, while Layer II contained ceramics of the type found at Karak-ni as well as Misong-ni upper layer ceramics and Mukpang-ni ceramics, while Layer II contained greyish,

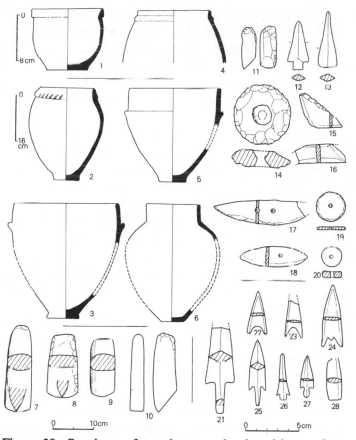

Figure 39. Specimens from the second cultural layer of the Sejung-ni site

straw-mat–impressed pottery plus bronze arrowheads, bronze daggers and sheaths, iron axes, and Ming-tao-ch'ien coins. Among the Karak-ni ceramics excavated from Layer II, the same two vessel forms—the jar with the constricted neck (Fig. 39:1–5) and the deep open jar (Fig. 39:6)—were found. The bottom part of the deep jar form was slightly larger than the base of the Top-Shape Pottery; however, it was still unstable compared to the upper portion of the body. The rim had a folded-over lip decorated with short slanting incisions reminiscent of Karak-ni Pottery. Among the jar-shaped vessels with constricted neck there were some which had a straight rim and a round, full shoulder, again suggesting the ceramics of Karak-ni.

Within this layer, there were other kinds of ceramics, such as those of the upper layer of Misong-ni, which belong to a different cultural tradition. The cultural contents and the dating of this site are very complex. From this same layer, a pedestal cup of black pottery was also found. Black pottery has been found on other Plain Pottery sites, as we have mentioned above.

Stone artifacts from Layer II included flat stone adzes, stone spears, daggers, arrowheads, crescent-shaped stone knives, stepped adzes, grooved adzes, stone sickles, spindle whorls, net sinkers, stone awls, stone saddle querns, disc-shaped stone artifacts, spoked mace heads, stone ornaments, and whetstones (Fig. 39:7–28). These stone artifacts generally accompany Plain Pottery; however, some of them seemed to be from different cultures and time periods. In addition, this cultural layer appears to contain a variety of forms of pottery, like those found in the upper layers of Misong-ni, Mukpang-ni, and Karak-ni.

More than 70 stone arrowheads were found. Most of them were either diamond shaped or near hexagonal in cross section. One exceptional specimen had a triangular cross section and was stemmed (Fig. 39:26), while another had two grooves on the back (Fig. 39:27). These two variations appear to belong to different cultures and time periods.

It is important to note that stepped and grooved adzes were found in the same cultural layer. Two stepped adzes, of the form with the bevel on the opposite side of the step (Fig. 39:10), were found. The stepped portion was poorly defined in both specimens. They were of average length (24 cm and 18 cm respectively). One notched adze was also recovered (Fig. 39:11); its length was only 9 centimeters. Four stone daggers were also unearthed. They were stemmed and had a diamond-shaped cross section; both blades were slightly convex. One stone sickle and a triangular-shaped knife were also recovered (Fig. 39:14, 15). Three comma-shaped stone pendants (termed *magatama* in Japanese) were also found. They were perforated in the upper portion.

As mentioned above, Layer II of the Sejung-ni site could be conjectured to fit into the Karak-ni Culture Period, judging from the ceramics and stone artifacts; however, there seems to be some diversity as well. One foreign trait is the appearance of handles on the ceramics. Both in Karak-ni and Sejung-ni, small nipplelike projections were seen to be attached to the body of the deep jars; however, they were too small for use as actual handles. They seem to be carried over from earlier periods. In addition to these small projections, large, functional handles were found in Sejung-ni. They were of a rounded rectangular shape and were attached either horizontally or vertically. These can also be seen from the upper layer of Misong-ni, although they are not known from Karak-ni. If I were to agree with the opinion of the writer of the report, that Layer II of Sejung-ni represents one component, I would have to recognize that two culture systems, those of Karak-ni and Misong-ni, are included.

## CENTRAL AREA

The middle and southern areas of the peninsula have produced slightly different forms of ceramics from the Top-Shape Pottery of the northwest. The following are some representative Plain Pottery sites of central Korea.

### KARAK-NI SITE

The Karak-ni site, Kwangju, Kyŏnggi Province was excavated by a group of specialists in 1963. Preservation of artifacts and stratigraphy was relatively good. Karak-ni is now within the limits of metropolitan Seoul, but I will use the historical name, Kwangju, for the location. The site is on the north slope of a low hill about 40 meters in elevation. A dwelling site consisting of a rectangular pit 10 meters long from east to west and 7 meters from north to south was excavated. Its depth from the surface varied from 10 to 50 centimeters. No post holes were found; the posts were probably set on the surface of the ground.

Four vessels unearthed from Karak-ni were completely restored, and an additional two were partially restored. These comprised three deep jars, two smaller jars, and one small plate. The paste of two of the vessels was mostly clay and sand and firing was done at a relatively low temperature. The vessels were either reddish brown or yellowish brown in color. The deep jar-shaped vessel form (Plates 14, 15; Fig. 40:1, 2) has a relatively small base (8 to 11 cm in diameter), which is, however, larger than the tiny base of northwestern

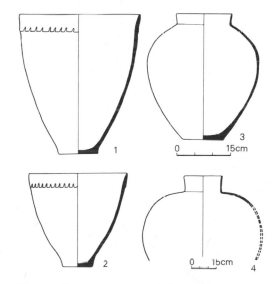

Figure 40. Pottery vessel forms from the Karak-ni site (see Plates 13, 14, 15)

Plain Pottery. The rim area has the same doubled-over lip with incised decoration. One of the complete specimens had a mouth diameter of 8.1 centimeters. A second example had a mouth diameter of 33.4 centimeters, a height of 38.1 centimeters, and a base diameter of 10.8 centimeters. This deep jar seems to be derived in part from the Geometric Pottery of sites such as Amsa-ri, while the incised decoration shows similarities with Geometric Pottery from Tongsam-dong, Pusan. The slightly larger base than those of the northwest seems to be part of a trend toward the enlarging of the base in later time periods.

The jar form with a narrow straight neck had a globular body. A completely restored example (Plate 16; Fig. 40:3) had a mouth diameter of 15 centimeters, a height of 33.9 centimeters, and a basal diameter of 11.4 centimeters. The base of these vessels seems very unstable in comparison to the full body, and the straight mouth does not have any decoration. Thickness of the vessel walls varied from 0.6 to 1 centimeter. This type of pottery, with a small mouth diameter, straight neck, and beautifully curved shoulders, shows greater development than examples from the northwest. This particular vessel form continues until the development of the white porcelain jar form of the Yi Dynasty, yet it is interesting to see how beautifully proportioned the jar form was even at this early date.

I would term the two forms—the deep open jar and the jar with constricted neck—the Karak-ni form of pottery and would consider it to be a diagnostic feature of the Plain Pottery of central Korea. Stone artifacts unearthed from Karak-ni include 1 sickle, 3 convex-bladed arrowheads, 1 awl, 2 spindle whorls, and 3 whetstones (Plate 17).

The stone arrowheads have concave bases, polished edges, and central grooves. The cross section of the arrowheads looks like a distorted hexagon, with concave front and back. This style seems to be a copy of the bronze arrowhead, and it appears after the Early Period of Plain Pottery. The bronze prototype has been found, along with a *pip'a* shaped bronze dagger, from the stone cist coffin of Lou-shang, located in Kan-ching tzu-chu, Lu-ta-shih, Liaoning-sheng (China). The *pip'a* shape refers to a Chinese stringed musical instrument, with a round, pear-shaped sounding board. The flaring sides are thus diagnostic characteristics. It is of interest that there are no stemmed stone arrowheads from Karak-ni up until this time, although they are the common form in the northwest. Two disc-shaped spindle whorls were also found. The Karak-ni site contained many of the most typical artifacts of the Plain Pottery Culture, yet it lacked stone adzes, crescent-shaped stone knives, and polished stone daggers, which are all typical of Plain Pottery sites in general. It is particularly regrettable that no stone daggers were recovered, since these might be useful in dating the site. Similarly, the Yŏksam-dong site did not produce any stone daggers.

## YŎKSAM-DONG SITE

The Yŏksam-dong site in Kwangju is a habitation site on a hill about 90 meters in elevation. It is located about 3 kilometers north of the ferry station on the Han River and is about 4 kilometers from the Karak-ni site. It was excavated in 1966. A rectangular-shaped house structure 16 meters long, 3 meters wide, and 50 to 60 centimeters deep was excavated. Post holes were found along the wall in 1- to 2-meter intervals, and there were burnt remains of posts. No fireplace was found (Fig. 41). The usual two jar forms of the Plain Pottery Period were recovered, and red-painted, polished pottery with a constricted neck was found.

Looking at the completely restored vessels, base forms seem to be about 8.5 centimeters in diameter, with a body which expands in a trumpet form (Plate 18; Fig. 42:2). The lip of the vessel is marked with depressions at intervals of 1 or 0.5 centimeter, and small holes were punctated at 3- to 4-centimeter intervals about 1 centimeter below the lip rim. The same method of marking the lip of the vessel appears in Yayoi pottery in Japan. The small punctates around the rim seem to be a carryover from Geometric Pottery. It is a common feature of the Plain Pottery of the Han River. A reconstructed example had a wide mouth diameter of 29 centimeters and a height of 28 centimeters. The color was reddish brown, and the firing was at a low temperature. The body consisted of clay mixed with coarse sand.

In the same manner as the ceramics found at Karak-ni, the base was formed by the addition of a round clay disc. A similar form can be seen in Yayoi ceramics. The paste con-

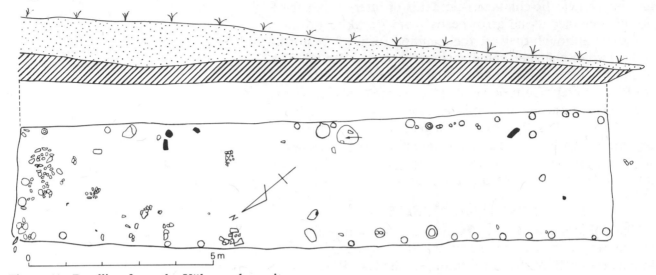

Figure 41. Dwelling from the Yŏksam-dong site

tained an admixture of sand grains, the thickness of the body wall was about 1 centimeter, and the pottery seems to have been fired somewhat harder than the ceramics of other sites. The overall color was greyish brown, with some yellowish-brown or dark brown areas.

A partially restored vessel had a slightly out-curving rim with a short constricted neck and a globular body (Fig. 42:3). Around the lip, decoration was produced by impression. The mouth diameter was 23.3 centimeters and the body diameter was 30 centimeters. The quality of the paste and the color was the same as that of the pottery mentioned above; however, the body wall was only about 0.5 centimeter thick. One small vessel with a short neck and slightly out-curving mouth had a round full body and a thickness of 0.5 centimeter. The mouth diameter was 12.7 centimeters; the body diameter, 17.2 centimeters. Very finely divided mica was mixed with fine clay, and oxidized iron was applied to the surface before it was polished (Fig. 42:5). Another red-painted, polished vessel had a clearly defined neck with a large mouth, slightly out-curving rim, and a globular body.

This is a typical shape for painted and polished ceramics found in cist coffins in central and southern Korea. The round bottom is also an important characteristic. The mouth

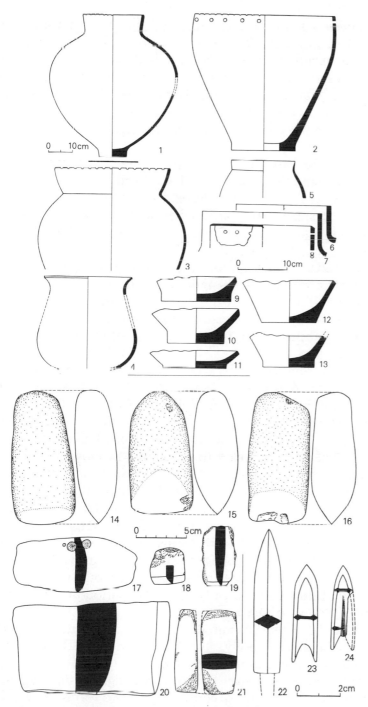

Figure 42. Specimens from the Yŏksam-dong site

diameter was 17.6 centimeters, and the maximum diameter was 20 centimeters. The method of decoration was similar to the jar mentioned above, but the body was slightly thicker (Fig. 42:4). Three examples from a total of five rim sherds were punctated (Fig. 42:6–8). The punctated examples all appear to have been fragments of deep jars, while the unpunctated examples, which are completely plain, appear to be rim sherds from jars with short necks.

From the base sherds, it appears that flat bottoms were predominant (Fig. 42:9–13). Two sherds, from a total of five, were slipped and polished. As for stone artifacts, 3 adzes, 2 small flat planoconvex adzes, 3 arrowheads, 1 crescent-shaped knife, and 6 whetstones were found. One whetstone is illustrated in Fig. 42:20.

The adzes had trapezoidal or rectangular cross sections and biconvex blades. Length was generally 12 to 13 centimeters (Fig. 42:14–16). One of the arrowheads had a diamond-shaped cross section and was stemmed (Fig. 42:22), while the other had a roughly hexagonal cross section and was stemless (Fig. 42:23, 24). The latter form had a groove removed from the center. One of the small, flat planoconvex adzes (Fig. 42:18, 19, 21) was only 3.6 centimeters long, while another was just 6 centimeters. (Plate 17.) These small examples have been termed chisels by the reporters. One rough example of a crescent-shaped stone knife was recovered. The shape appears to be almost rectangular and the blade is poorly finished. Two central holes were only partially perforated (Fig. 42:17). From this site we can see most of the usual assemblage of stone artifacts which accompanies Plain Pottery, with the exception of stone daggers and the stepped and grooved adze forms. The grooved, stemless, hexagonal-sectioned stone arrowheads appear to be copies of bronze arrowheads. The arrowhead form would indicate that the site belongs to a slightly later time period than the Top-Shape Pottery of the northwest.

Materials from Yŏksam-dong appear to resemble those of Karak-ni rather closely. The same two vessel forms were found; the doubled-over rim of Karak-ni, however, was not seen in Yŏksam-dong. At Yŏksam-dong, the lip had impressed and punctated decoration. The two forms of decoration seem to be equivalent.

Both sites yielded stone arrowheads of the stemmed and grooved form, and both lacked stone daggers and stepped and grooved adzes. The absence of the doubled-over rim may show a difference in time period. These two sites could be considered to be representative of the central Korean variant of the Karak-ni Culture.

Karak-ni ceramics can also be found in southern Korea, as exemplified in Location D of the Hoehyŏl-li shell mound, Kimhae (Fig. 49:1, 2). Jar burial seems to be later than Karak-ni ceramics; I have termed the jar coffins Karak-ni Type III. Grave goods from the jar burials, particularly the narrow bronze dagger, would substantiate this relative dating.

## RELATIONSHIP WITH YAYOI POTTERY

If one makes a comparison between the various forms of Karak-ni ceramics in southern Korea and the earliest Yayoi Pottery of Japan, Itatsuke I of Kyushu, it would seem that Karak-ni ceramics might be the origin of Yayoi ceramics. Itatsuke I ceramics have two shapes—the deep jar and the short constricted neck form; in addition, they share the small unstable base and lip incision with Karak-ni. The short-necked form is not found in Jōmon ceramics; it definitely appears to be a foreign introduction into Japan.

In Japan, the established idea in archaeological circles is that Yayoi Pottery developed from Jōmon ceramics. The Yusu ceramics of the Final Jōmon are often cited as a transitional type. However, we can definitely see the strong influence of the Plain Pottery Culture of southern Korea in ceramics, stone artifacts, and burial systems in Late and Final Jōmon communities in northern Kyushu. Therefore, the Yayoi Culture seems to be the product of foreign influences on Late and Final Jōmon. The two ceramic vessel forms of the Plain Pottery Culture can be seen in the Kurokawa, Yusu, and Yamanotera types of Japanese ceramics. Particularly the narrow base and lip incision appear to be characteristic of the jar form of pottery of Karak-ni. Yayoi Pottery appears to have its roots in the Late and Final Jōmon as a result of influence from Korea. Another instance of southern Korean influence can be seen in the dolmens, which appear at the end of the Jōmon Period in northern Kyushu.

In addition, the stone tools which accompany Yayoi ceramics—the crescent-shaped knife, the planoconvex adze, and the arrowheads—are the same shapes as those found with the Plain Pottery of Korea.

## *OKSŎNG-NI SITE*

The house site found from the lower layer of Dolmen B1 of Oksŏng-ni of P'aju in Kyŏnggi Province is an important discovery. On a hill about 82 to 100 meters in height behind Oksŏng village, about 20 northern-style dolmens have been located. These are relatively small in size, for their type.

Dolmen B1 was located on the ridge of the hill and was the largest example in Location B (Fig. 43). The cover stone was split in two and the long axis ran parallel to the ridge in a southeast direction. The dimensions were 3.30 meters by 1.90 meters by 4 centimeters. The side wall of the cist under the cover stone had fallen into the earth and was buried; however, the four supporting stones remained intact. Inside the stone cist, at a depth of about 50 centimeters from the ground surface, a planoconvex adze was found.

In the course of the investigation of Dolmen B1, a portion of a house site was uncovered under the dolmen. The first discovery was that of a fire pit, showing burned earth along the side; after the discovery of this feature, a house site was uncovered. The floor surface of the house site was 15.7 meters long and 3.7 meters wide; the size was similar to the example from the Yŏksam-dong site (Fig. 41). The four corners of the house were at right angles and the wall was perpendicular to the floor. The depth of the house pit was 60 centimeters to the northeastern corner, and less than 30 centimeters in the other areas. Clay was spread over the floor to a depth of about 3 to 4 centimeters. No remains of posts could be found in the center of the house; yet along the walls there were holes for small pillars. The same form can be seen in the house site at Yŏksam-dong.

Two fireplaces, each consisting of an oval pit 60 centimeters by 40 centimeters with a depth of about 10 centimeters, were found to the east of the center. It appears that considerable time elapsed between the burning and desertion of the house pit and the construction of Dolmen B1. There is no trace of the actual destruction of the house site through the construction of the dolmen.

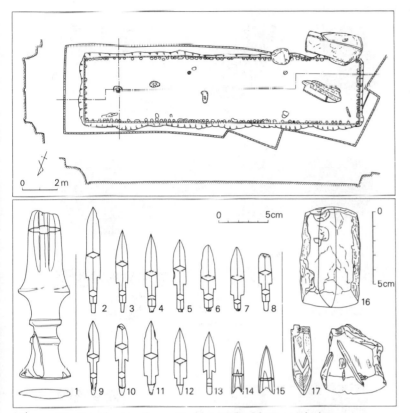

Figure 43. Specimens from Dolmen Bl, Oksŏng-ni site

Artifacts were relatively few, considering the size of the house site. A polished dagger, stone arrowheads, spindle whorls, and the lower portion of a saddle quern were also found.

More than 120 potsherds, red or brown in color, with quartz or feldspar temper, were found. A few of the sherds were comparatively harder than the others, and contained fewer grains of sand temper. The sherds were 0.85 to 1.25 centimeters thick and were relatively coarse, with parallel striations on their interior faces.

Ten of the eleven rim sherds were decorated with small punctates around the lip. This is a frequent motif on Plain Pottery in the Han River Basin. The same pottery is seen from Dŏkp'ung-ni in Kwangju (Fig. 44) in addition to the Yŏksam-dong ceramics. In addition to the ceramics at Dŏkp'ung-ni, there were crescent-shaped stone knives, planoconvex adzes, diamond cross-sectioned arrowheads,

Figure 44. Pottery sherds from the Han River Basin
(Dŏkp'ung-ni site)

disc-shaped spindle whorls, and saddle querns (Figs. 45, 46). I expect that Yŏksam-dong and Dŏkp'ung-ni are both of the same general time period, preceding Oksŏng-ni.

A flat base from a deep jar-shaped vessel, apparently with straight sides, was also found. A similar vessel was found from Tangdong-ni, about 6.5 kilometers distant from Oksŏng-ni. The latter example also had a punctate decoration around the lip. A polished dagger, slightly chipped on the tip and with a length of 16.8 centimeters, had two parallel grooves along both sides of the central ridge and a handle of the two-stepped style.

Twenty-two polished stone arrowheads were recovered (Fig. 43:2–15). Fourteen of them were stemmed and had a diamond cross section. In addition to a number of fragments, two arrowheads with a distorted hexagonal cross section, lacking stems, were found. All of the stemmed examples had a hexagonal cross section in the basal and stem portions. The stems were short, being less than 1 centimeter in length. The stemless forms had a polished cutting edge around the perimeter of the arrowhead with the exception of the concave base. Of the two complete specimens, one was 5 centimeters long and the other 5.5 centimeters. Two of the spindle whorls were flat and disc shaped. The central hole was perforated from one side. One was 6.4 centimeters in diameter, while the other was 5.9 centimeters.

In addition, the broken portion of a stone mace head was recovered. The radius, from the central hole to the edge, appeared to be about 5.5 centimeters (Fig. 43:17).

Two flat planoconvex adzes were also found. One was 7.1 centimeters long and 1.1 centimeters thick (Fig. 43:16), while the other, which was incomplete, was 0.9 centimeter thick.

Three fragments of the lower portion of saddle querns were also found. The material appears to be micaceous schist. The reconstructed size of one specimen was 26 centimeters long, 13.5 centimeters wide, and 2 to 4 centimeters thick.

The two forms of arrowheads and the polished stone dagger suggest that the site may date to some time after the initial portion of the Plain Pottery Culture, since the grooved arrowheads and the stepped-handle type of the stone dagger (Fig. 43:1) appear to be copies of bronze prototypes. Char-

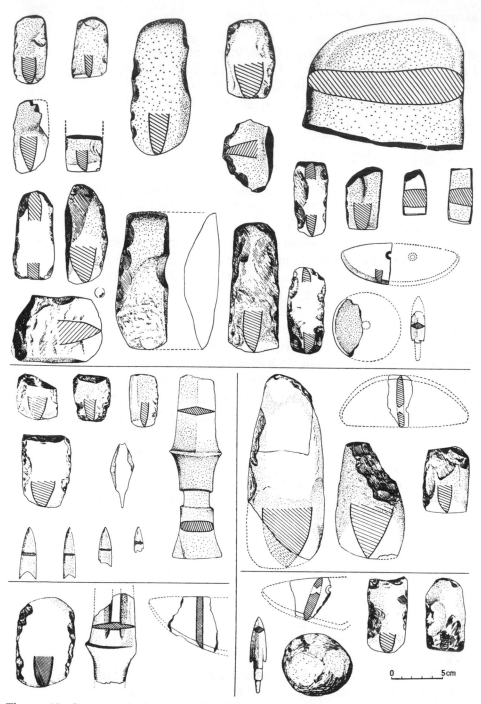

0        5cm

Figure 45. Stone tools from the Han River Basin (1): top section, Dŏkp'ung-ni site, Kwangju; left middle, Myŏngil-li, Kwangju; right middle, Nonhyŏn-ni site, Kwangju; lower right, Munjong-ni site; lower left, Kodŏng-ni site, Kwangju

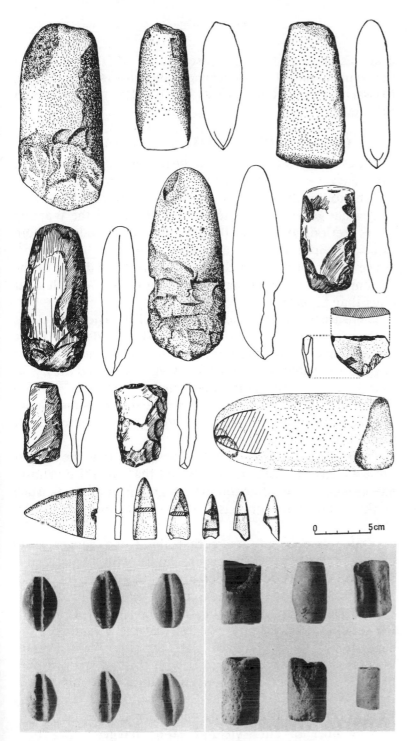

Figure 46.  Stone tools from the Han River Basin (2)

coal was unearthed from House Site B1 of Oksŏng-ni, and the result obtained by Geochron Laboratories, Cambridge, Massachusetts (GX–0554) was 2590 ± 105 B.P., or about 640 B.C.

## CHRONOLOGY OF THE STONE DAGGER

The established opinion up to the present has been that the stone dagger was a copy of the bronze and iron dagger. According to this theory, the earliest date of the slender bronze dagger has generally been set toward the end of the Warring States Period, about the third century B.C., judging from associated iron remains and also Ming-tao-ch'ien coins. However, problems immediately arise from the dating of the Oksŏng-ni site to about the seventh century B.C., which is far older than the earlier posited dates.

There are two approaches to this problem. The first relates to the original prototype of the polished stone dagger. There are a number of possibilities, such as stone spears, bronze daggers and halberds, and bronze dagger axes, and the *pip'a*-shaped dagger (termed the "Liaoning bronze dagger")—with flaring sides. The Liaoning-style bronze dagger is older than the narrow dagger in Korea, and should be considered as the most likely prototype.

The second point which must be made is that the slender bronze dagger is older in time period than the third century B.C. It is often found in contexts lacking iron artifacts, such as the rectangular stone cist coffin of Koejŏng-dong, Taejŏn.

While there is no doubt that the stone dagger from Oksŏng-ni is a copy of the bronze dagger with a handle, it is not clear whether the slender bronze dagger or the *pip'a*-shaped dagger (with the blade convex near the handle) was copied. Depending on which form is the prototype, the dating should differ. I would suggest that the seventh century B.C. should be a standard date for the Plain Pottery associated with the stone dagger with the two-stepped handle. The same stone dagger was used until quite late in particular areas; for example, the P'onam-dong site, Kangnung City, of Kangwŏn Province.

A number of sites yielding stone daggers have been radiocarbon dated. Dolmen No. 13, of the so-called southern

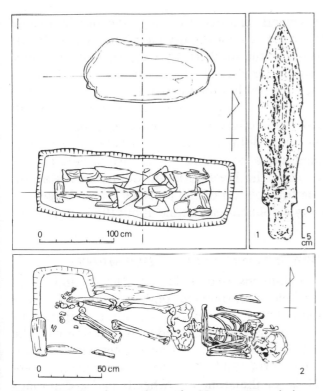

Figure 47. Specimens from the Hwangsŏng-ni site,
Dolmen No. 3

style, at Hwangsŏng-ni, Chech'ŏn-gun, Ch'ungch'ŏng Province, was surveyed in 1962 (Fig. 47). The stone cist, covered by a relatively small stone, contained an almost complete human skeleton (Fig. 47:2). The associated grave goods consisted only of a single polished stone dagger. A fragment of bone was sent to Geochron Laboratories and a date of 2360 ± 370 B.P. (GX–0555) was obtained. The range of error of 370 years seems exceptionally large; however, it reflects the smallness of the sample. The calendrical date should be about 410 B.C.

The polished stone dagger (Fig. 47:1) was a small example fashioned of slate. The lower portion of the body is concave on both sides, suggesting the notched portion of the slender bronze dagger. While is is not certain that the slender bronze dagger is a prototype, it would be appropriate to date the dagger to the fifth century B.C. The Oksŏng-ni house site was dated to the seventh century B.C., and the northern-style dolmen over it must be of a slightly later date. The dolmens of Hwangsŏng-ni of the southern style appear to be of a later date than that of Oksŏng-ni. The basis for this kind of reasoning is the general hypothesis that the southern style of dolmen, consisting of large stones sitting on very small stones or resting directly on the ground, is a degenerated form of the northern dolmen, which consists of a table form, with side stones and a large "lid." The carbon date for the human bones from the Hwangsŏng-ni dolmen gives an indication of the time period of the polished stone dagger, or the southern-style dolmen—sometime about the fifth century B.C.

## HWANGSŎNG-NI SITE—DOLMENS

Some of the dolmens (No. 1, No. 2, No. 7, and C) at Hwangsŏng-ni yielded red-painted, polished ceramics as well as Plain Pottery. From Dolmen No. 1 a stone dagger, with broken tip and handle, was unearthed in association with the ceramics. From Dolmen No. 2, a stone dagger with the two-stepped handle form and ten stone arrowheads were unearthed. Three of the stone arrowheads had a diamond-shaped section and stem, while seven arrowheads were stemless with a hexagonal section. From Dolmen No. 7, a stone dagger with a single-stepped handle and six stemmed arrowheads with a diamond cross section were found (Plate 24). Of this last group of arrowheads, the lower body and stem portion of one example was hexagonal in cross section. From Dolmen C, a restorable Plain Pottery vessel and two red-painted polished vessels were recovered.

Like all of the other dolmens at Hwangsŏng-ni, Dolmen C was of the southern type. The cover stone of Dolmen C was 1.8 meters long from east to west, 1 meter wide from north to south, with a thickness of 30 centimeters. The stone cist was constructed of a number of slabs set upright into the earth, the floor being constructed of two slabs with stones piled up around the coffin. The interior length of the cist coffin was 1.35 meters from east to west, 50 centimeters from north to south, and the depth was 40 centimeters. The ceramics appear to have been in their original location, which was on the eastern edge of the coffin.

The paste of the Plain Pottery contained sand temper and the surface was well polished, while the neck was almost straight and the mouth rim was curved slightly outward. The body was roughly globular in shape, and the bottom was small and flat. This kind of unstable base seems to follow the tradition of Plain Pottery. The height of the vessel was 24 centimeters; the mouth diameter, 10 centimeters; the bottom diameter, 9.3 centimeters; and the thickness, 0.7 centimeter. The shape is typical of the later Plain Pottery of the southern portions of the peninsula; connections can particularly be seen with Koejŏng-dong in Pusan.

The paste of the red-painted polished pottery was fine clay, and the thickness was 0.4 centimeter. The base was rounded and the lip portion curved outward from a constricted neck. (Plates 19, 20.) The shape is typical of the red-painted polished pottery of the central and southern portions of Korea, and examples of these from dolmens or box-shaped stone cist coffins in South Kyŏngsang Province have the same characteristics. It is particularly interesting to see the rounded bottom of the red-painted polished pottery in association with the flat-bottomed Plain Pottery. Other objects from Hwangsŏng-ni are shown in Plates 21–24.

### P'ONAM-DONG SITE

The P'onam-dong site, Kangnŭng City, Kangwŏn Province, is important because it confirms that the Plain Pottery was still being used in central and southern Korea after iron was introduced in the fourth and third centuries B.C. P'onam-dong was discovered by accident in 1963. The site, situated on a small hill, yielded stone celts, planoconvex adzes, crescent-shaped stone knives, stone arrowheads, polished stone daggers, stone sickles, grindstones, spindle whorls, foot-shaped adzes, whetstones, discs, nephrite ornaments, bronze arrowheads, and iron fragments, in addition to Plain Pottery (Fig. 48). The Plain Pottery vessels could not be reconstructed. The sand-tempered sherds are soft and reddish brown in color.

With the exception of the foot-shaped adze (Fig. 48:13), all of the stone artifacts were of types associated hitherto with Plain Pottery. Of the stone daggers found, four had the two-stepped handle, and one was stemmed. Six of the eight

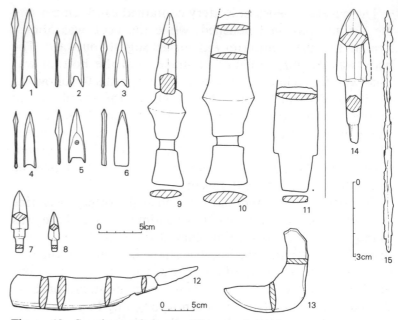

Figure 48. Specimens from the P'onam-dong site

stone arrowheads had a hexagonal cross section, while two had a diamond-shaped cross section and were stemmed (Fig. 48:7, 8). One of the stemmed arrowheads had a hexagonal cross section in the portion near the stem, indicating that it is a copy of a bronze example. The bronze examples from the site had the same shape. All of the bronze arrowheads (Fig. 48:14) were very badly disintegrated; one specimen had an octagonal cross section while the stepped stem was round.

The P'onam-dong site was not scientifically excavated, and the exact location of the iron artifacts (Fig. 48:15) is uncertain. If the association of iron with the artifacts previously mentioned is secure, it would seem that the site could be dated to the Late Plain Pottery Period of central Korea.

## SOUTHERN AREA

Two or three important Plain Pottery sites have been found in the Pusan area since independence. These are Sajik-dong, Tongnae, and Koejŏng il[one]-dong and i[two]-dong. In addition, jar burial sites which appear to be part of the Plain Pottery Culture are the Nangmin-dong site, Tongnae, the Hoehyŏl shell mound, Kimhae, and the Sinch'ang-ni site, Kwangsan-gun, South Chŏlla Province.

### KIMHAE SHELL MOUND, LOCATION D

The Kimhae shell mound has been famous ever since its excavation in 1920 by Sueji Umehara and Kosaku Hamada. The most recent period of site occupation appears to be about the first century A.D., judging from the discovery of Wang Mang coins. The date seems to be appropriate, judging from the similarities with artifacts from the Ungch'ŏn shell mound of Ch'angwon-gun, South Kyŏngsang Province, which has been excavated three times since 1959. That site was dated to the first century A.D. by radiocarbon.

From 1934 to 1945, Tojin Kayamoto excavated Location D, the top area to the east of the location excavated by Hamada and others, and discovered dolmens, box-type stone cist coffins, and jar burials from which a bronze dagger and bronze planing tools were found.

Three jar burials, numbered 1 to 3, were found (Fig. 49:1, 2). Although they were broken, it was possible to reconstruct the original shape. The jars were made after the tradition of Karak-ni Pottery. This would appear to substantiate the idea that the Yayoi Pottery of Kyushu was somehow derived from the Karak-ni–type ceramics of southern Korea.

Burial No. 1 of Location D, Kimhae, contained bronze artifacts; however, they were too disintegrated for the original shape to be reconstructed. From Burial No. 3, 3 pipe-shaped pieces of dark nephrite (Fig. 49: 6–8), 2 bronze daggers (Fig. 49:1, 2) and 8 bronze planing tools were recovered (Fig. 69:3–14). The bronze daggers will be discussed later. The bronze planing tools were very badly disintegrated; but they very much resembled the examples found in association with a red-painted polished jar and bronze dagger from a stone cist grave surrounded with cut stones, from Saro-ri, Yangju-gun, Kyŏnggi Province, or the remains of a bronze planing tool which were found in association with bronze daggers and bronze mirrors with geometric decoration and two knobs for suspension, from Panch'on-ni, Taedong-gun, South P'yŏngan Province.

The bronze planing tool was used in the Ch'un Ch'iu (Spring and Autumn Annals) Period of the Warring States

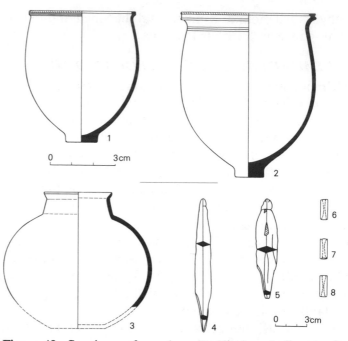

Figure 49. Specimens from Area D, Kimhae shell mound

Period of China, and should be dated to the Bronze Age of Korea. The Korean examples (Fig. 74:3) have been discovered in association with iron adzes, mirrors with fine decoration and knobs for suspension, and slender bronze daggers from stone tombs in Songsan-ni, Pongsan-gun, Hwanghae Province. In addition, iron planing tools have been found together with Ming-tao-chi'ien coins under stone piles at the site of Yongyŏn-dong, Wiwŏn-gun, North P'yŏngan Province. From the association of iron wares and Ming-tao-ch'ien coins, a dating of the fourth and third centuries B.C. is probably appropriate.

The western slope of the Kimhae shell mound, excavated by Hamada and Umehara, probably belongs to the first century A.D., from crossdating with the Ungch'ŏn shell mound. However, the burial area in Location D of the eastern top area can be estimated to be before the second century B.C. at the latest, judging from the styles of the bronze daggers that were found. The cultural contexts of the two areas of the Kimhae site are different, and two occupations of different periods should be recognized.

In the report, the ceramics from the western slope are classified into three categories: bluish-black ceramics, reddish unglazed pottery, and dark brown unglazed pottery. These are the same as the ceramics from the Ungch'ŏn shell mound and are distinct from the earlier Plain Pottery in their shape and method of manufacture. The reddish unglazed ceramics appear to be part of the tradition of Plain Pottery from earlier periods; but various new styles appear to have developed. No bronze artifacts were found from the western slope area, yet many iron arrowheads, iron knives, and antler knife handles were found. These were the same as the specimens from the Ungch'ŏn shell mound. Both of these components fall completely within the Iron Age.

As mentioned earlier, the Hoehyŏl shell mound of Kimhae had two kinds of occupation from different time periods. Location D may be termed Kimhae I while the site on the western site on the western slope of Kimhae can be termed Kimhae II.

The term "Kimhae Pottery" should be used only for the ceramics from the Iron Age site on the western slope. However, Iron Age sites contain a variety of different wares, including soft red or black ceramics and bluish-black hard wares. It is not clear which of these should be included in the term "Kimhae Pottery." In Location D, red-painted polished pottery and Karak-ni Pottery showed the tradition of the Plain Pottery Culture before the Christian era. These types should not be included within Kimhae Pottery.

### SAJIK-DONG SITE

Sajik-dong, Tongnac, was found by accident in 1964, and the site was mostly destroyed. Although there was little indication of other cultural remains, a cist coffin, with its long axis running east-west, was discovered. The four walls and cover stone were constructed of slabs, and small pebbles were spread to create a floor. No dolmen was found over the cist coffin; it is impossible to determine whether one previously existed. A large and small Plain Pottery vessel were located near the north wall; the large vessel was restorable. It is said that two stone daggers were placed in the large jar.

The same method of construction, using single slabs for the walls and lid, was seen in the cist under Dolmen C of

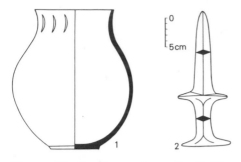

Figure 50. Specimens from the Sajik-dong site (see Plates 25, 26)

Hwangsŏng-ni and was a common means of construction in the southern part of Korea. A similar stone coffin was found at Sŏngmun-ni, Ch'angwŏn-gun. It contained a stone dagger with a one-step handle.

A Plain Pottery vessel from the Sajik-dong site, Tongnae, is preserved in the Pusan National University Museum (Plate 25, Fig. 50:1). The body was roundish, full in the upper portion rather than in the middle, and the mouth was curved slightly outward. The base was small and flat.

Decoration consisted of short slanting lines which resemble nail impressions. The paste contained an admixture of sand, and the body was thin (0.4 to 0.6 centimeter). The decoration technique seems reminiscent of Karak-ni Pottery. The pottery was fired at a low temperature, and was soft and reddish. The height was 24 centimeters, the mouth diameter 13.5 centimeters, and the base diameter about 8 centimeters. The shape was distorted, apparently through tilting of the vessel during firing.

Both stone daggers were of the style with the one-step handle. In one of the reports on the site, it was recorded that one of them had a two-step handle, but according to Yong-ki Kim, who collected the artifacts, the two-step example came from another site. One of the specimens, which is in the Pusan National University Museum, is 22.7 centimeters long and is made of clay slate stone. The top of the handle and the guard have the same width (Plate 26, Fig 50:2).

The gradual widening of the dagger guard and the top of the handle appear to be special features of central and southern Korea. A good example of this type is the dagger with the one-step handle from Dolmen No. 6, Hwangsŏng-ni; other examples of this extreme kind of development have been found in the stone cist coffin from Mugye-ri, Kimhae and a stone cist coffin from Koejŏng-i-dong, Pusan.

## KOEJŎNG-I-DONG SITE, PUSAN

Koejŏng-il-dong, Pusan City yielded one almost perfect Plain Pottery vessel, and Koejŏng-i-dong, of the same area, yielded red-painted polished pottery, a polished stone dagger, and polished arrowheads.

The Koejŏng-i-dong site is located on a hill at the foot of Mount Ch'onma. The stone cist coffin was found accidental-

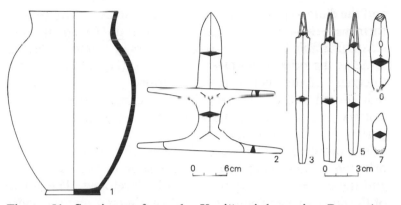

Figure 51. Specimens from the Koejŏng-i-dong site, Pusan (see Plates 27, 28)

ly in the course of construction. Although portions of the cist were destroyed, a portion of the side wall of the chamber was found intact. It consisted of cut stones about 20 centimeters in diameter. In addition, a floor slab was also found. A slab which appeared to be the lid had a length of 1.6 meters, a width of 0.5 meter and a thickness of about 20 centimeters. Around the stone cist there was a pile of cut stones varying from 5 to 20 centimeters in diameter. From the remnant of the side wall, it seems that the original length of the coffin was about 1.8 meters, and the depth, 70 centimeters. The upper stone of the dolmen could not be found in this site; thus it is not clear whether this stone cist coffin was the lower portion of a dolmen or an independent stone cist grave.

From the site of Koejŏng-i-dong, 1 red-painted polished vessel, 1 polished stone dagger, and 5 polished stone arrowheads were unearthed. The red-painted polished vessel (Plate 27; Fig. 51:1) was made of fine clay, and the surface of the vessel and the inside of the rim were painted with oxidized iron and polished. The oxidized iron remained on most of the surface except for some portions where it had peeled off; it was noteworthy to find that the oxidized iron was painted even inside the rim. The vessel was not of the typical shape of red-painted polished ceramics usually found in the stone cist graves in South Kyŏngsang Province, such as Dolmen C of Hwangsŏng-ni. Instead, it resembled the Plain Pottery from Dolmen C of Hwangsŏng-ni or Koejŏng-il-dong. The height was 33.1 centimeters, the mouth diameter 15.2 centimeters, and the diameter of the flat base, 10 centimeters. The general form was that of a deep jar, with an out-curving lip. The small, unstable bottom of 10 centimeters in diameter was the same as the other examples of Plain Pottery. However, the thickness of the sherds and the refined paste resemble the red-painted polished pottery. The vessel resembles the Plain Pottery tradition in its shape and the red-painted polished pottery in paste and body.

The polished stone dagger (Plate 28, Fig. 51:2) was of the one-step–handle type; however, the style of the handle top and the dagger guard were unusually developed. The length of the dagger when found was 14.1 centimeters and the width of the guard was 22.6 centimeters. The restored width of the upper portion of the handle was 25.2 centimeters. If one compares this specimen with one from a cist coffin at Mugye-ri, Kimhae, it appears that the blade was refashioned before interment and was not intended for actual use. The example from Mugye-ri had a handle 11.5 centimeters long, with a blade of 46 centimeters; the width of the top of the handle was 27 centimeters. Two of the five polished stone arrowheads (Fig. 51:3–7) were only partially completed. Three of them were of the stemmed type, with a diamond-shaped cross section. All three specimens are broken on the top and are unusually long. They were not intended for practical use.

## KOEJŎNG-IL-DONG SITE, PUSAN

This site is on the same ridge as Koejŏng-i-dong,* and was also found in the course of road construction. The site did not yield any stone cists or accumulations of pebbles; it was probably a habitation area. The only find consisted of Plain Pottery, which is useful in defining the typical shape of ceramics in the southern part of the peninsula (Plates 29, 30; Fig. 52).

The paste was not as fine as that of the red-painted polished ceramics, the firing having taken place at a lower temperature. The body was slightly thicker than the former (0.9 to 1.2 centimeters) and the color was reddish. The form of the vessel was almost the same as that of the red-painted

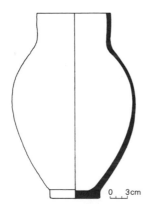

Figure 52.  Pottery vessel from the Koejŏng-il-dong site, Pusan (see Plate 29)

0   3cm

*[Translators' Note: The term il-dong refers to No. 1 "dong" in Koejŏng, and i-dong to No. 2 "dong." The reader should take care not to confuse these separate sites.]

polished ceramics with the exception of the rim, which curved outward from the straight neck. The height was 32.8 centimeters, which is almost the same as that of the former vessel; perhaps they were made by the same artisan. The silhouettes of both vessels show the same curving lines. The site yielded no remains other than pottery; it is difficult, therefore, to establish its chronological position, but the technique and shape of the pottery indicate the same date as that of the former.

The structure of the stone cist chamber of Koejŏng-i-dong is similar to that of the Mugye-ri site in Kimhae, and the styles of the grave goods—stone daggers and arrowheads—are the same from both sites (Fig. 53); therefore, we can assume that the two sites are of the same relative date. From the stone cist chamber of the Mugye-ri site of Kimhae, red-painted polished potsherds were recovered. These finds belong to the later period of the Bronze Age, before the introduction of such iron objects as iron arrowheads.

### NANGMIN-DONG SITE

This jar burial site, near Tongnae, was accidentally exposed when the end of the hill of Nangmin-dong was cut during railway construction. A total of four jars was found. Two reddish jars were placed in the ground with their mouths together. One of the vessels was a red-painted polished jar. The shape of the other three jars is not clear because they were broken; however, they appear to be close to the vessel types found in Koejŏng-il-dong and i-dong. From one of these broken jars, a glass pipe-shaped ornament and an iron ring were recovered.

It appears that Plain Pottery was in general use in this area for burials. Considering the style of the vessels and the associated grave goods, the ceramics appear to belong to the Late Period of the Plain Pottery Culture of the southern portion of the peninsula. It seems that Plain Pottery continued to be used for a long time in the southern portions of the peninsula, judging from the number of examples found in association with iron objects. The P'onam-dong site of Kangnŭng appears to be an example. Among the burial jars from Nangmin-dong, a large jar with a pair of handles placed near the middle of the vessel appears to be similar to

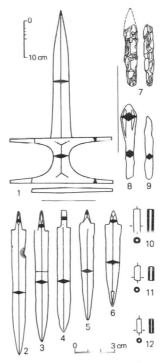

Figure 53. Specimens from the Mugye-ri site, Kimhae

the example from Sinch'ang-ni, Kwangsan-gun, South
Chŏlla Province; in addition, these sites all contain iron objects. The latest date of the burial jars from Nangmin-dong
should not be later than the first century B.C., considering
the style of the Plain Pottery.

## CHRONOLOGY AND EVOLUTION
## OF THE PLAIN POTTERY CULTURE

Heretofore I have been trying to systematize the origin,
formation and development of the Plain Pottery Culture by
citing representative sites in each area. In addition to the sites
previously mentioned, there are also a number of somewhat
divergent Plain Pottery sites from South and North Hamgyŏng Province; for lack of space, however, I have not included them. The Plain Pottery Culture appears to be earliest
in the northwest of the peninsula. One of the diagnostic characteristics is the so-called Top-Shape vessel, which is a deep
jar form. The other form, which is always found in association, is a jar with a constricted neck. The two forms together
are characteristic of the Plain Pottery Culture, and their appearance together in Yayoi Pottery must reflect influence
from southern Korea.

The two vessel forms seem to have different origins. The
deep jar form seems to have originated through the attaching
of a small flat base to the pointed bottom of Geometric Pottery; the relation with Geometric Pottery can also be seen in
the placing of punctate decoration or short slanting lines
around the mouth rim. On the other hand, the jar form with
the short constricted neck appears to have originated in the
northern or northeastern parts of China. The new form,
semiglobular with a constricted neck and flat bottom, marks
the end of the hemispherical shape of the Geometric Pottery
and the beginning of the Plain Pottery Culture.

### EARLY PERIOD

Artifacts which accompany the Top-Shape ceramics of the
northwest include stone celts, stepped adzes, thin planoconvex adzes, crescent-shaped stone knives, and stone arrowheads. These are almost the same as the examples from
northern China, indicating that the Plain Pottery Culture of
northwestern Korea had deep affinities with the prehistoric

cultures of northern China. In particular, the crescent-shaped stone knife resembles Lungshan prototypes rather than Yang Shao; it would seem that the Top-Shape Pottery Culture of the northwest is contemporary with Lungshan. Since Lungshan is not dated scientifically, we can only estimate the general time period. From the Top-Shape Pottery Culture of Sinhŭng-dong, bronze buttons may be comparable to similar objects from the Karasuk Culture in Siberia. The dates for the Karasuk have been estimated to range from 1300 to 700 B.C.; the Top-Shape Pottery component of Sinhŭng-dong, therefore, could date as early as the end of the second millennium B.C., or as late as the first part of the first millennium B.C. From Mound No. 2 of the Shih-erh-t'ai-ying-tzu site of Ch'ao-yang Hsien in Liaoning, a bronze button was found together with the Liaoning-style bronze dagger (*pip'a* style); the site was estimated to have been occupied in the first half of the first millennium B.C. at the latest. House Site No. 1 of the Wŏnam-ni site, in which a spear-shaped stone dagger with a short stem was found, could be considered to belong to the Early Period of Plain Pottery; no bronze object was found in it. However, Dwelling Site No. 2, which yielded a stone dagger with grooves on the blade and a two-stepped handle, belongs to a different period from House Site No. 1. The Top-Shape Pottery sites of the northwest, which belong to the Early Period of Plain Pottery Culture, must date from the end of the second millennium to the early first millennium B.C.

## MIDDLE PERIOD

Pottery of the Karak-ni type appears to be the diagnostic feature of the Middle Period of the Plain Pottery Culture. One notable characteristic is that the base is slightly larger than that of the Top-Shape Pottery. This can be seen through a comparison of a vessel from House Site No. 2, Sŏkt'al-li, in which the ratio of mouth to the base is 7:1, and a vessel from Karak-ni, in which the ratio is about 3:1. Both Top-Shape Pottery and Karak-ni Pottery have a doubled-over mouth rim and short slanting lines of decoration on the rims. The neck of the jar form, which is associated with Top-Shape Pottery, is only slightly constricted, in contrast with the longer, constricted straight neck of Karak-ni Pottery.

Karak-ni also possesses a number of stone artifacts, such as stone sickles and arrowheads with a flat hexagonal cross section, which are never found in sites of the Top-Shape Pottery.

Although there is no means of estimating the absolute date of sites of the Karak-ni type, they appear to fit into the Middle Period of the Plain Pottery Culture. The associated stone arrowheads appear to have been influenced by bronze arrowheads; however, bronze artifact production appears to have been limited at that time period.

The Yŏksam-dong site of Kwangju appears to belong to almost the same period as the Karak-ni site. The same two vessel forms, and the same ratio of mouth to base, prevail. However, the doubled-over rim is not present at Yŏksam-dong. Instead, lip incision is present on the jars with short constricted necks, and punctate decoration was applied on the lip of the deep jar form. The latter appears to be a carry-over from the Geometric Pottery tradition. The neck portion is narrow and vertical in the same style as Karak-ni Pottery.

Two red-painted polished vessels were found with the Plain Pottery at Yŏksam-dong. This association of the two types is common on other sites from the north to the south of the peninsula.

Stone arrowheads from Yŏksam-dong were of the same two styles as Karak-ni. In both sites, stone daggers were absent. Since the Yŏksam-dong site did not produce the folded-over rim which was found at Karak-ni, it may be from a slightly later time period. I would like to call the ceramics of Yŏksam-dong Karak-ni II and the ceramics of Karak-ni itself Karak-ni I.

The jar coffins of Location D of the Kimhae shell mound have many characteristics of Karak-ni Pottery, including the very small base and the ratio of mouth to base diameter. In addition, Kimhae pottery has a well-developed rim and incised horizontal decoration either immediately below the rim or on the body. The innovations represent a departure from the original Karak-ni Pottery, and should be called Karak-ni III. All three of the Karak-ni styles have great similarities with Yayoi Pottery, such as those from the Itatsuke and Tateyashiki sites of Fukuoka Prefecture. In particular, the method of thickening the lip instead of doubling it over, the

incised horizontal decoration on the body, and the small foot
are shared characteristics.

As mentioned previously, bronze objects of undefined
shape were found in Jar Coffin No. 1, Location D, Kimhae
shell mound; in addition, a pipe-shaped ornament, a bronze
dagger, and a bronze planing tool were found in Jar Burial
No. 3. I have termed this particular style of bronze dagger
Style IIBb (see chapter 4), which is estimated to date around
the second century B.C. by a similar dagger in the grave of
Pujo Yegun. In Japan, jar burials containing slender bronze
daggers are thought to date to the end of the Early Yayoi.
The jar coffins at Location D, Kimhae shell mound resemble
those from the beginning of Yayoi, and their dating must be
relatively similar.

In northwestern Korea, sites dating to the fourth and third
centuries B.C. contain bronze objects such as daggers and
dagger axes (termed *ko* in Chinese) together with iron artifacts; also found in these sites are greyish ceramics
decorated with straw mat or checked mat impressions. This
pottery was slightly harder and finer than Plain Pottery;
however, it is not as hard as the ceramics of the first century
A.D. or the early forms of Kaya ceramics, illustrated in Plates
31 and 32. The same type of mat or checked impression was
used extensively on the ceramics of the Warring States
Period of China; these ceramics must be the predecessors of
the Korean examples. A decorative motif was carved on a
paddle, which was used to shape the ceramics as they were
being formed. The type of soft grey impressed pottery diffused to central and southern Korea rather late. Although
sherds have been found from a number of locations, other
"attributes" of this culture are as yet unknown, and no truly
representative sites have yet been found.

In the central and northern portions of the peninsula, the
grey impressed ceramics were perhaps used together with
Plain Pottery until the first century B.C. These two kinds of
pottery were mixed in the shell mounds of Ungch'ŏn and
Kimhae, which date from the first century A.D.

## LATE PERIOD

Characteristics of the Late Period Plain Pottery include
the lack of doubled-over rim, the degeneration of the incised

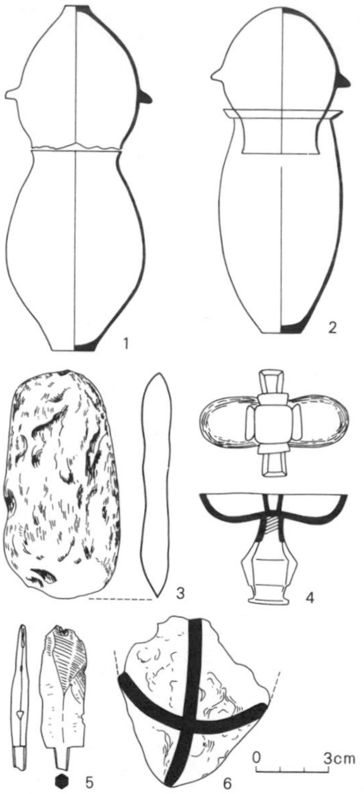

Figure 54. Specimens from the Sinch'ang-ni site

decoration, and the addition of handles. Some ceramics of the central region have an outward-turned lip. These can be seen in the ceramics of the Han River Basin and at Koejŏng-dong, Taejŏn (Plates 33, 34) (not to be confused with the Koejŏng-dong sites in Pusan). In the ceramics from the Sajik-dong site, the doubled-over rim is absent but the tradition of incision on the lip remained. In the central and southern districts, including the Han River Basin (Fig. 44, lower), the handles are of the so-called ox horn shape. This kind of handle persisted into the greyish impressed ceramics and finally into the early Kaya ceramics. The handles attached to the jar coffins from the Nangmin-dong site and the handles of the jar coffins of Sinch'ang-ni, Kwangsan also show this tradition (Fig. 54). The "ox horn" type of handles appear to be a local invention of the Plain Pottery Culture of Korea; they are not seen in neighboring countries. There are a number of variants, which include the elongation of the handles or, in some cases, the joining of the end of the handle to the vessel wall so that a ring is formed.

The Plain Pottery Culture appears to have persisted for a long time. The earliest dates may be somewhere in the range of the end of the second millennium B.C. or the beginning of the first millennium. The terminal date for the Plain Pottery Culture varies in each area. In the northwest, it appears that iron is found in sites from about the fourth or third centuries B.C., at about the same period as impressed soft grey ceramics. Therefore it appears that Plain Pottery began to decline in the fourth and third centuries B. C. in the northwest. However, in the central and southern areas, the change seems to be later. Even up to the first century B.C., the major metal artifacts were made of bronze, and the production of iron artifacts seems to have been very limited. The total length of the Plain Pottery Period must have been over a thousand years. This long period can be divided into Early, Middle, and Late divisions. Further time divisions can be created as more knowledge is accumulated. The following reference points can be used to initiate the establishment of a chronology of the Plain Pottery Culture. The Lungshanoid Culture of northern China and the Karasuk Culture of Siberia are important for comparison. A number of dates are also available. House Site No. 4, Hogok, Musan, has been dated at 2430 ± 110 B.P. (about 480 B.C.) and two samples from House Site No. 3 at Susŏng-ni have been dated at 2340 ± 120 B.P. and 2230 ± 280 B.P. This Susŏng-ni site appears to date from the beginning of the third century. Another reference point is the beginning of the Yayoi and the end of the Jōmon in Japan. From the Ukikunden site of Karatsu, the Yusu pottery layer was dated to 405 B.C., the Itatsuke pottery layer was dated to 275 B.C., and the Itatsuke II pottery layer was dated to 215 B.C. Roughly, the radiocarbon dates show that the Plain Pottery Culture existed in the first millennium B.C. Future research will allow for more detailed chronological divisions.

# CHAPTER 4

# Origin and Development of Bronze Age Culture of Korea

In what time period and from what direction did metal production come to the Korean peninsula? One of the most widely held datings for this period has been the time of the Warring States Period of China. For example, Ryosaku Fujita has written:

> While most of Korea was still in the Stone Age, in the northwest, coins such as the Ming-tao-ch'ien were imported, and bronze and iron wares began to appear in North and South P'yŏngan Provinces. The dates for these would be the time of the Warring States Period in China. Moreover, the discovery in various parts of Korea in addition to these two provinces—of such artifacts as bronze daggers, dagger axes *(ko)* and spears, small bronze bells of two distinct forms, bronze containers, iron swords and axes, would prove that the so-called Aneolithic Culture spread very rapidly over the whole peninsula.

The main points of this argument can be summarized.

1. In the Korean peninsula, bronze and iron artifacts and Ming-tao-ch'ien coins were contemporary with each other.
2. This time period must be about the end of the Warring States Period, or about the third century B.C., judging from the presence of Ming-tao-ch'ien coins.

3. This period could be called Aneolithic to indicate the coexistence of Neolithic and metal-using cultures.

This opinion has had great impact on local archaeology and is still currently held by a number of scholars.

The early excavation of sites dating to the beginning of the metal culture, however, was unscientific, and the number of excavations was limited. In recent years, the accumulation of new knowledge from northeastern China and the Korean peninsula has made possible the correction of many earlier hypotheses.

Because few sites were scientifically excavated, the early studies concentrated on the typology of bronze artifacts, particularly daggers and mirrors. Sites in which they have been found are indicated in Figure 55. A particular gap lay in the lack of ceramic data. Typology is doubtless an important aspect of research; equally as important, however, are the investigation of the total assemblage from each site and the restoration of life patterns. I will introduce representative sites from each period in an attempt to examine the total range of the culture.

## THE BEGINNING OF THE BRONZE AGE

Metal objects are not known from the Geometric Pottery Culture of the Korean peninsula. They appear in the Plain Pottery Culture for the first time, the earliest examples of which are the Top-Shape Pottery sites.

### *SINHŬNG-DONG SITE*

The Sinhŭng-dong site of Pongsan-gun, Hwanghae Province, is a typical Top-Shape Pottery site. Seven house sites, numbered 1 to 7, were excavated. Each yielded Top-Shape sherds, together with stone daggers, stone arrowheads, stone celts, thin planoconvex adzes, crescent-shaped stone knives, spindle whorls, stone spears, disc-shaped stone adzes, stone perforators, net sinkers, large disc-shaped stones, saddle querns, pestles, and whetstones (Fig. 32). The only metal object found was a bronze button from House Site No. 7.

House Site No. 7, about 3 meters west from House Site No. 3, was already destroyed along the eastern wall. The size of the pit dwelling was comparatively small, the length from

Figure 55. Locations of finds of bronze daggers in Korea

South Hamgyŏng Province
1. Pukch'ŏng-gun, Chŏnghae-myŏn, T'osŏng-ni
2. Sinch'ang-gun, Hasŏdong-ni
3. Hongwŏn-gun, Unp'o-ri
4. Hamju-gun, T'aesŏng-ni
5. Hamhŭng City, Hoesang kuyŏk, Ihwa-dong
6. Hamhŭng City, Panyong kuyŏk, Ch'isan-dong
7. Hŭngnam-gun, Hosang-dong

North P'yŏngan Province
8. Kapsŏng

South P'yŏngan Province
9. Maengsan-gun, Pongil-myŏn
10. Kaech'ŏn-gun, Yŏnghŭng-ni
11. P'yŏngyang, Sŏg'am-ni
12. Taedong-gun, Yongang-myŏn, Sang-ni
13. Kangnam-gun, Tongson-ni
14. P'yŏngyang, Yongsan-ni
15. Taedong-gun, Taebo-myŏn, Panch'ŏn-ni
16. Kangsŏ-gun, Taesŏng-ni
17. Taedong-gun, Yulli-myŏn, Changch'ŏn-ni
18. Taedong-gun, Mirim-ni
19. P'yŏngyang (vicinity)
20. P'yŏngyang City, Tongdaewŏn kuyŏk, Tongdaewŏn-dong, Hŏsan
21. P'yŏngyang City, Nangnang kuyŏk, Chŏngo-dong
22. P'yŏngyang City, Chŏngbaek-dong
23. P'yŏngyang City, Man'gyŏngdae kuyŏk, Man'gyŏndae-ri

Hwanghae Province
24. Hwangju-gun, Hŭkkyo-ri
25. Unyul-gun, Unsŏng-ni
26. Hwangju-gun, Ch'ŏngyong-ni, Chŏngch'on
27. Hwangju-gun, Ch'ŏnju-ri
28. Pongsan-gun, Songsan-ni
29. Pongsan-gun, Songsan-ni, Tang-ch'on
30. Unp'a-gun, Kalhyŏn-ni
31. Chaeryŏng-gun, Pudŏng-ni, Suyŏk-tong
32. Sŏhŭng-gun, Ch'ŏngong-ni
33. Suan-gun

Kyonggi Province
34. Yangju-gun, Kuri-myŏn, Saro-ri
35. Yongin-gun, Mohyŏn-myŏn, Ch'obu-ri
36. Yangyang-gun, T'osŏng-myon
37. Ch'unch'ŏn (vicinity)

South Ch'ungch'ŏng Province
38. Asan-gun, Tunp'o-myŏn, Tunp'o-ri
39. Tangjin Pyegok-ni
40. Sŏch'ŏn-gun, Changang-ŭp, Wŏnsu-dong
41. Puyŏ-gun, Kyuam-myŏn, Kombok-ni
42. Puyŏ-gun, Ch'och'ŏn-myŏn, Yŏnhwa-ri
43. Nonsan
44. Taejŏn City, Koejŏng-dong
45. Kongju
46. Yŏn'gi-gun, Sŏ-myŏn, Pongam-ni

North Chŏlla Province
47. Wanju-gun, Kosan-myŏn, Nambong-ni
48. Chŏnju, Ch'op'o-ri

South Chŏlla Province
49. Kwangju
50. Yŏngam-gun, Yŏngam-myŏn
51. Kohŭng-gun, Tuwŏn-myŏn, Undae-ri

North Kyŏngsang Province
52. Yŏngdŏk-gun, Sach'ŏn-ni
53. Sangju (vicinity)
54. Taegu City, Pisan-dong
55. Taegu City, Manch'ong-dong
56. Yŏngch'ŏn-gun, Sillyŏng (vicinity)
57. Yŏngch'ŏn
58. Kyŏngju City, Naedong-myŏn, Paeban-ni
59. Kyŏngju City, P'yŏng-ni
60. Kyŏngju City, Kujŏng-ni
61. Kyŏngju City, Ipsil-ni

South Kyŏngsang Province
62. Ulsan City, Changhyŏn-ni
63. Miryang
64. Kimhae-gun, Kimhae-ŭp, Hoehyŏl-li

north to south being 5.8 meters and the depth along the west side 40 centimeters. The floor surface was made of clay hardened by firing. Artifacts were found near the surface of the wall. In addition to the bronze button recovered from the floor surface of the northern side, slightly toward the west, 1 stone dagger, 1 stone celt, 2 stone arrowheads, 1 planoconvex stone adze, 1 stone spear, 1 stone pestle, 2 pestles for saddle querns, 1 fragment of a stone disc, and ceramics were unearthed from this site.

Only the tip of the blade of the stone dagger was recovered; it had a biconvex cross section. In general, stone daggers from Top-Shape Pottery sites are either biconvex or diamond shaped in cross section. The stone adzes were almost oval in cross section with a bifacial blade. One stone adze had a charred portion of the wooden handle attached to the poll, showing the original method of hafting. The stone arrowheads were of the stemmed type with a diamond-shaped cross section. One variant had a pointed tip like the nib of a pen. The flat planoconvex adzes had the same shape as others found in house sites. Because of their small size, they may have been used for scraping, even though the term "adze" has been used. The tip of the stone spears had a diamond-shaped cross section; morphologically, it is the same as the stone arrowheads or swords from Top-Shape Pottery sites. The term "spear" has been used for artifacts that are intermediate in size between arrowheads and daggers. For instance, a stone dagger from House Site No. 2 was 20 centimeters long and 3.5 centimeters wide, while an arrowhead from House Site No. 7 was 5.5 centimeters long and 1.6 centimeters wide. A complete stone spear was 8.2 centimeters long and 2.3 centimeters wide (Fig. 32:19). Stone daggers from Top-Shape Pottery sites in the northwest generally follow the shapes of arrowheads or spears. They seem to have developed from stone artifacts (rather than from bronze prototypes).

Similar bronze buttons to the example from Sinhŭng-dong were found in the box-shaped stone cist grave of P'ungnyong-ni, Kanggye-gun, North P'yŏngan Province, the Sinam-ni site of Yongch'ŏn-gun, North P'yŏngan Province (Fig. 56:1), and the Ch'ŏdo site of Najin, North Hamgyŏng Province (Fig. 88). There is no doubt that these sites in North

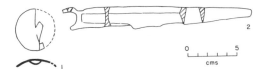

Figure 56. Bronze objects from Cultural Layer 2, Area 3, of the Sinam-ni site

P'yŏngan Province belong to the Plain Pottery Culture; however, their ceramics differ from those of the Top-Shape Pottery sites of Hwanghae Province. They seem to be related in part to the undecorated pottery sites of northeastern China.

In the northwest of Korea (with the exception of North P'yŏngan Province), sites yielding Top-Shape Pottery appear to be the earliest in the Plain Pottery Culture, exhibiting the simplest forms of Plain Pottery; the stone artifacts seem to show influence from the Lungshan of China. The influence of metal-using cultures on these sites seems to be slight indeed. One might expect that stone daggers and stone arrowheads, the forms which are easily influenced by metal technology, might show strong influences; however, the daggers and arrowheads in these areas retained completely the aspects of stone weapons. Only at a later date can clear influence from bronze daggers and arrowheads be seen.

House Site No. 7 from Sinhŭng-dong contains typical Top-Shape Pottery. However, the bronze button found in House Site No. 7 is completely divergent from artifacts found in the Lungshan or Lungshanoid Culture. Similar buttons have been seen in sites of stone cist coffins in northeastern China and also in the Karasuk Culture of Siberia. The Sinhŭng-dong example must have travelled overland to reach Korea from northeastern China. Many of the stone artifacts of Sinhŭng-dong, such as planoconvex adzes, stone chisels, crescent-shaped stone knives, and disc-shaped stone adzes, are almost the same as artifacts of the Lungshanoid Culture on the eastern coast of China, or the Ch'ing-lien-kang Culture; therefore, the cultural tie between the two seems strong. The route of such cultural diffusion probably went along the east coast of Kiangsu and Shantung and north along the coast of the Yellow Sea to the northwest of Korea.

### SINAM-NI SITE

From Layer 2, Location 3, of the Sinam-ni site, Yongch'ŏn-gun, North P'yŏngan Province, a ring-handled bronze knife and button were found (Fig. 56). The Sinam-ni site, as mentioned in earlier sections, covers a wide area and is composed of a number of cultural layers, including the Hondungmale site (Location 1), the Moresan (Location 2) site, and a site in front of the farm and barn, termed Location 3. The remains at Location 1 belong to the end of the Geometric Pottery Culture. In the ceramics as well as in the stone artifacts, the influence of the Plain Pottery Culture can be seen clearly. From Layer 2, Location 2, the so-called Misong-ni Pottery and stone artifacts were unearthed. From Layer 1 of Location 3, artifacts similar to those from the Hondungmale site were recovered; from Layer 2 of Location 3, the bronze button and ring-handled knife mentioned earlier were found in Pit No. 4. The ceramics from Layer No. 2 were undecorated, but for Plain Pottery they had some unusual shapes. The dominant shape of the pottery was the jar form with a long constricted neck. However, a substantial number of elevated stands was also seen. The jar-shaped vessels had a doubled-over rim, and incision was applied on the doubled-over portion or on the edge of the lip in the same manner as the Plain Pottery. However, the neck form and the absence of handles separates these wares from the Misong-ni ceramics (Fig. 38). Appliqué decoration or linear incision was applied in many cases; this kind of pottery is found among the ceramics of northeastern China. As for stone artifacts, there were adzes, crescent-shaped knives, and stone arrowheads—all of the kind found generally in the Plain Pottery Sites. All of the stone arrowheads had a cross section in the form of a flattened hexagon and were stemless; one stone arrowhead had grooves in the body that suggested it was a copy of a bronze specimen.

A bronze knife from Pit No. 4 of Layer II had a ring handle with a convex back and a concave blade. This type of knife is typical of the Karasuk Culture and is also known from the Sui Yuan area and from Yin (Shang) and Chou bronzes.

Half of the bronze button found with the bronze knife was missing. On the surface of the convex side there was no decoration, and on the center of the concave side there was a semicircular loop for attachment (Fig. 56). This is the same as in the Karasuk examples.

What, then, is the time period for Sinhǔng-dong House Site No. 7 and Pit 4, Location 3? It would seem that the beginning of the first millennium B.C. would be an appropriate dating. At first, this might seem surprisingly old, but the Top-Shape Pottery is definitely the oldest stage of the Plain Pottery. This site was occupied at the end of the Neolithic and the beginning of the Bronze Age. Lungshanoid influence seems evident in the stone artifacts, while the dates for Karasuk which seems to be the nearest connection for the bronze artifacts have been estimated at 1300 B.C. to 700 B.C.

From Layer 2 of Location 3 of the Sinam-ni site, long-necked vessels, in the tradition of the undecorated pottery of the northeast of China, were found in addition to a bronze knife and button. Once again, some of the stone arrowheads were grooved, suggesting that metal and stone tools existed side by side.

In later periods, sites yielding bronze buttons are relatively common in the northeastern part of China and in the Korean peninsula. For example, bronze buttons from the cist coffin of Shan-chu-tzu, adjacent to the Ma-tao-kou site of Kirin Province, exhibited traces of iron rust; a fragment of iron was also found. In addition, Pit 9, Location 1 of the Ch'ōdo site in Korea yielded iron objects as well as bronze buttons. These sites are slightly later in time period than Sinhŭng-dong House Site No. 7, Location 3 or Layer 2, Location 3 of the Sinam-ni site.

The bronze button from Sinhŭng-dong marks the earliest appearance of bronze in the Korean peninsula; in addition, the bronze knife and button from Sinam-ri must be almost from the same period. The artifacts and ceramics from both sites show clear differences from the artifacts associated with the slender bronze dagger, the bronze spear, and the bronze dagger axe *(ko)*. This division is corroborated by the situation in Liaoning, in which the so-called *pip'a* style of bronze dagger, with a wider blade, was found with bronze knives and bronze buttons. The Liaoning (or *pip'a*) bronze dagger is older than the slender bronze dagger.

## MISONG-NI CAVE (UPPER LAYER)

In addition to the bronze knife and bronze button of the Early Bronze Age, the bronze axe has been found in Korea. A representative example comes from the upper layer of the cave at Misong-ni. Since the upper layer of Misong-ni has already been discussed, I will only dwell on the details relevant to the finding of the bronze axe.

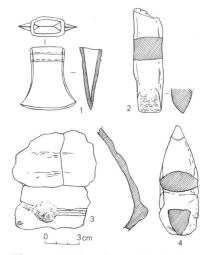

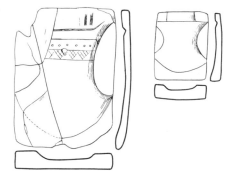

Figure 57. Specimens from the stone chamber tombs of Ta-huo-fang, Fou-shun, Manchuria

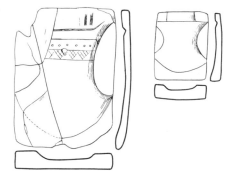

Figure 58. Baked clay molds of bronze adzes found at Yŏnghŭng-up

Two examples were found. The blade of one example had flaring edges (Fig. 38:19), while the other example was narrower. These are similar to the two types of bronze axes found in the stone cist of Lou-shang, Lu Ta City, Liaoning Province (Fig. 85:6, 7). The wide-bladed bronze axe was found in the sites of Shih-erh-t'ai-ying-tzu of Liaoning (Fig. 83:5) and in the stone cist of Ta-huo-fang, of Fou-shun, in northeastern China. From this site, the ceramics appear similar to those from the upper layer of Misong-ni; in addition, the same kinds of stone chisels were also found (Fig. 57). One of the special features of bronze axes found in these sites was the square socket with a convex band around the edge. Additionally, the blade was flaring. This type is widespread in Eurasia, in the Sui Yuan area, in the northeast of China, and in the Korean peninsula.

In Korea, the bronze axe appears to have become narrower through time, probably through influence from the narrower iron axe of the Chinese. The broad form of the axe was found in the Yŏnghŭng-up site of Southern Hamgyŏng Province (Fig. 58), while the narrower form was found in the stone grave of Songsan-ni, Pongsan-gun, Hwanghae Province (Fig. 74:5) as well as from the site of Sŏbyŏn-dong, Taegu City (Fig. 93:1).

Special features of the ceramics from the Upper Layer of Misong-ni are the long neck, the technique of applying a "belt" or a horizontal line on the body, and the lump-shaped handles. These are characteristics of the undecorated pottery of northeastern China and can be seen in the ceramics of North P'yŏngan Province. The Misong-ni Pottery of North P'yŏngan Province is different from Top-Shape Pottery, the center of which is South P'yŏngan and Hwanghae Provinces.

From the Upper Layer of Misong-ni, 16 stone arrowheads, 1 stone chisel, 1 spindle whorl, and 1 pipe-shaped ornament of dark green nephrite show the general range of artifacts which accompany Plain Pottery. Yet there are differences between those sites and the Top-Shape Pottery sites in the Taedong Basin and the Hwanghae District. Stone artifacts which might be used for agriculture, such as the crescent-shaped stone knife, are missing, suggesting that perhaps there was a greater dependence on hunting and livestock farming than on agriculture.

Most of the arrowheads were of the type with the flattened hexagonal cross section and a concavity on both sides, which is a copy of the bronze arrowhead. In addition to the bronze axes, the arrowheads give some indication that the site fits into the early metal period of Korea.

## DEVELOPMENT OF THE BRONZE DAGGER AND ITS STYLISTIC CHANGES

As representative remains of the Bronze Age, we have so far mentioned the bronze dagger, the bronze spearhead, the bronze *ko* (dagger axe), and the bronze mirror, which has a fine geometric decoration and plural knobs apparently used for attaching strings for suspension. These bronze artifacts are found in association with iron artifacts and are often considered to mark the beginning of the Iron Age. However, the concept of the beginning of the Metal Age has changed with the accumulation of new data.

Most of the bronze daggers found in the Korean peninsula are of the so-called slender type. One of the characteristics of this type of dagger is the narrowing of the lower blade by the creation of indentations on both sides. The ridge has nodes, a feature that appears to be limited to the Korean peninsula. Although the prototype of the bronze dagger was the Liaoning or *pip'a* dagger, the technique of making scooped-out portions on the lower blade is not known from that area. [Translators' note: The name *pip'a* refers to the Chinese stringed musical instrument, known in Japanese as the *biwa,* which has a wooden sounding portion much like that of a violin. The curved sides distinguish the early prototypes from Liaoning from the later examples.]

A number of Liaoning daggers have been discovered in Korea, although they are by no means common. The lower portion of the blade is wide, and the central portion has a protuberance; the central ridge does not extend below the protuberance. The Liaoning dagger seems to have changed little through time. It appears to have become somewhat narrower, and the protuberance gradually to have become closer to the handle. Examples of later forms are shown in Plates 35–46, and other forms of bronze artifacts from unknown provenience are illustrated in Plates 47–51.

In attempting to establish a typology of bronze daggers, I

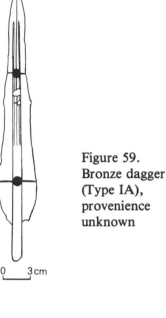

Figure 59.
Bronze dagger
(Type IA),
provenience
unknown

0    3cm

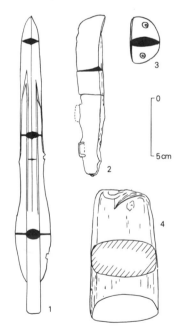

Figure 60. Specimens from
the Yŏnghŭng-ni site

have termed the Liaoning dagger Bronze Dagger Type I, and
have divided it into three subtypes—A, B, and C. I would
label the slender bronze dagger Type II, with subdivisions A,
Ba, Bb, and C. The following are representative examples.

### BRONZE DAGGER TYPE IA

The oldest *pip'a*-shaped dagger is one which the National
Museum bought from a dealer in Seoul (Fig. 59). The protuberance is slightly to the upper part of the blade, and the
proportions of the blade are similar to examples from Shih-
erh-t'ai-ying-tzu and Kangshang.

Although it appears to have come from the southern part
of Korea, the provenience of this dagger is not known. Unfortunately, no reliably documented examples of this type
are known from Korea.

### BRONZE DAGGER TYPE IB

A representative site for this type of dagger is Yonghŭng-
ni, Kaech'ŏn-gun, South P'yŏngan Province, accidentally
discovered in 1939. A whole group of artifacts found together with the dagger is now in the National Museum. Although
these artifacts are very important, no local survey was carried out and no report was published, and the original conditions of the find are thus unknown. The group of artifacts
comprised 1 bronze dagger (Fig. 60:1), 1 bronze knife (Fig.
60:2), 1 semicircular jade ornament (Fig. 60:3), and 1 stone
adze (Fig. 60:4).

The bronze knife had a convex blade and three protuberances at the handle; one was missing. The protuberances apparently served for attaching the handle. Bronze knives with
similar projections on the handle were found in the stone
slab tombs of Tsao-ta-kou, Kirin Province; Tung-chia-ying-
tsu, Jehol; and Nan-shan-ken, Ning-ch'eng-hsien, Chao-wu-
ta-meng. Also from the hill of Pao-shen-miao, T'ang-shan
City, Hopei Province, 5 molds of bronze knives similar to
the one from Yonghŭng-ni, 1 bronze axe, and 4 bronze
spears were found (Fig. 86).

The stone decoration was made from amazonite. Holes
were pierced on each side of the semicircular shape. Similar
ornaments were discovered at Koejŏng-dong, Taejŏn, South
Ch'ung-ch'ŏng Province and also Yŏnhwa-ri, Puyo-gun.

These latter two had a semicircular shape with the central portion removed; only one hole was made for suspension. The stone adzes maintained their traditional shape. The blade is slightly wider than the poll, and the bit is biconvex or clam shaped (termed the *hamaguri* type in the Japanese literature). Stone artifacts appear to decline with the advent of bronze artifacts. A number of tools should be mentioned specifically.

A bronze dagger, with protuberances on both sides slightly closer to the handle than to the tip, was found, as mentioned previously. This dagger might be called the Yonghŭng-ni type. It is important to note that bronze spearheads or dagger axes were absent in Yonghŭng-ni. This is the usual situation for Type IA, and IB, even in the Liaoning area. Yonghŭng-ni appears definitely to be an early site, from the style of the bronze dagger and the lack of spears or dagger axes.

The knife recovered from Yonghŭng-ni differed from the example found at Sinam-ni. Instead of a ring handle, the knife had a lugged tang. The back of the blade was slightly curved, and the tip of the blade pointed up. It seems that both of these kinds of knives were used in the Yin (Shang) Dynasty. A stone mold from Pao-shen-miao, T'ang Shan (Fig. 86) is important for tracing relationships between these knives, and will be discussed later.

The semicircular jade ornament was pierced on each edge; its form appears to be antecedent to the example from Koejŏng-dong, Taejŏn (Fig. 65:10; Plate 56).

A bronze dagger (Plate 38), said to be unearthed in the P'yŏngyang area, seems to be Type IB; it has the same features as the example from Ssu-erh-pao-hsiang, Liaoning Province (Fig. 61:2). The reduced protuberance on the blade looks almost vestigial, while the lower part of the blade maintains the full curve. The actual site location and associated artifacts are unknown.

## BRONZE DAGGER TYPE IC

An example of this type is kept in the collection of the Kyŏngbuk University Museum (Fig. 62). The protuberance on the side is relatively developed, and the ratio of the upper blade portion to the lower portion is about 4:3. Another example from P'yŏngyang has the same style, which comes

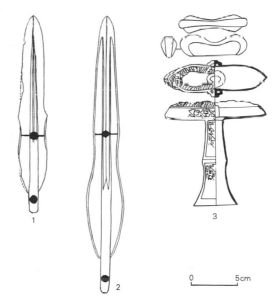

Figure 61. Types of bronze daggers: 1) Example of Type IC, reported to have come from P'yŏngyang; 2) example of Type IB, from Ssu-erh-pao, Manchuria; 3) handle parts, also from Ssu-erh-pao

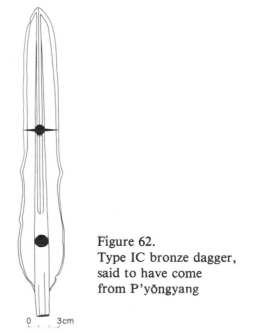

Figure 62. Type IC bronze dagger, said to have come from P'yŏngyang

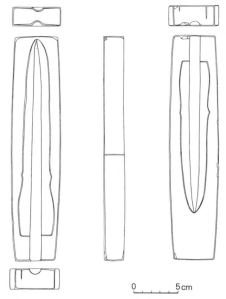

Figure 63. Stone molds for bronze daggers (Type IC) from the Ch'obu-ri site

close to the slender bronze dagger and marks the final time division of the Liaoning dagger (Fig. 61:1).

Three pieces of stone molds for bronze daggers which are similar in style to the above were found from the slope of a hill at Ch'obu-ri, Yongin-gun, Kyŏnggi Province (Plate 52, Fig. 63). Two of the three pieces are part of the same mold (upper and lower portions). The rounded sides of the blade near the handle have become narrower, and the protuberances on the blade are reduced. The body of the blade ends with a right angle to the stem, a characteristic feature of slender bronze daggers of the Korean peninsula.

The final product of this evolution, the slender bronze dagger, is not known from the Liaoning area.

## BRONZE DAGGER TYPE IIA

In contrast to earlier types, the slender Korean bronze dagger lost the protuberances on the blade while the entire blade became narrower. The upper and lower portions of the blade are now separated by a concavity or indentation. This type, with many temporal variations, is the most numerous in the Korean peninsula and was used for the longest period of time.

The oldest style of the slender bronze dagger is an example unearthed from the Koejŏng site of Taejŏn. This site, located on a low hill at Koejŏng-dong, was found accidentally by the land owner during cultivation, in 1967. It consists of a grave surrounded by piled stones; a roughly oval pit was excavated, and natural cobbles about 10 centimeters in diameter were piled up to make a rectangular stone cist about 2.2 meters long and 50 centimeters wide. Natural large stones were used as a cover. The total accumulation of stones was huge (Fig. 64), amounting to the contents of several horse carts. The overall shape of the stone pile was an oval, which is the typical form of the northern type of piled stone grave. Rotted wood, about 2 centimeters thick, was found on the floor of the cist; it may have been the remains of a coffin or bier. The associated remains appear to be almost in their original context.

A bronze dagger (Plate 54, Fig. 65:1) was made of a whitish copper which may have nickel inclusions. The blade was ridged from the top down to the concavity, and the portion between the concavity and the handle was relatively full. This is the oldest form of the slender bronze dagger. It was 32.4 centimeters long.

Two geometric decorated mirrors, with loops for attachment, were also found. The mirrors were 11.3 centimeters and 8 centimenters in diameter (Plates 57, 60, 61; Fig. 65:2). Both had two loops and a rather roughly executed decoration.

The back of the former was decorated with a series of triangles filled with slanting parallel lines, while the back of the latter was divided into three concentric circles, the innermost of which was filled with short parallel lines, while the other two contained triangles filled with slanting parallel lines. The section of the rim was planoconvex, which is characteristic of this type of mirror.

Two bronze bells were also found (Plates 58, 59; Fig. 65:4,5), both of the same style and almost the same size. Attachment was accomplished by a semicircular loop on the top. Two round holes were perforated in the top of the bell. The center portion of the loop was worn, showing that the bells had actually been used for a long time. The full length of one specimen was 11.4 centimeters while the other was 11.2 centimeters.

The horse mask (Plate 53, Fig. 65:7) was decorated with a checkered relief pattern, while the back side was plain. On the upper side, four holes were pierced in a straight line, and the upper portion of the holes showed wear; therefore, strings were placed through these holes to suspend the ornament. This kind of bronze ornament has not been previously encountered. Two similar bronze "masks" were found from the Sŏgam-ni site, P'yŏngyang City in 1962, together with a slender bronze dagger. Both had a long triangular form with rounded corners (Fig. 87:3). The horse mask from Koejŏng-dong differed in its form somewhat. It was 16 centimeters long.

The three bronze "leggings" (Plates 62–67; Fig. 65:8,9) are unknown from previous excavations. They are almost planoconvex in section; there is a kind of node in the central portion which resembles a split section of bamboo. The decoration was divided into an upper and lower section, each being decorated with two double lines parallel to the edge. In

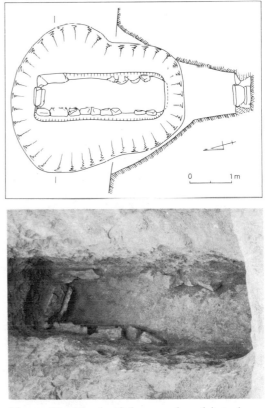

Figure 64. The burial mound and interior chamber from Koejŏng, Taejŏn

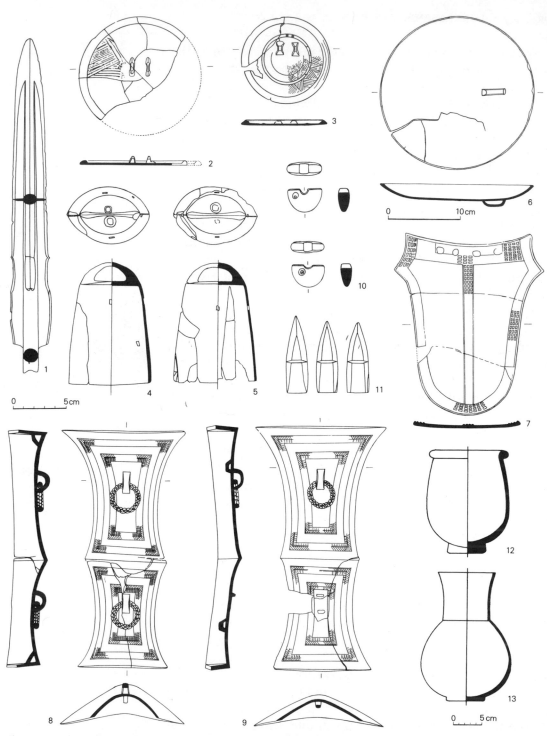

Figure 65. Specimens from the burial mounds of Koejŏng, Taejŏn (see also Plates 33, 34, 53–67)

the central portion of the upper and lower registers were loops, from which ropelike rings were suspended. On the back sides, loops were found for attachment. One example was 23.3 centimeters long; the other was 22.7 centimeters. They appear to be too small for practical use; it seems that they were ritual objects for use in burial.

The third legging had the same style as the other two. It was slightly smaller, however, and the decoration was a little different. In addition to the slight variations in the decoration, the hooks on the back were placed on the corners of the upper and lower edges. There does not appear to be any functional difference. In size, it was slightly smaller (22.1 centimeters).

These "leggings" have a rough outline of dagger handles. However, they seemed to have functioned as leggings to protect either the legs of humans or of horses. From later periods, there are leggings from Mound 34 of Talsŏ and from the Gold Crown Tomb. These appear to be comparable to the examples from the Koejŏng-dong site.

One plain circular bronze object, with a loop for attachment, was also found. The location of the attachment loop was off center. The diameter was 20.6 centimeters and the thickness was 0.25 centimeter; the side with the loop was convex. I would regard it as a variety of the bronze button with single attachment loop which seems to have had the same origin as the plain mirror with single attachment loop, to be discussed later.

Three polished stone arrowheads were also found (Plate 55; Fig. 65:11). They were stemless, with flat bases, and were roughly triangular in shape. In section they were roughly hexagonal, and they were made of greyish-brown slate. In length they varied from 6.8 to 7.4 centimeters.

The two ornaments of amazonite were semicircular in shape, with a "bite" taken out of the upper straight-line portion (Plate 56; Fig. 65:10). About fifty of these small ornaments were found in the entire site.

One Plain Pottery vessel was also excavated (Plate 34; Fig. 65:12). Its shape was almost cylindrical, with a slightly narrower upper portion. On the rim, a rounded band of clay was attached. This method of appliqué can be seen in many Plain Pottery vessels in the Han River Basin. The flat bottom was created by attaching a thick clay disc to the round bottom.

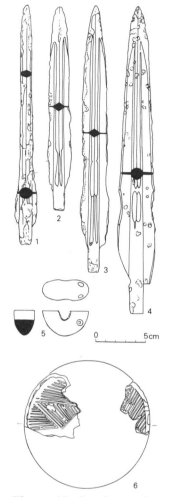

Figure 66. Specimens from the stone burial chamber at Yŏnhwa-ri (see also Plate 68)

The vessel was not wheel made, and the paste did not contain any large grains of sand. The height was 17 centimeters; the mouth diameter, 13 centimeters; and the base diameter, 6.5 centimeters. The thickness of the body varied from 0.4 to 0.7 centimeter.

One black pottery vessel was also recovered (Plate 33; Fig. 65:13). To the lower portion of the body, which was rounded, a long neck was attached. The neck had a slight flare, which showed the tradition of early Plain Pottery. The paste was a refined clay, and the body was quite thin (0.3 to 0.4 centimeter). The surface was well-polished and lustrous, and the black shiny color could be seen even inside the body. The height was about 22 centimeters; the mouth diameter, 9.5 centimeters; and the base diameter, 6.5 centimeters.

The burials and associated artifacts of Koejŏng-dong show the culture complex of the Korean Bronze Age. The custom of constructing a rectangular stone cist and covering it with numerous cobbles to create a cairn is related to the customs of the Bronze Age of Liaoning and the southern part of Siberia. In the Liaoning area, the graves of Kang-shang and Lou-shang in Lu Ta City are examples of this kind of burial, which is completely different from the burial system of the proto-Chinese.

For dating the Koejŏng-dong site, the associated bronze dagger is important. The flaring protuberance is absent, and a concavity has taken its place. However, the portion from the concavity to the handle is slightly flaring. This type can be considered to be the oldest type of slender bronze dagger (Type IIA) and could be called the Koejŏng-dong type.

### YŎNHWA-RI SITE

The stone cist coffin of Yŏnhwa-ri, Puyŏ-gun, South Ch'ungch'ŏng Province is similar to Koejŏng-dong. Four bronze daggers (Plate 68; Fig. 66:1–4), fragments of mirrors with rough geometric decoration (Plate 68; Fig. 66:6), and amazonite ornaments (Fig. 66:5) were unearthed. All of the bronze daggers had broken blades; their typological position is thus not very clear. One of the daggers had a central ridge which ran only from the tip to the first indentation, while the other three had ridges running the entire length of the blade, indicating that they belong to a later period. The mirror and amazonite ornaments appear to be very similar to those from the Koejŏng-dong site. Considering the style of the bronze dagger, this site might date from a slightly later period than the former.

The so-called Type IIA dagger is distinguished by the width below the indentation on the blade; Type IIB has straight sides between the indentations and the handle. Until now, these two types have been included in the general grouping of slender bronze daggers. The chronological ordering of these two subtypes seems to be borne out by the example from Koejŏng-dong, since the excavated grave goods are of an older date than those found with subtype IIB. Type IIB daggers are often found in association with bronze spearheads and dagger axes *(ko)*. The spearheads and dagger axes are types which originated in the Chung Yuan and Yangtze areas, and appeared in Korea in association with Type IIB daggers for the first time. Even in the Liaoning district, the bronze spear and dagger axe *(ko)* are not found in association with Type IA bronze dagger, while in Korea they have not been found with Type I or Type IIA daggers yet.

The loop on the mirror from Yŏnhwa-ri is missing, but the decoration was of the same rough type as that on the large mirror from Koejŏng-dong. The design composition on the back of the mirror resembles that of one found at Sorok-do, South Chŏlla Province (Fig. 94:6). A more similar format can be seen on the mirror with two loops for attachment found at Okŭm san, Iksan gun, North Chŏlla Province, and other examples of mirrors with coarse geometric decoration (which are different from those with fine geometric decoration) are illustrated in Figure 94.

## BRONZE DAGGER TYPE IIB

Type IIB is the traditional slender bronze dagger. It represents a further refinement of Type IIA. In Type IIA, the area below the notches is flared, and was not polished for cutting, as seen in the Koejŏng-dong dagger. The ridge, therefore, did not extend below the indentation. With the narrowing of the portion between the indentation and the handle, the lower portion was polished and the ridge extended to the handle. It may be useful to divide Type IIB into IIBa and IIBb, the former being the type with the ridge extending to the indentation, while the latter has a ridge extending directly

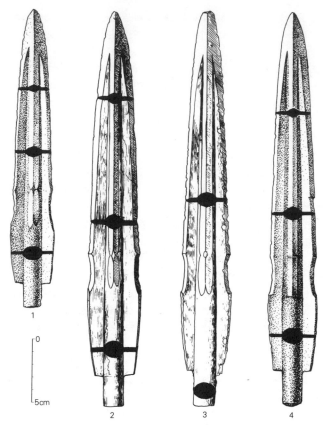

Figure 67. Bronze daggers (Type IIBa) from Yŏngam
(see also Plate 69)

to the handle. Very few Type IIB daggers have been scientifically excavated. Often they were found accidentally or
were dug up independently, so that many of them cannot be
considered to be reliable archaeological specimens.

### PUKCH'ŎNG SITE

A bronze dagger dug up accidentally inside the earth wall
at T'osŏng-ni, Chonghae-myon, of Pukch'ŏng-gun, South
Hamgyŏng Province may be considered to be one of the best
examples of the Type IIB dagger. From this earth wall adzes
and arrowheads have been unearthed before, but the stratigraphic relationship of these artifacts to the Type IIB bronze
dagger is not known. The blade displays a clear indentation,
and the polished ridge extends to the portion of indentation;

the tip portion is very short, showing that the dagger belongs to an early part of Type IIB.

Another example of Type IIBa was found at Mirim-ni, P'yŏngyang. Several mounds were destroyed during construction, and many objects were scattered. Some objects were recorded in the Japanese publication *Chosen Kobunka Sokan [A Synthesis of Korean Ancient Culture]*. Included were bronze daggers, a mirror with semicircular decoration near the center, bronze chariot parts, a bronze dagger handle attachment, bronze dagger guards and a bronze ring. One of the two bronze daggers recovered was of Type IIBa, while the other was of Type IIBb. The mirror with semicircular decoration near the center does not appear to be from the same period as the daggers.

A group of daggers from Yŏngam, South Chŏlla Province should be mentioned (Plate 69; Fig. 67). Three of them had a flaring portion below the indentations. They belong to Type IIBa. Various bronze objects and stone molds were also found from Yŏngam; however, it is not known whether they came from the same site (Plates 70–75).

### PONGAM-NI SITE

Another find of a dagger and a dagger axe or halberd, for which the exact provenience is not known, comes from Pongam-ni, Yŏn'gi-gun, South Ch'ungch'ŏng Province. The blade of the bronze dagger (Plate 76; Fig. 68:1) was eroded; it is therefore difficult to place the dagger typologically. It appears to be Type IIB, or possibly IIBa. Other dagger axes from central and northern Korea are shown in Plate 77.

Although its blade was partially damaged, the halberd or dagger axe retained its shape. The length was 27.1 centimeters; the width, 6.7 centimeters. The cross section of the ridge was circular.

Other stray finds of daggers include an example (length 22.7 centimeters) from Nambong-ni, Wanju-gun, North Chŏlla Province (Fig. 68:3) and a dagger (length 23.6 centimeters) from Miryang, South Kyŏngsang Province (Fig. 68:4). Both appear to be Type IIBb.

### KIMHAE SHELL MOUND, LOCATION D

As previously mentioned, Jar Burial No. 3, Hoehyŏl-li shell mound, Kimhae, yielded 3 pipe-shaped ornaments of

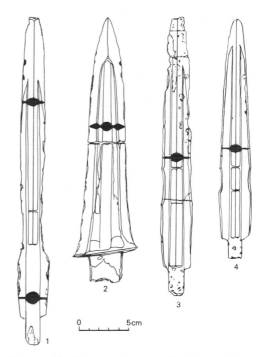

Figure 68. Bronze daggers (1, 2, and 3, Type IIBb) and bronze halberd: 1 and 2, from Pongam-ni; 3, said to have come from Nambong-ni; 4, said to have come from Miryang

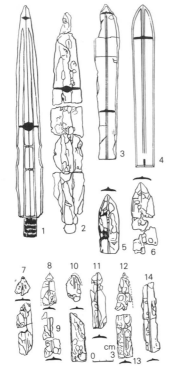

Figure 69. Specimens from Area D, Kimhae shell mound

dark green nephrite, 8 bronze planing tools, and 2 bronze daggers.

The blade of one of the daggers was not polished (Fig. 69: 2). From the width of the blade, it appears to be of the slender type. The length when found was 27 centimeters, and the restored length was 28 centimeters. The width was 3.3 centimeters at the widest part.

The other bronze dagger (Fig. 69:1) was almost intact, with clear indentations on the sides. The total length was 28.85 centimeters, and the width was 3.3 centimeters. Associated artifacts consisted of a pipe-shaped ornament of jade, and a bronze planing tool.

### YANGYANG SITE

In 1967, from an earthen wall in Yangyang-gun, Kangwŏn Province, a slender bronze dagger was found with a fine geometric decorated mirror which had multiple attachment loops. The exact provenience is unknown. The dagger (Plate 78; Fig. 70:2) was almost intact, and appears to be Type IIBb.

The mirror had two loops slightly above the center. The surface was flat instead of curved, and the back was divided into four concentric circles. Each area was decorated with parallel and triangle arrangements. The site is a good example of the association of the slender bronze dagger with the mirror with fine-line geometric decoration.

### IPSIL-NI SITE, KYŎNGJU

During the construction of the railroad (in the Kyŏngju area) in 1920, a good many artifacts were found. Although many of the remains disappeared into the hands of collectors, some were bought by the Museum of the Government General of Korea and are now in the collection of the National Museum. These objects include slender bronze daggers (Fig. 71:1), bronze spearheads (Fig. 71:2), bronze dagger axes, two geometric decorated mirrors with multiple attachment loops, bronze bells (Fig. 71:3, 4, 5, 6), small bronze horse bells, bronze handle heads with bells (Fig. 71:7), bronze handle fixtures, bronze bells with attached handles, a bronze anchor-shaped fixture with an attached bell, a bronze decorative tack, a bronze ring, a fragment of an iron sword, an iron axe, and pottery. (Plates 79, 80, 81.)

One of the daggers, collected by Jiro Ichida, is 38 centimeters long and seems to belong to Type IIBb. Another example, collected by Takenosuke Ogura, was smaller than the former, but the style was the same.

The bronze dagger axe had a long *hu* ( 胡 ) with grooves on the right and left side of the ridge. The length was 26.8 centimeters; the width, 10 centimeters.

One of the spears was very long (40.9 centimeters); the handle portion was decorated with a raised band and a semicircular attachment loop was placed on one side. The other specimen had two grooves along the blade, with ten grooves carved vertically on each side of the handle. There was a protuberance on each side near the division between the blade and the handle. The style of this example is particularly unusual.

This site yielded a number of other unusual specimens, including a bronze handle top with a bell and a bronze anchor-shaped fixture, also with a bell.

The former appears to have been a decorative handle for a dagger. Inside each portion of the top, a small bronze bell was placed. The pierced hole on one side of the handle may have been used in attaching it to the blade of a dagger. The surface was decorated with short parallel lines and sawtooth decoration. Four similar examples are known from the Naktong Basin, and a more elaborate form is illustrated in Plate 82.

The anchor-shaped fixture had a flat handle about 13 centimeters long and 1.5 centimeters wide. Branches were attached to each side of the handle, and a bell was attached to each side. The handle and both branches were decorated with a parallel curving design and raised band on the surface. One round hole was pierced on the top edge of the handle, apparently for suspension. The object was probably some kind of horse gear.

The uniqueness of the bronze objects of Ipsil-ni and their marked contrast with the Bronze Age of China should be stressed.

The daggers appear clearly to be Type IIBb. Judging from the dagger found in the grave of Pujo Yegun, to be discussed

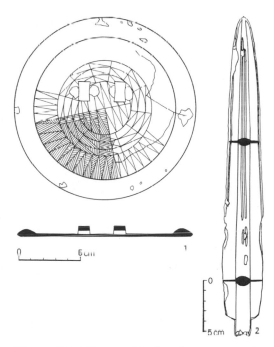

Figure 70. Mirror with fine-line geometric decoration and bronze dagger (Type IIBb) from the ruins of T'osŏng, Yangyang-gun, Kangwŏn Province (see Plates 78, 106)

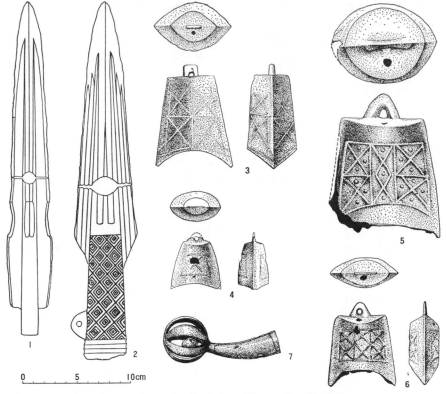

Figure 71. Specimens from Ipsil-ni (see Plates 79, 80, 82)

in the next section, the date should be slightly earlier than the second century B.C. The Ipsil-ni site appears to have more Scytho-Siberian characteristics than the Pujo Yegun grave site.

## THE PUJO YEGUN GRAVE

A pit chamber tomb was found in Chŏngbaeng-ni, P'yŏngyang City during construction in 1958. The tomb was already partially destroyed. The site location was a hillside, sloping to the south and east. One layer of wooden blocks was located as if it might have been under the coffin, on the floor of the pit, but there was no trace of the outer box of the coffin. The grave goods include 1 slender bronze dagger, 1 stone dagger handle top, 1 bronze spear, 15 bronze arrowheads, 2 bronze chariot hubcaps, 4 bronze chariot fixtures, 7 bronze hat-shaped fixtures, 12 bronze bells, 18 bronze attachments for chariot canopy, 2 iron swords, 1 iron spear, 1

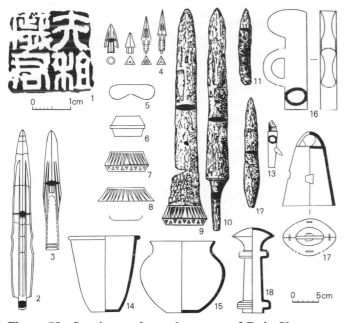

Figure 72. Specimens from the grave of Pujo Yegun

iron knife, 1 iron axe, some iron horse trappings, and some ceramics. In addition to these, the most notable object was a silver-carved seal of Pujo Yegun (Fig. 72:1).

The slender bronze dagger had clear indentations (Fig. 72:2) and was of the IIBb Type. The dagger length was 39.6 centimeters. It seemed to have been kept in a wooden sheath, but only the metal attachments of the wooden sheath were found. The head of the dagger handle was fashioned of stone in the shape of a pillow (Fig. 72:5).

The bronze spearhead (Fig. 72:3) had grooves on both sides of the blade, and along the edge of the socket were two raised bands. A hole was pierced in the side of the socket. The total length was 24 centimeters.

The bronze chariot fixture, hubcap, hat-shaped metal fixture, chariot canopy attachment, and bell are typical of the horse chariot equipment of Korea in the Late Bronze Age. While they show influence from the Warring States of China, there are many distinct features, some of which may have come to Korea from the north.

Although they are relatively rare, a few iron artifacts were also found.

The iron daggers appear to have been kept in wooden

sheaths. Some remains of the wood can still be seen, and some had dagger guards similar to those of the bronze ones. The sides of the blade appear to have been almost parallel, and the cross section of the blade was biconvex. The bodies and handles of these daggers were cast separately, and the bronze fixtures attached to the wooden sheaths obviously followed the tradition of the slender bronze daggers of the Korean peninsula. However, the lack of indentations or grooves on the blade seems to show the influence of Chou Dynasty swords. The two ubiquitous vessel forms of ceramics were recovered—the deep jar-shaped vessels and the jars with short constricted necks. The paste of the deep jar forms contained sand and asbestos, and the color was brown. The paste of the jar with the short neck was more refined, and the pottery was harder. The color was yellowish brown. The surface of the body was decorated with mat impressions. This type of pottery came to the Korean peninsula late in the Bronze Age together with the introduction of iron artifacts.

The pottery with straw mat impression is harder than Plain Pottery but did not reach the level of stoneware. It later became the pottery used by Kaya after the first century A.D. in the southern part of the peninsula.

The silver seal of Pujo Yegun (Fig. 72:1) contained four characters engraved in two lines in the small *chuan* character form; the seal was 2.2 centimeters square and had a small handle in the shape of an animal.

Pujo is mentioned in the section concerning the 25 prefectures attached to Lolang (read in Korean as *Nangnang*), in the geographic history section of the *Han Shu*. In the *Han Yuan,* the character for Pujo was written as ( 夭租 ): Hiroshi Ikeuchi considered this to be an error, however, and suggested that the characters should be (沃沮). I agree with this view that Pujo should be the present Hamhŭng of South Hamgyŏng Province. According to the discussion of Eastern Okchŏ in the *San Kuo Chih* or the *Hou Han Shu,* when the first four counties were set up by Han Wu-Ti, in 108 A.D., the Okchŏ castle was put under the administration of Hyŏnt'o County. However, after a rebellion of the local people, Hyŏnt'o County was moved to the Liaotung District, and Okchŏ was placed under the direct administration of Lolang.

The name of Yegun appears for the first time in the *Wu ti* chronicle in the entry: ''In the autumn of the first year of

Yuan-shuo (128 B.C.), Yegun, one of the Eastern Barbarians (Tung-i) led by Namyro and others, surrendered [to the Chinese] with about 280,000 people, and the area was called Changhae County." *Ye* was written in the same way as *Ye Maek* ( 穢貊 ) in the economic history section of the *Han Shu,* and after the *San Kuo Chih,* it was written as *Ye Maek* ( 濊貊 ) or *Yei.* In the Puyŏ article of the "History of the Eastern Barbarians" of the *Wei Shu* in the *San Kuo Chih,* there is mention of an old seal, "the seal of the king of Ye," in Puyŏ. The castle was called Ye Fortress, and it appears that the Puyŏ area belonged to the Ye Maek. From the description of the Puyŏ article, it appears that the seal of the king of Ye was given by the Han. However, there is no direct historical evidence that Puyŏ belonged directly to Han. Most likely it is the case that when Puyŏ established diplomatic relations with the Han Dynasty, a seal was given to the king of Ye in the usual manner of treating bordering ethnic groups.

The same kind of relation existed between some of the Japanese states and the Han Dynasty, through Lolang, as seen from the gold seal found in Shiga-jima, Kasuya-gun, Fukuoka prefecture. The seal, if taken literally, could mean that these states were subordinates of Han; that was not, however, the actual case. They certainly were not in a situation of dependent statehood in relation to the Han.

In the Han bureaucracy, there were the ranks of Chunshou, T'ai-shou, Ta-yin, Ch'eng, and Chang-shih in the county—and Ling, Chang, Ch'eng, and Wei in the prefecture. Many seal impressions in mud were found in an earth wall near the Taedong River in P'yŏngyang. Among them were the Lolang T'ai-shou seal, the Lolang Ta-yin seal, the Choson Ling seal, the Tung-i Chang seal, the Tung Ch'eng seal, and the Pujo Ch'eng seal, indicating official rankings within Lolang.

The seal of Pujo Chang, from the grave of Ko Sang-hyon, which will be discussed later, was the seal given to the head of Pujo Prefecture. However, the term *Yegun* as such cannot be seen on the seals of Lolang. The title *Yegun* was not conferred on the top person in Pujo Prefecture. The Chinese, who considered ranking and ordering very important, never would have given the title *Yegun* to the head of a prefecture which belonged to Han. The title *Ye Wang* was given to the heads of larger countries, and the title *Yegun* was given to the heads of smaller countries. Therefore, the title *Yegun* was conferred before Okchŏ belonged to Lolang County. The Pujo Yegun seal was conferred on the king of Okchŏ before the four administrative divisions of the Han were established in Korea.*

We should therefore assume that the date of the grave of Pujo Yegun is the third to second century B.C. This date seems to be appropriate, judging from the associated artifacts and particularly the bronze Type IIBb daggers.

## BRONZE DAGGER TYPE IIC AND III, AND THE PUJO CHANG SEAL GRAVE

In 1961, a wooden chamber grave was found 100 meters to the east of the grave of Pujo Yegun. From this site, two silver seals were recovered. These were the seals of Pujo Chang together with bronze artifacts, including a black-lacquered pole for supporting a canopy, which was inscribed "Made in December, the third year of Yung Shih in the reign of Chao Ti." Although these are very important materials, unfortunately no detailed report has been published yet. According to Takashi Okazaki, who received a report from Jaroslav Barinka, a participant in the excavation, there were two wooden coffins within the wooden chamber, and in the western coffin a female was interred. In the northern part of the wooden coffin, lacquerware was found along with a soft grey pottery jar that had been fired in a reducing atmosphere. To the west of the coffin was a small space in which were placed a slender bronze dagger, a mirror, a horse mask, a bell, a crossbow, a chariot fixture, and a black-lacquered canopy pole. There is no mention of iron artifacts, which seems peculiar for this kind of site. It would seem that they may have been missed in the record.

The concave portion of the slender bronze dagger (Fig. 73) has been reduced to a formality, and the width of both por-

---

*[Translator's note: The Okchŏ were tribes living in what is now South Hamgyŏng Province. They were controlled at one time by the Hsüan-t'u "commandery" of Lolang County but came under the power of the Puyŏ from 268 A.D. The Puyŏ lived to the northeast of the Okchŏ. See K. H. J. Gardiner, *The Early History of Korea* (Honolulu: University of Hawaii Press, 1969) for an introduction to this period. Gardiner, however, seems to take too literally the accounts of Chinese control over the peninsula, particularly in the south.]

tions of the blade is almost the same. The ridge on the blade extends the whole length of the blade to the stem. This style is identical with a dagger from Mound No. 10, T'aesŏng-ni, which can be classified as Type IIC.

No photographs are available of the other materials. The inscription of "December, the third year of Yung Shih, in the reign of Chao Ti," seen on the pole of black lacquer, indicates that the upper date for this site should be 14 A.D. The style of the slender bronze dagger also corresponds with this time period.

The seal of Pujo Chang almost certainly belonged to the head of Pujo Prefecture, Lolang County. In the government of the Early Han Dynasty, the *Ling* was the head of a large prefecture of more than 10,000 houses, and the *Chang* was the head of a smaller prefecture of less than 10,000 houses. The head of Pujo Prefecture, when it was under the administration of Lolang County, was given the seal of Pujo Chang.

Pujo Yegun and Pujo Chang were both governing officials of Pujo or Okchŏ. The Okchŏ area, however, is quite far from Lolang, the capital of which was located in the P'yŏngyang area; the question thus arises as to why these two personages were buried near P'yŏngyang after their death.

In the records mentioned previously, the *San Kuo Chih* or the *Hou Han Shu,* Imdun was abolished after a local revolt, in the fifth year of Chao Ti (82 B.C.). The administration of Hyŏnt'o was then shifted to Liaotung (75 B.C.), and Okchŏ was transferred to Lolang. Tung-pu-tu-wei was placed in control of the seven Prefectures of Yŏndong. The local people were against domination by a different ethnic group from the outset. Therefore, Pujo Yegun and Pujo Chang were local people living in the P'yŏngyang area, using false titles and seals, who were bribed through the assigning of lucrative positions to assist in the domination of their people by the Han Dynasty. The associated grave goods indicate that they were definitely Korean people; the slender bronze daggers and the other associated grave goods are immediately distinguishable from the grave goods found in the Han tombs of Lolang. The grave of Pujo Yegun was a pit tomb, but the grave of Ko Sang-hyŏn was a wooden chamber grave, which shows the influence of the burial system of the Han Chinese. The latter tomb could be distinguished from Chinese examples by the presence of slim bronze daggers.

Figure 73. Bronze dagger (Type IIC) from the Tomb of the Seal of Pujo Chang

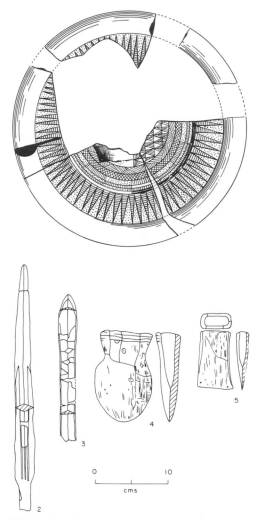

Figure 74. Specimens from the Songsan-ni stone chamber tomb

The bronze dagger unearthed from this site was Type IIC, as mentioned earlier. From the inscription on the chariot canopy pole, it is known that the dagger should be dated to about 14 B.C. This gives a standard for dating Type IIC daggers.

## SONGSAN-NI SITE

The Songsan-ni site of Pongsan-gun, Hwanghae Province, located on the southern slope of a hill, was found during construction in 1957. The stone cist was 2.3 meters long and 1 meter wide; it was covered with a low mound about 20 centimeters high, of pebbles. The north wall and the northern portion of the west wall were already destroyed, and pebbles were piled up about 70 centimeters from the south wall to create a separate space for grave objects. From this small chamber, 1 bronze dagger, 1 bronze axe, 1 bronze planing tool, 1 bronze chisel, 1 bronze hoe, 1 mirror decorated with fine geometric design, and 1 iron axe were unearthed.

It is difficult to establish the type of the bronze dagger (Fig. 74:2), since both sides of the blade near the indented area were severely damaged. It would seem that the type might be IIC rather than IIB. The polished ridge reached from the tip to the handle, and the tip portion of the blade was unusually long. It should be placed in a relatively late period of the development of the slender bronze dagger. The total length was 33 centimeters. The mirror with fine-line geometric decoration (Fig. 74:1) was broken, and almost half was missing. The portion holding the loops for attachment was not recovered; we cannot be sure, therefore, of the exact number of loops. The surface diameter was 13.8 centimeters.

The presence of the iron axe would indicate that the site belongs to the later part of the Bronze Age.

## KUJŎNG-NI SITE

From the Kujŏng-ni site of Kyŏngju, bronze artifacts such as a bronze dagger, bronze spear, bronze dagger axe, small bronze bell, and large bronze bell were unearthed, together with iron artifacts such as iron axes, iron sickles, and iron knives, in 1951. Since the site was exposed through road construction, it is not clear that they all came from the same layer.

Once again, part of the bronze dagger is damaged (Fig.

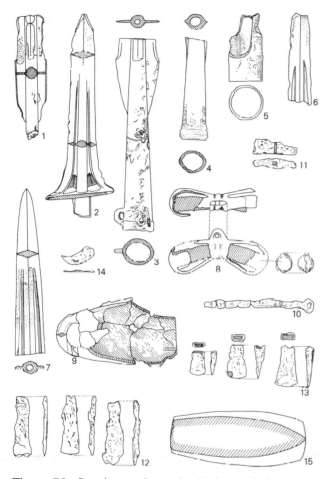

Figure 75. Specimens from the Kujŏng-ni site

75:1) particularly near the indented portion; however, it probably belongs to Type IIC. A similar dagger was found during the Japanese occupation at Sang-ni, Yongang-myŏn, Taedong-gun, South P'yŏngan Province. The ridge on this example, and on a dagger from Kujŏng-ni, Kyŏngju, extended only to the indentation. They seem to be of an earlier type of IIC.

The bronze dagger axe (Fig 75:2) showed slight development of the lateral extensions near the base of the blade in what is called the dewlap. A herringbone decoration was cast on the lower edges of the grooves of the blade; it appeared to belong to a relatively late time period and resembled an example from Ipsil-ni.

The bronze spearhead (Fig. 75:3) was broken on the tip; it had a protruding band along the base, and a semicircular loop for attachment was placed on one side. This also resembled an example from Ipsil-ni.

The most unusual object from Kujŏng-dong was a double-headed bronze bell (Fig. 75:8). This particular style resembles examples from areas of northern Asia; it was probably a horse bell. A similar kind of bronze bell was found in Chŏng-baeng-ni, P'yŏngyang during the Japanese occupation, while another example was recently found near Kongju, South Ch'ungch'ŏng Province.

Among the iron artifacts, a dagger with a ring handle (Fig. 75:10) should be mentioned. A similar ring-handled dagger was found from the Sang-ni site of Taedong-gun; in addition, both sites yielded the same kind of bronze dagger.

The iron axe (Fig. 75:13) had a widened blade, and resembled the iron axe unearthed from the Sang-ni site. Both sites are also similar in yielding bronze and iron artifacts in association with each other.

The bronze dagger appears to be Type IIC. At the end of the time period of the dagger sword, iron objects were appearing with increasing frequency.

### P'YŎNG-NI SITE

From the P'yŏng-ni site, on a hill near Kyŏngju City, 2 slender bronze daggers, 2 dagger axes or halberds, and 3 bronze spears were recently found (Plate 83). However, the site was destroyed during construction and the context of the artifacts is not clear at all.

The portion near the handle of one of the bronze daggers was damaged, but it seems to be Type IIC. The indentations were very shallow, indicating that this dagger should be placed near the end of the period for Type IIC. The blade was originally sharpened from the tip to the handle, and the ridge on the back extended the whole length of the blade. The entire length was 33.3 centimeters. A second bronze dagger (Fig. 76:1) was almost the same as the former; its chronological position is not entirely clear, because it was damaged.

Two bronze dagger axes were of the same type (Fig. 76:3, 4). Grooves on the right and left of the back were decorated with triangle motifs comprised of seven parallel slanting

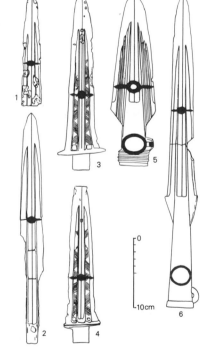

Figure 76. Specimens from the P'yŏng-ni site (see Plate 83)

lines. The trait of applying decoration to the halberds or dagger axes appears to be a relatively late characteristic. The base of the bronze halberd had tips to the right and the left (the dewlaps) which were somewhat developed. The length of these two projections was 2.4 centimeters and 2.2 centimeters.

One of the bronze spears was 24.1 centimeters long and 6.8 centimeters wide (Fig. 76:5); there were three parallel grooves on each side of the blade, however, which suggest a slightly later time period. A convex band was present on the base of the socket and a semicircular attachment loop was present. The second bronze spear (Fig. 76:6) was 43.6 centimeters long and 4.7 centimeters in maximum width. This long slender form appears to be of a later time period. It also possessed the attachment loop on the side and the sharp ridge along the blade. Another example with a broken tip was very similar to this second specimen. The spears and dagger axes belong to a later period, which is compatible with the Type IIC bronze sword with which they were found. The bronze artifacts showed traces of iron rust, suggesting that they are definitely from the later Bronze Age.

### HASŎ-DONG SITE

In 1958, bronze artifacts, including a slender bronze dagger, were found at Hasŏ-dong, Sinch'ang-gun, South Hamgyŏng Province during construction of an irrigation system. In addition to the dagger, 1 bronze spear, 1 dagger axe, and 1 bronze bell were found.

The bronze dagger (Fig. 77:1) was similar to Type IIC. The indentations or concavities on the blade were shallow, and the ridge extended from the tip to the indentation. The total length of the spear was 17 centimeters (Fig. 77:2).

The bronze spear (Fig. 77:2) had a short tip and body, and the raised band around the bottom of the socket. A hole was pierced in the side of the socket for attachment, apparently in place of a semicircular loop.

The bronze dagger axe (Fig. 77:3) had relatively long projections from the base. The total length was 26.5 centimeters. This site is important for the particular association of artifacts—the Type IIC bronze dagger, the bronze dagger axe, and the bronze spearhead.

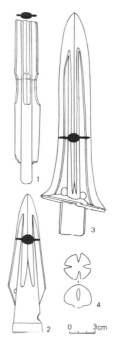

Figure 77.
Specimens from
the Hasŏ-dong site

## IHWA-DONG SITE

In the course of collecting fill on the southern flank of Ch'imat'ae, which is the main peak of Mt. Panyong-san, Hamhŭng City, the Ihwa-dong site was found. From later formal investigation, the site appeared to be a pit tomb 2.2 meters long and 70 centimeters wide. The bottom of the tomb, which was 1.27 meters below the ground surface, was covered with flat stones. It seems that subsequent to the tomb construction, soil eroded from the slope and accumulated over the grave.

The burial yielded 2 bronze daggers, 1 cross-shaped head of a sword handle, 2 slender bronze spears, 1 bronze dagger axe, 1 mirror with geometric fine-line decoration and three loops for attachment, 1 iron axe, and 2 ceramic vessels. The two bronze daggers were slightly damaged; however, the forms were perfectly recognizable. The smaller one, which was broken around the indentation (Fig. 78:1), appears to be Type IIB. The ridge originally reached to the indentation, suggesting that it might belong to a slightly earlier period. It appears to be of a slightly different time period than the larger example that I will mention next. The total length was 27 centimeters, and the greatest width was 3.4 centimeters. The larger example (Fig. 78:2) had a long, parallel-sided blade with a ridge extending from the tip to the handle. This is definitely Type IIC, belonging to the end of the period of the slender bronze daggers. The total length was 33 centimeters, and the greatest width was 3.2 centimeters.

The bronze spear (Fig. 78:3) had perforations on the side of the socket with the usual ridge at the bottom. The rotted remains of a wooden handle were also detected. The total length was 22 centimeters, and the greatest width was 4.4 centimeters. The bronze dagger axe had two grooves along the ridge of the blade (Fig. 78:4). The entire length was 27 centimeters, and the width at the center was 3.8 centimeters.

The bronze mirror with fine geometric decoration had three loops for attachment (Fig. 78:7). Although it was broken into six pieces, it was completely restorable. The back of the mirror was divided into two parts by a circle, and the triangular decorations were filled with fine parallel lines. The three loops for attachment were placed in a triangular ar-

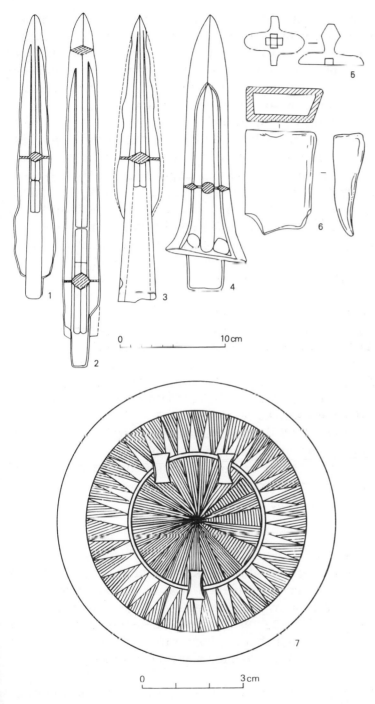

Figure 78. Specimens from the Ihwa-dong site

rangement at the boundary of the inner and outer circles. This mirror, with the three loops for attachment, is the first of its kind to be found in the Korean peninsula. A three-looped example was found from Shih-erh-t'ai-ying-tzu Mound No. 1. However, its decoration consisted of geometric motifs around the outer portion near the rim, while the inner portion was plain. This arrangement of decoration is thought to be older than the arrangement of the Korean example. A similar mirror with three attachment loops was found in a box-shaped cist at Kajikurihama, Yasuoka-cho, Shimonoseki City, Japan. [I believe that] this mirror is much older in the Liaoning Area than in the Korean peninsula. The pattern of its diffusion is an interesting problem.

The iron axe had a large socket area and a narrow blade. Once again, its association with bronze artifacts seems to indicate that the site is of a relatively late date in the Bronze Age.

Two potsherds were found with the bronze artifacts from the Ihwa-dong site. One was a sherd of the bottom of a reddish-brown vessel, made of clay mixed with fine sand. The basal diameter was 6.3 centimeters. The other was a dark brown sherd, with inclusions of large sand grains. In form and paste they resembled Plain Pottery very closely. The thickness was 0.5 centimeter.

The Ihwa-dong site is important for showing the range of artifacts association with the pit tomb form of burial. The association of iron artifacts and the particular types of bronze objects indicate that the pit tomb form of burial is a phenomenon of the Late Bronze Age.

## T'AESŎNG-NI SITE

After the Japanese occupation, many groups of mounds were found at T'aesŏng-ni, Kangsŏ-gun, South P'yŏngan Province during the construction of irrigation facilities, and about 14 pit tombs were recognized through archaeological survey. The T'aesŏng-ni site is located on the eastern slope of a long, narrow hill about 25 meters in elevation. I will discuss Tomb No. 10, which yielded a relatively wide range of artifacts.

Tomb No. 10 consisted of two burials, the western one of which appeared to be earlier. The western grave was 1.55

meters from east to west and 3.15 meters from north to south. In these pit tombs, traces of wooden coffins were recognized.

From the western grave, 1 bronze dagger, 1 bronze spear, 2 bronze chariot axle heads, a number of differently shaped chariot fixtures, 3 chariot canopy poles, 3 bronze discs, 2 cylindrical chariot fittings, 1 iron spear, 1 iron chisel, 1 iron sickle, and 1 deep pottery jar were recovered. From the eastern grave, 2 bronze axles, 20 chariot fixtures, 4 pipe-shaped stone ornaments, 1 silver disc, and 2 pottery vessels—a small-necked jar and a deep jar—were found.

The bronze dagger (Fig. 79:1), Type IIC, was found in the remains of a lacquered wooden sheath, associated with a bow-shaped handle. The indentations on the blade were only barely recognizable, indicating a late stage in the development of the slender dagger. Once again, the range of bronze artifacts and the assocation of iron objects suggests a Late Bronze Age date.

### PISAN-DONG SITE

Two important Late Bronze Age sites have recently been found in the Taegu area. The Pisan-dong site was first investigated in 1956; the second site, Manch'on-dong, was investigated in 1966. Both yielded bronze daggers and dagger axes of similar types. The Pisan-dong site, at the foot of Mt. Waryong, was washed out by heavy rains. About fifty items were found in a circular area 5 to 6 meters in diameter in which slate chips were scattered. It seems likely that the site originally contained a stone cist or some other buried structure.

Most of the remains were scattered by dealers; however, a number of the bronze artifacts were kept in the Hoam collection. Objects from Pisan-dong in the Hoam collection include 5 slender bronze daggers, 2 bronze spears, 1 bronze dagger axe, 2 chariot fittings possibly for a canopy, 1 tiger-effigy belt hook, and some metal sword fittings. In addition, 1 bronze dagger and 1 dagger axe in the collection appear to have come from other sites. I will restrict my comments only to the bronze artifacts from Pisan-dong. (Plates 87–96.)

Bronze Dagger No. 1 (Plate 86; Fig. 80:1) is a rare specimen, having complete attachments, such as the ornament for

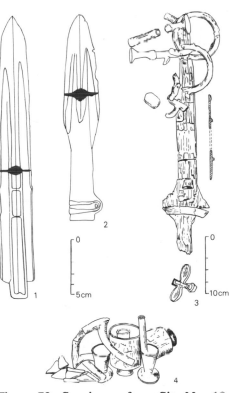

Figure 79. Specimens from Site No. 10, T'acsŏng-ni

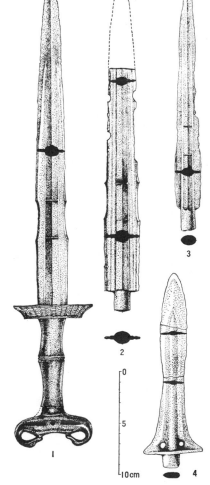

Figure 80. Specimens from the Pisan-dong site (see Plates 86, 87, 90, 91)

the top of the handle, a blade guard, and metal fixtures for the sheath. The indentations on the blade were shallow, and the portion near the handle was narrow, suggesting that the dagger should be classified as Type IIC. The handle decoration consisted of a realistic pair of ducks, placed back to back, with the heads bending to face each other. The side of the handle ornament contained two opened portions in the shape of long triangles, with a hole pierced in the center. The entire length was 45 centimeters, and the width was 3.2 centimeters.

Bronze Dagger No. 2 (Plate 87; Fig. 76:2) was damaged, so the style was not very clear; from the form of the blade, however, it seems to be Type IIC. The length was 23.5 centimeters, and the maximum width was 3.4 centimeters. Bronze Dagger No. 3 (Plate 88), although slightly damaged, can be recognized as Type IIC. The length was 24 centimeters; the width, 2.5 centimeters. It is similar to two examples from Manch'on-dong.

Bronze Dagger No. 4 had a metal decorative fixture on the top of the handle, a metal blade guard and a fixture at the base of the blade, and a metal attachment on the sheath. The indentations on the side of the blade were shallow, and the portion between the indentations and the handle were narrow, suggesting Type IIC. However, there were two lines of grooves on the blade, and they extended to the base. This is the same type as Bronze Dagger No. 5 as well as one of the examples from the Manch'on-dong site. While it is obviously a variant of the slender bronze dagger, it should be classified as Type III. Type IIC and Type III overlap chronologically. The length was 32.2 centimeters; the maximum width, 3.2 centimeters.

The handle head decoration is extremely damaged. However, it can be called pillow shaped, with round bulges on both edges. Other examples are illustrated in Plate 84, and different forms are shown in Plate 85. The metal fixture seen at the bottom of the dagger is a kind of sleeve for connecting the body of the blade to the handle. Very few of these have been found.

Bronze Dagger No. 5 (Plate 86, Fig. 80:2) can also be considered to be Type III. The upper portion of the blade was cut. A metal fixture at the top of the sheath was also found.

The length when found was 23.5 centimeters, and the greatest width was 3.5 centimeters.

Two of the bronze narrow daggers had narrow top portions, with a ridge around the base of the socket and a semicircular car or lug on the inside. One example was the longest yet recorded—46.7 centimeters, while the greatest width was 5.1 centimeters. The other was 40.05 centimeters long and 4.2 centimeters wide. The trend in the later part of the Bronze Age appears to have been toward greater length. These daggers were no longer made for practical use.

One bronze dagger axe (Plate 91; Fig. 80:4) had a wide blade tip in relation to its length; again, it seems to show the process of becoming a ritual weapon. The blade was not sharpened. It was 19 centimeters long and 2.5 centimeters wide.

A belt hook in the form of a crouching tiger with open mouth (Plate 95) has an extension from the front leg with a hook that fits into a ring. The design is similar to other tiger-effigy belt hooks in the Korean peninsula. The design of the tail, which bends back to attach to the body, is the same as that of the one from Ŏŭn-dong, Yŏng'hŏn. The reverse side was flat, and a flat flange was added for attachment to a leather belt. This type of animal design, as well as the belt hook in the form of a horse figure, is characteristic of the Scytho-Siberian cultures. Horse figure belt hooks from Sangju, North Kyŏngsang Province, are illustrated in Plates 97 and 98. The length of the tiger figure was 10 centimeters; the total length of the object was 14 centimeters and the diameter of the ring was 4 centimeters.

Two chariot fittings (Plate 94) were in the form of a long cylinder with an attached hook. The pair were apparently used to hold poles of the canopy of the chariot. Wood fibers were found around the inside of the cylinders. The length of each was 8.5 centimeters and 8.7 centimeters. These artifacts lead one to suspect that other chariot fixtures may have been associated at Pisan-dong, when the site was first found. In addition, it was said that many iron artifacts were found.

Specimens of Bronze Dagger Type III found since the Japanese occupation include the two from Pisan-dong and a single specimen from Manch'on-dong. In the Japanese occupation, they were also found at Hŏsan, Tongdaewol-li,

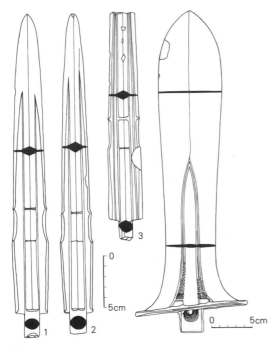

Figure 81. Specimens from the Manch'on-dong site (see Plates 99, 100)

P'yŏngyang City and Hŭkkyo-ri, Hwangju-gun, Hwanghae Province. The parallel edges of the blade and the grooves on the right and left of the ridge suggest a new style, Bronze Dagger Type III. A further type with a T-shaped dagger handle will be discussed in a later section.

## MANCH'ON-DONG SITE

The Manch'on-dong site of Taegu, located on a low slope area of the bank of Kumho River, was destroyed during construction. According to the original finder, the site did not have any notable surface features. The remains included 3 bronze daggers, 1 handle-top decoration, 1 blade guard fixture, 4 metal sheath attachments, and 1 broad-bladed dagger axe.

Bronze Dagger No. 1 (Plate 99; Fig. 81:1) had clear indentations on the blade and can be included in Type IIBb. The entire length was 30.8 centimeters, and the greatest width was 3.5 centimeters. Another example of the same style of dagger was found at Wonsu-dong, Sŏch'ŏn-gun, South Ch'ungch'ŏng Province.

Bronze Dagger No. 2 (Plate 99; Fig. 81:2) had shallow indentations compared to No. 1. It can be classified as Type IIC. In the same manner as No. 1, the lower portion of the blade tapers from the indentation to the stem. The entire length was 30.1 centimeters, and the greatest width was 3.2 centimeters. Bronze Dagger No. 3 (Plate 99; Fig. 81:3) was damaged near the tip of the blade. The sides of the lower portion of the blade were almost parallel and the indentations were relatively slight; were it not for the grooves along the ridge, this example would fall into Type IIC. However, it might better be considered Type III. This dagger is similar to the example from Pisan-dong.

The wide-bladed bronze dagger axe (Plate 100; Fig. 81:4) is the largest example yet found in the Korean peninsula. The enlarged portion near the top of the blade was 7.8 centimeters wide. The flat, unsharpened blade would indicate that it was a ritual object, not fabricated for actual use. On the lower part of the grooves on the back of the blade, there was a herringbone decoration. In addition, the relief design of five concentric semicircles on the stem was particularly rare. A similar example belongs to the collection of the Kusumi

Shrine, Kusumi-cho, Oita Prefecture, Japan. The large, non-functional type of dagger axe belongs to the end of the Bronze Age. This dating is supported by the direct association with Bronze Dagger Type III.

### YANGDONG-NI SITE, KIMHAE

Local children found pottery exposed by a landslide on a slope behind the village of Kagok, Yangdong-ni, in 1969. Digging was carried out subsequently near the ceramics and many metal objects were found. The artifacts were scattered by dealers, but a few were documented. These included 2 bronze spears, 1 bronze handle-top decoration, 2 iron daggers, 2 iron spearheads, and a mirror with a decoration motif of a square and four gods (Plate 102). Since a bronze handle decoration was found, there must also have been a dagger; however, we do not have any direct record of it.

Two bronze spears had similar styles. One had a belt around the socket, with a semicircular loop on each side. There was also a ridge running down the blade to the socket and a herringbone motif on the grooves of the blade. On the other example the belt on the socket was absent and two holes were pierced in the sides. The total length was 38.5 centimeters and 39.5 centimeters respectively (Plate 103; Fig. 82:1, 2).

A handle-top decoration (Plate 101; Fig. 82:7) had a cruciform shape with a central stick in the middle of the cross. On the long axis of the cross, four simplified horse figures were found. The longer axis was 10.5 centimeters, the shorter was 4.3 centimeters.

The iron daggers were diamond shaped in cross section, and the blades had short stems. The sheath of the dagger was made of wood, and the grain of the wood can be seen on the upper part of the sword and the stem. On one of the iron daggers there was a thread mark on the stem portion, and on the center of the top part of another example there was something like a woven design impression. The total lengths were 36.5 centimeters and 30.5 centimeters respectively.

The cross section of the iron spears was also triangular (Fig. 82:3, 4) in the same manner as the iron dagger. The sockets were cylindrical, and the total lengths were 29.5 and 28.8 centimeters respectively.

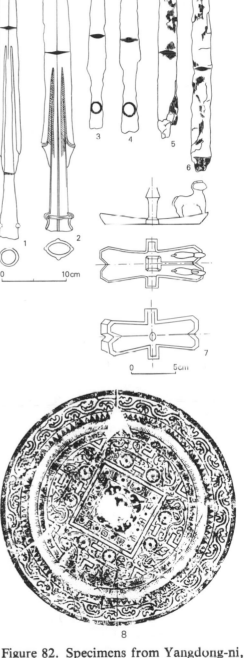

Figure 82. Specimens from Yangdong-ni, Kimhae (see Plates 101, 102, 103)

The bronze mirror (Plate 102; Fig. 82:8) had a diameter of 20 centimeters. It is a typical example of the so-called TLV Chinese mirror. The inner area of the decoration was composed of twelve small circles in relief, inside a square field. Symbols, which have the form of angular T, L, and V, were arranged in four areas within the middle circular field, and animal motifs were drawn in fine relief between them. The inscription, consisting of 28 characters in relief, reads:

> The mirror made in the Imperial Factory is very good and large. There is a magical hermit carved, who does not get old; when he is thirsty he drinks from the pure fountain, and when he is hungry, he eats the fruit of the jujube tree. He can fly all over, and is proud of being a hermit.

The ceramics appear to have been broken up or lost. Kyŏng-won Pak asked the original finder about pottery; he was told that it was soft, blue grey, with mat-impressed decoration.

The association of the bronze spear, the bronze dagger handle, the dagger handle-top decoration, the iron sword, and the iron spear suggest that the site was occupied at a relatively late date. The chronological position is supported by the presence of herringbone decoration in the grooves on the top part of the bronze spear and the presence of loops on either side of the socket. The horse figures on the top of the dagger handle seem to reflect the northern tradition of Scytho-Siberian culture, which is often evident in bronze artifacts from Korea. However, the best indicator of the date is the mirror with the square motif with four gods, the so-called Han Dynasty Shang-fang-ching Type. This style of mirror was made by artisans directly attached to the royal family. The date, which should be either first century B.C. or first century A.D., fits well with the styles of the bronze spears and iron artifacts.

## RELATIONS BETWEEN THE BRONZE CULTURE OF KOREA AND THE CULTURES OF LIAONING AND THE GREAT WALL REGION

The bronze culture of the Korean peninsula was directly connected to that of the Liaoning area, which in turn was related to the culture of southern Siberia. The connection appears to be by way of the Great Wall region. To understand the Bronze Culture of Korea, it is necessary to make direct comparisons with the Liaoning area, and also to make indirect comparisons with Sui Yuan and southern Siberia. On the other hand, the bronze center of north China must also be considered, since it is an important center of the Bronze Age in northeastern Asia. However, until recently too much emphasis was placed on the Bronze Culture of the Chung Yuan (Yellow River Plain) as the source of the so-called Bronze Culture of the Korean peninsula and Liaoning. The Bronze Culture of the Chung Yuan has been studied most extensively, and the presence of inscriptions has been an immense aid in establishing absolute dates. Nevertheless, the accumulation of current data makes it necessary to reconsider the idea that the Bronze Culture of Korea or Liaoning originated directly from the Chung Yuan. Part of this assumption seems to be based on racial prejudice. Korea and Liaoning are border areas, where the so-called Eastern Barbarians lived. A similar notion is that all eastern Asian ancient culture originated in the Chung Yuan. It would seem that the influence from the Chung Yuan began relatively late in the Bronze Culture of the Korean peninsula and Liaoning.

The most important sites of the Early Period of the Bronze Culture of Liaoning are Shih-erh-t'ai-ying-tzu and the stone cist cemetery of Kang-shang.

## SHIH-ERH-T'AI-YING-TZU SITE

This site consists of a number of mounds, and was found during construction of irrigation facilities in 1958. Mound No. 2 and Mound No. 3 were destroyed beforehand; only Mound No. 1 was excavated and studied archaeologically. The contents of Mound No. 2 were almost completely preserved; it is therefore a very important site.

The grave in Mound No. 1 was constructed by the piling up of about six layers of natural rocks and pebbles, and the entrance on the western side of the chamber was shut by a large slab. Three big slabs were used for a ceiling. Pebbles were placed on the floor surface of the grave chamber which was 1.8 meters long, 1 meter wide, and 1.2 meters deep. A large pebble was placed in each corner of the chamber to support the wooden board on which the deceased was placed.

Bones from two individuals were found; probably they were those of a couple. The bodies appear to have been placed on a reed mat.

The contents of Mound No. 1 included the following: 2 bronze daggers, 2 mirrors with coarse geometric decoration and plural loops for suspension, 1 bronze Y-shaped fixture, 1 bronze axe, 2 bronze arrowheads, 2 bronze knives, 1 bronze chisel, 3 bronze perforators, 9 pieces of bronze plate, 3 bronze fishhooks, 6 bronze bridle-shaped fixtures, 6 bronze tools, and 12 bronze joints, 59 pipe-shaped artifacts, 2 stone artifacts (including 2 microblades) and some ceramics, including 1 spindle whorl and 2 sherds.

It is particularly interesting that all of the artifacts were of bronze; no iron artifacts were found at all. It is also important that none of the artifacts appears to be directly related to types from the Chung Yuan (Yellow River Plain).

The two bronze daggers were of Type IA (Fig. 83:1). The protuberances on the upper portion of the blade were well developed, and the lower part near the handle was fully curving. Remains of textiles and wood fragments were found on the stem, suggesting that a wooden handle was attached. A pillow-shaped handle-head decoration was also found.

The two mirrors (Fig. 83:2) were of the same size (20.4 centimeters in diameter) and type; it is probable, therefore, that they were cast from the same mold. The reverse side was slightly concave; and large, coarse decoration was applied in two rows, the inner row consisting of a square thunder pattern, and the outer row of a variation of the thunder pattern with additional slanting lines. The three loops for attachment were arranged in a triangle form near the rim of the reverse side.

The bronze axe (Fig. 83:5) had a flaring blade with two belts on the socket. A surface decoration of square motifs and slanting lines was cast on the square portion of the socket. The entire length was 9.3 centimeters; the blade width was 5.8 centimeters.

The two bronze knives had curved backs and concave blades (Fig. 83:7, 8). The decorations on the handle of one of the knives consisted of two nostrils (probably a simplified animal face design) and a geometric design consisting of squares, triangles and rectilinear slanting motifs. The entire length was 13.8 centimeters; the blade width was 1.3 to 1.5

Figure 83. Grave goods from the burial site of Shih-erh-t'ai-ying-tzu, and their original arrangement

centimeters. The other example had a slightly wider blade and a portion of the handle top missing.

One of the potsherds was brown in color, and the paste was composed of fine clay and sand. The other example was thicker and was composed of a grey paste. The firing temperature seems to have been low in both cases. Both sherds were so small that the vessel shape could not be reconstructed.

The construction workers were able to describe the location of the artifacts in Mound No. 2 even though it had been destroyed before the arrival of the archaeologists. The structure of the grave chamber was almost the same as that of Mound No. 1. The wall was made by setting up slabs, and the roof was composed of a double layer of large slabs; the floor was also composed of a single slab. Once again, two skeletons were also found, probably those of a couple. The entire length of the chamber was about 2.3 meters, while the width was 1 meter and the depth about 0.7 meter.

The grave goods consisted of 2 bronze daggers, 2 bronze mirrors with multiple attachment loops, 1 bronze Y-shaped fixture, 10 bronze axes, 14 bronze arrowheads, 1 bronze knife with a ring handle, 2 rectangular bronze fixtures with rings attached, 1 bronze fixture of two combined vipers, 5 bridle-shaped fixtures, 5 long pipe-shaped fixtures, 12 cross-shaped bronze fixtures, 7 bronze belt attachments, about 20 bronze joints, 10 bronze circular buttons, and 1 bronze awl. No iron artifacts were recovered. There were probably a few stone artifacts or ceramics as well, as in Mound No. 1, but these were not collected.

The two bronze daggers were almost the same as the one from Mound No. 1. That is to say, they belong to Type IA. The entire length was 36 to 36.8 centimeters; the greatest width was 6.4 to 6.6 centimeters. The stone pillow-shaped decoration was the same as the examples from Mound No. 1.

The two bronze mirrors with multiple attachment loops were of the same style as the examples from Mound No. 1. The only difference lay in the arrangement of the four loops in a square near the rim, on the reverse. Disintegrated fragments of rope were found on the attachment loop. The diameter was about 20 centimeters.

The bronze axe had the same style and decoration as the one found from Mound No. 1. It had a ridge on the bottom of the socket. The entire length was 7.7 centimeters; the blade width was 3.2 centimeters. The bronze knife had a ring handle, with a convex back and a concave blade, resembling closely the example from the house site at Sinam-ni (Fig. 56:2). The entire length was 18.2 centimeters.

Ten round buttons of bronze were found; each had an attachment loop on the concave face. The diameter was 4 centimeters.

Mound No. 3 was destroyed during construction. Only a mirror with multiple attachment loops and a stone pillow-shaped handle-head decoration were collected. The mirror (Fig. 95) was decorated with a zigzag motif with short lines used as space fillers. Three attachment loops were arranged in a single line. The mirror seemed very distinctive compared to those from the other two mounds; however, all of the mirrors had the same kind of decoration on the outer rim and the same kind of attachment loops.

In the Shih-erh-t'ai-ying-tzu site, all of the tools were made of bronze; in addition, almost no agricultural tools could be found. From the number of artifacts associated with horses, it seems that the people were largely nomadic, although some hunting and fishing may also have been carried out.

The reporter on this site stated that it belonged to the Spring and Autumn or Warring States Period. He assumed that at this time the Ch'ao Yang region in which the site was located was inhabited by the Yen-kuo, San-jung, and Tung-hu tribes. However, this hypothesis is proven neither by the archaeological remains nor by the historical documents. Among Chinese archaeologists the idea is strong that remains of the Bronze Culture, such as the stone coffins of Kang-shang in Lu Ta, and Lou-shang in the Liaotung area, belonged to the Tung-hu ethnic group. The term *Tung-hu* is an ambiguous label for an ethnic group; it is used to designate the people who lived to the east of the Hsiung-nu people. The area which they occupied varied in different time periods; however, they were primarily Mongoloids who lived mostly in the northwestern area of Liaoning. There are no historical documents stating that they moved to Ch'ao Yang or to the southern part of the Liaotung peninsula. The Liaoning district, including these areas, was inhabited by the so-called Tung-i ("Eastern Barbarians" in the Chinese documents) or the Ye Maek and was the place of origin for people who were ethnically the same as Koreans. This seems to be proven by the distribution of the Liaoning bronze dagger, which is directly connected to the Bronze Culture of the Korean peninsula.

## STONE CIST COFFIN SITES OF KANG-SHANG AND LOU-SHANG

Groups of stone cist coffins were found on the western hill of Huo-mu-ch'eng-i, comprising a large grave area of about

28 meters from east to west and 20 meters from north to south. Within this area, about 20 grave pits were arranged. The burial area was covered with small cobbles, which seem to indicate the tradition of cairn burial that we have seen previously. The grave goods consisted of 6 bronze daggers, 1 bronze spear fragment, 2 bronze arrowheads, 4 bronze bracelets, 1 bronze hairpin, 1 bronze ring, 7 fragments of bronze decoration, 1 lump of bronze metal, 2 stone handle-top decorations, 4 molds, 3 stone mace heads, 30 arrow-heads, 8 spindle whorls, 2 whetstones, 1 bone needle, 1 bone perforator, 3 bone hairpins, 771 beads, 1 stone ring, 8 pendants, 2 shell pendants, and 15 ceramic vessels. No iron artifacts were found. Of the six bronze daggers which were recovered, three could be typed, falling into the IA category. The molds included those for making chisels (Fig. 84:8–12). The bronze axe had a flaring blade. The ceramics were brown and had protruding handles resembling those of the second cultural layer of Sinam-ni and the upper layer of Misong-ni.

The reporter mentioned a broken bronze spear fragment, but in fact the object has a hexagonal cross section and looks like a fragment from the top of a dagger (Fig. 84:4). From all of the other sites found so far, bronze spears and dagger axes were not recovered with the Liaoning Type dagger. The bronze spearhead and dagger axe are elements of the Chung Yuan Bronze Culture.

The stone cists of Kang-shang seem to fit best into the Early Period of the Bronze Culture, judging from the association of stone, bone, and bronze artifacts. In particular, it is important to note that all three of the bronze daggers belong to Type IA.

I should also mention the groups of stone cist coffins from Lou-shang (Fig 85). These are situated about 450 meters to the east of the Kang-shang graves. The area of the cemetery was as large as that of Kang-shang. The graves contained bronze artifacts from a number of different periods. Among the bronze daggers there are examples of Type IA (Fig. 85:3, 4) and IB (Fig. 85:1), and Type II (Fig. 85:5). There were also bronze axes with flaring as well as narrow blades (Fig. 85:6, 7). The burials thus date to different time periods. In particular, Ming-tao-ch'ien coins and iron artifacts were found

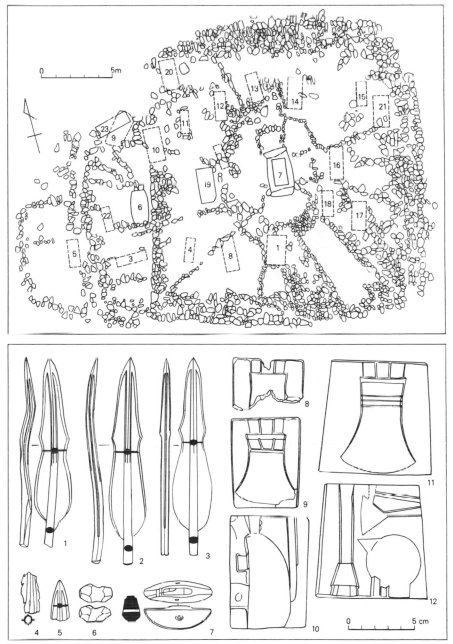

Figure 84.   Arrangement of stone coffins in the Kang-shang site with their grave goods

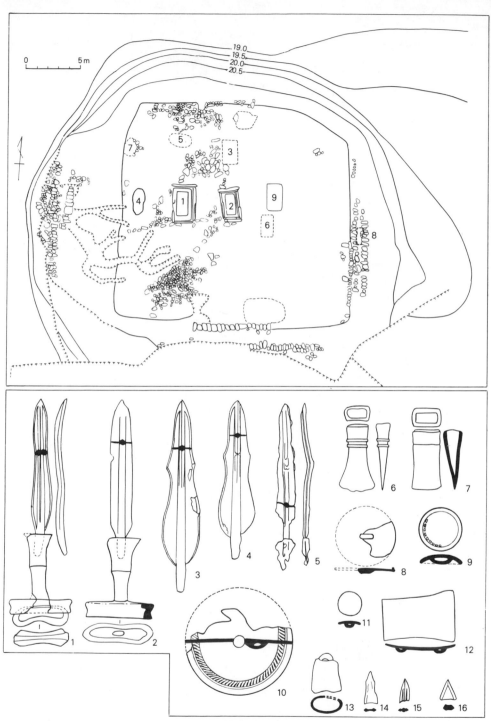

Figure 85. Arrangement of stone coffins in the Lou-shang site with their grave goods

from this site; some of the burials, then, must date from a relatively late time period.

Contrary to this evidence, however, stone molds for bronze axes from the Kang-shang graves, which had flaring blades, belonged to the same type as those from Mound No. 1 of Shih-erh-t'ai-ying-tzu.

For the following reasons, Shih-erh-t'ai-ying-tzu Mounds No. 1 and No. 2 and the groups of stone coffins of Kang-shang appear to be of the same period.

1. Both had stone cist graves and the same burial system.
2. Type IA bronze daggers were unearthed from both sites.
3. The bronze axe from Mound No. 1 of Shih-erh-t'ai-ying-tzu and the stone mold for the bronze axe from the graves of Kang-shang were of the same style.
4. The bronze dagger axe was absent from both sites.
5. Horse equipment was relatively well developed in both sites.
6. Neither site produced iron artifacts.

The stone cist coffin was the characteristic burial type of Liaoning, Sui Yuan, and Siberia in the Bronze Age, and the tradition extended into the Korean peninsula. It seems that people may have subsisted through the raising of livestock and that relatively little agriculture was carried on.

In recent times, stone cist graves and jar burials have been found in Hopei Province, attracting attention because of their potential relationship with Liaoning and the Korean peninsula. It seems that this area, near the Great Wall, was out of the control of the Chung Yuan for a long period of time, not only in the Shang Dynasty but also in the later parts of the Chou Dynasty (Spring and Autumn Annals Period). The inhabitants of the area at that time were the so-called northern group, which was different from the so-called Han Chinese. Since these people had affiliations further to the north, it seems that the Chung Yuan area provided little influence during that period.

## PAO-SHEN-MIAO SITE

Stone molds for producing spears or knives were found in 1952 from the Pao-shen-miao site, Tang-shan City, Hopei Province. Discovered accidentally in the course of quarrying

Figure 86. Stone molds for bronze tools from the Pao-shen-miao site

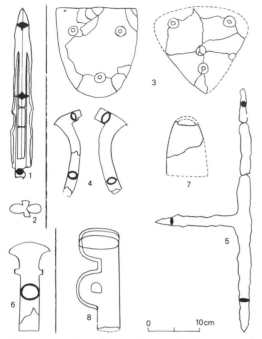

Figure 87. Specimens from the Sog'am-ni site

Figure 88. Artifacts from the Ch'o-do site

and completely destroyed, the site was located on a slope on the western bank of the Chih River. Since a large number of stone molds was found, it is thought to have been a dwelling site or a production center for bronze artifacts. The objects which were collected included 1 polished stone adze, 2 stone molds for bronze knives, 2 stone molds for bronze spears, and 1 stone mold for a bronze axe.

The stone molds for bronze knives constituted a pair (Fig. 86:2). The back was convex and the blade concave; on the handle were a number of protuberances which appear to be vestiges of lugs that were used to bind the handle. The function of the knives seems to have been for chopping or cutting.

The two stone molds for spearheads (Fig. 86:3, 4) were not an actual pair; each one was missing its mate. Both of them had relatively short blades with hollow central ridge and handle portions. In one of the molds there was a semicircular loop on one side of the socket; on the other mold four loops were attached to the socket.

A stone mold for a bronze axe was also recovered (Fig. 86:1). The head was wide and the blade portion was slightly narrower. It appears that the blade became gradually narrower in later periods. There are two parallel protuberances on both sides of the socket; also in the middle portion of the axe are two ridges. The axe seems to belong to a late period.

The writer of the Pao-shen-miao site report stated that the styles of artifacts seen in the stone molds were different from those of the Warring States Period, although the site is not far from the Chia-ke-chuang site, which dates to the Warring States. It would be appropriate to date Pao-shen-miao not later than the Spring and Autumn Annals Period. A bronze knife in the same tradition as the example from Pao-shen-miao was found in the Yonghŭng-ni site of Kaech'ŏn-gun, as we have mentioned before, along with a bronze dagger of Type IB. The Spring and Autumn date suggested by the Chinese archaeologists seems to fit our dating of the Type IB dagger very well.

The Metal Culture of the Chung Yuan diffused from the Great Wall area to southern Siberia, the Liaoning area, and the Korean peninsula at about the end of the Warring States Period and into the Han Dynasty (Figs. 87, 88, 89). The animal motifs in the bronze artifacts of the Yin-Chou, the

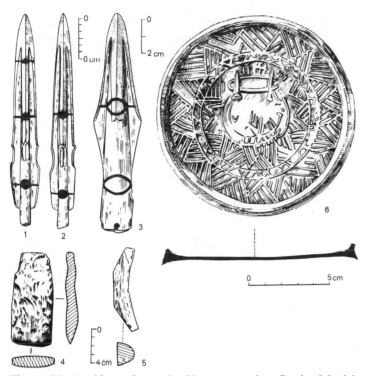

Figure 89. Artifacts from the Yeswestov site, Soviet Maritime Province

bronze swords (of Chou), bronze spears, knives, socketted axes, and mirrors were influenced mainly from the so-called northern Scytho-Siberian culture. In fact, the mirror developed from the bronze buttons of Siberia. The dagger, spear, knife, and axe forms are already known from the Andronovo Culture, while the button form was seen in Karasuk (Fig. 90). The bronze dagger was not known in the Yin (Shang) Dynasty, but appeared in the Chou Dynasty. On stylistic grounds, it seems that the dagger developed under influence from the north.

## THE SOURCE OF KOREAN BRONZE CULTURE

The oldest style of the *pip'a* or Liaoning dagger, with the violin-shaped sides, is found in the examples from Mounds No. 1 and No. 2 of Shih-erh-t'ai-ying-tzu and in the cemetery of Kang-shang, Lu Ta City. No handle parts for these daggers have been found. From Shih-erh-t'ai-ying tzu, organic

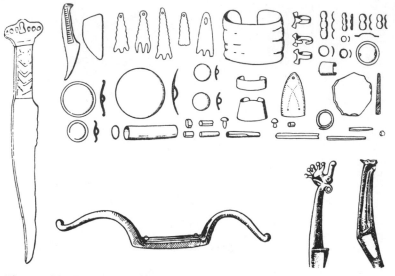

Figure 90. Bronze artifacts of the Karasuk Culture, southern Siberia

remains from near the stems of the blades would suggest that the original handles might have been wood. From later sites in the Liaoning region, bronze handles have been found with blades in many cases. Regardless of whether the handle was wood or bronze, the handle, handle-head decoration, and dagger body were separately cast. This tradition is probably derived from the bronze daggers of northern Eurasia. They present a contrast to the Hallstat and Akenakes daggers, in which the body and the handle were cast together.

The Chinese swords and daggers of the Chou, and the daggers of the Ordos, were cast in one piece; the bronze daggers of the Korean peninsula, however, were cast in several pieces, in the same manner as those of Liaoning. Liaoning thus appears to be the center for this kind of bronze dagger.

The ring-headed bronze knife and the animal-headed bronze knife, excavated from Mounds No. 1 and No. 2 of Shih-erh-t'ai-ying-tzu, can be seen in Karasuk, Shang, and Chou. As for the origin of this style, there are differences among various scholars.

There seems to be little doubt that the Bronze Culture of the world diffused from Egypt or Mesopotamia. The Bronze Culture of southern Siberia, the Sui Yuan area, the Chung Yuan, the Liaoning area, and the Korean peninsula originated ultimately in the Near East and diffused through central Asia. The animal style was known from the Iranian plateau from an early period and seems to have developed particularly quickly in northern Eurasia. It must have appealed to the forest and steppe nomads of southern Siberia, Sui Yuan, and Liaoning.

In the Chung Yuan, agriculture was developed from an early date, and the pattern of cultural evolution diverged from that of the northern areas. Bronze chariots and horse trappings did not develop very much in the Chung Yuan. Other artifacts and the animal motif appear to be products of influence from the north. Thus the ring-handled or animal-headed bronze knives of the Shang and Chou could be considered to be the products of northern influence. The definite connections between the ring-headed or animal-headed knives in the Liaoning area and the Korean peninsula can be considered to have originated under influence from the north.

The early bronze sites of Shih-erh-t'ai-ying-tzu or Kang-shang all had rectangular stone chamber graves or stone cist coffin graves. The bronze grave goods are dominated by horse equipment, with almost no agricultural tools. This is similar to the bronze culture of southern Siberia or Sui Yuan. The *pip'a*-shaped or Liaoning bronze daggers from these sites had their origins in the bronze daggers of the northern culture; at this time, there were no true daggers in the Shang Dynasty. In southern Siberia, however, daggers, knives, spears, and axes had already appeared in the Andronovo Period. In Karasuk, the combination of the bronze knife and button is notable, and the close relationship between those unearthed in Liaoning and the Korean peninsula is undeniable. The buttons from Karasuk (Fig. 90), Liaoning, and the Korean peninsula are all the same; they have a semicircular loop on the reverse face, with short parallel lines around the circular edge.

## THE ORIGINAL FORM OF KOREAN GEOMETRIC DECORATED MIRRORS

I would regard the bronze mirrors with roughly executed decoration and two loops for suspension presumed to have been found in south Ch'ungch'ŏng and the P'yŏngyang area (Fig. 91:2) as the most primitive form yet found in the

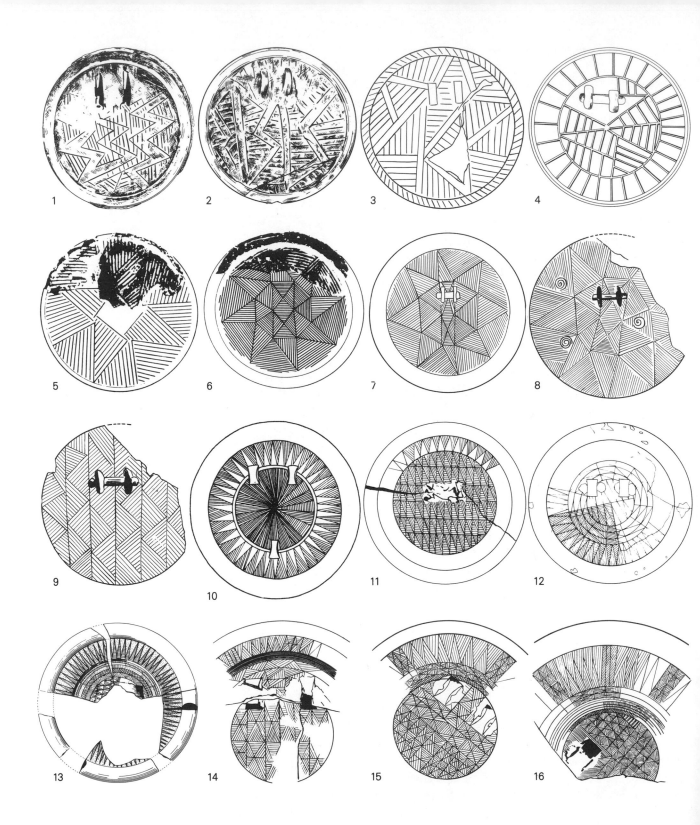

Korean peninsula. This mirror was decorated with rough, zigzag motifs, with the intervening spaces filled with rough parallel lines. The mirror from Shih-erh-t'ai-ying-tzu seems to be the prototype of these. From Mound No. 1 of Shih-erh-t'ai-ying-tzu, 2 mirrors with geometric decoration, each with three attachment loops (Fig. 83:2), and from Mound No. 2, 2 mirrors with geometric decoration, each with four hooks, were found. Mound No. 3 yielded 1 mirror with zigzag decoration and three hooks (Fig. 95). The example from Mound No. 3 was decorated with a lightning motif; parallel lines filled up the intervening spaces and a circular narrow rim was left. The rim decoration looked like the conventionalized thunder pattern which was used to decorate the mirrors from Mounds No. 1 and No. 2.

The distorted thunder pattern seems to have been simplified to make the zigzag motif seen in a mirror assumed to be from Sŏngch'ŏn (Fig. 91:3). The mirror from Mound No. 3 with three attachment loops in a straight line seems to be more primitive than the mirrors with two hooks, such as the one from Sŏngch'ŏn or South Ch'ungch'ŏng. The examples from Mounds No. 1 and No. 2 appear to be older than that from Mound No. 3. The arrangement of the attachment loops in a triangle or square seems to be related to a different function of the mirrors than as a reflecting surface for seeing oneself.

Namio Egami once wrote that the origin of the mirrors

Figure 92. Bronze mirror with geometric decoration and multiple attachment loops from Shih-erh-t'ai-ying-tzu site No. 3

Figure 91. Mirrors with geometric decoration and multiple attachment loops (not all drawn at the same reduced scale)

1. Reported to have come from South Ch'ungch'ŏng Province
2. Reported to have come from P'yŏngyang
3. Reported to have come from Sŏngch'ŏn
4. Reported to have come from Iksan
5. From Yŏnhwa-ri
6. From Sorok-to
7. Reported to have come from Chonghwa
8. Mold for mirror reported to have come from Maensan
9. Mold for mirror reported to have come from Maensan
10. From Ihwa-dong
11. Reported to have come from South Kyŏngsang Province
12. From P'yŏngyang
13. From Songsan-ni
14. From Panch'on-ni, Mirror No. 2
15. Reported to have come from southern Korea
16. Presumed to have come from P'yŏngyang

with two attachment loops was the horse mask in the Sui Yuan bronze assemblage. This seems to be an important opinion, which is worthy of reconsideration; I would suggest, however, that the mirror developed from the decorative bronze button, which was also an element from the north. The horse mask always has a long narrow shape. The horse armor mask from Koejŏng-dong (Fig. 65:7) of Taejŏn, for instance, had a long narrow shape, similar to the one from Sog'am-ni (Fig. 87:3) of P'yŏngyang City. These examples had three or four holes for attachment. Among the bronze wares from the stone cist of Lou-shang there seems to be one with two hooks which looks like a horse mask; its upper part is wider, however, and it is also relatively long in shape (Fig. 85:12). This example is close in shape to the horse mask from Koejŏng-dong.

The bronze button is one of the chief characteristics of the Karasuk Culture (Fig. 90). There is a great deal of variety of shapes and sizes; however, the circular button is distinguished by its semicircular attachment loop, and in some cases by incised lines on the rim of the face. The example from Sinhŭng-dong did not have any decoration, but the button from the stone coffin of P'ungnyong-ni had a linear decoration around the edge of the face. The button from Pit No. 9, Location No. 1 of the Ch'o-do site, Najin (Fig. 88) had the same kind of attachment loop on the reverse side as the Karasuk examples; the area of decoration around the edge was set off by a row of dots. Chin-hui Lee, who described this find, described it as a bronze mirror instead of a bronze button, probably because it was slightly larger than the usual buttons (the diameter was 5 centimeters). The bronze button from P'ungnyong-ni was about 3 centimeters in diameter. The bronze mirrors with multiple attachment loops from Koejŏng-dong, Taejŏn ranged from 8 centimeters to 11.3 centimeters in diameter (Fig. 65: 2, 3). Since the button from Ch'o-do seemed close to the small mirror from Koejŏng-dong in size, it might be appropriate to call it a mirror. The bronze buttons from the stone cists of Lou-shang were both plain and decorated; in each case they had a single attachment loop. One example was much larger in diameter, and the single attachment hook was placed off center. Once again there was a slanting line decoration around the rim (Fig. 94:10). The off-center location of the single attachment loop may represent a transitional stage to the use of multiple attachment loops.

The bronze mirrors from Shih-erh-t'ai-ying-tzu Mounds No. 1 and No. 2 were clearly distinguishable from the buttons because of their large size (diameter about 20.4 centimeters). Except for the presence of multiple attachment loops, they maintained the same form as the buttons.

Since the hooks were attached to the concave side of the mirrors from Shih-erh-t'ai-ying-tzu, it appears that the mirrors were not attached to flat objects, but to a convex surface. Perhaps they were attached to belts used on horses, or some other type of horse equipment, by strings. In fact, the mirror from Mound No. 1 did have the remains of some leather on it, and the mirror from Location No. 1, Cheng-chia-chia-tzu, had marks of either cloth or hemp on the reverse. The opinion that these mirrors or buttons were used as decorations on clothes has a great deal of merit; I would suggest, however, that originally they might have been used as decoration for horse equipment. With the increasing elaboration of the mirror form, did the function change? For instance, the attachment loops on the mirrors from Shih-erh-t'ai-ying-tzu Mound No. 3 were decorated all over on the same surface as the three attachment loops that were now arranged in a straight line. From what point was the mirror used as a reflecting surface? It seems that the mirrors from Mound No. 3 show the beginning of the change from the ornament on horse equipment to the mirror as a reflecting instrument. On the other hand, the mirror with three loops attached in a triangle from the Ihwa-dong site, which was found with daggers of the Late Bronze Age (Fig. 81:4), does not seem to have actually been used for reflection. These mirrors may have been used as magic tools with special power, in which case they were buried together with the deceased. It is unfortunate that Mound No. 3 was destroyed and that the distribution of artifacts within the grave could not be recorded. Moreover, there are few independent means of dating this particular burial.

The zigzag motif on the mirror from Mound No. 3 (Fig. 92) was the most popular motif, along with the triangle and parallel-line decoration, seen on the mirrors with many attachment loops. These are common motifs on the ceramics and bronzes in the area of northern Asia.

Figure 93. Bronze mirror with multiple attachment loops and undecorated surface found at Shen-yang

Figure 94. Bronze axes: 1) from Sŏbyŏng-dong, Taegu City; 2) from Kongju, South Ch'ungch'ŏng Province (Songjŏn University Museum collection, Seoul City)

The dating of Shih-erh-t'ai-ying-tzu through comparison of decoration with Chinese bronzes of the Warring States Period should be reconsidered, since Mounds No. 1, 2, and 3 have virtually no Chung Yuan elements at all. Similarities of decoration between the bronze artifacts of the Warring States Period and mirrors from these sites are not unequivocal indications of direct relationships between the two; rather, they reflect influence from the Eurasian bronze culture of the north on both the bronzes of the Warring States and the Liaoning bronzes. The same northern influence can be seen on the early Chou mirror with the animal motif from the Kuo-kuo grave of Shang-ts'un-ling. The mirror with the single attachment loop apparently developed into a form with multiple loops. An example of part of this development can be seen in the specimen found a long time ago in Shen-yang (Fig. 93). An earlier dating seems to be compatible with the similarities seen in bronze axes from sites such as Shih-erh-t'ai-ying-tzu (Fig. 83), Songsan-ni (Fig. 74), and sites in the southern Korean peninsula (Fig. 94).

The mirror was undecorated. Through a comparison of the shape of the attachment loops, their method of attachment, and the cross section of the rim, it seems clear that this plain form later developed into the decorated form. Thus the pattern of evolution seems to be the following: undecorated button with one attachment loop ⟶ undecorated mirror with one loop ⟶ undecorated mirror with many loops ⟶ mirror with rough geometric decoration and many loops ⟶ mirror with fine geometric decoration and many loops. (Plates 104–106.)

From Koejŏng-dong, Taejŏn, there is clear evidence that the rough geometric mirror with many attachment loops existed at the same time as the older undecorated mirror with one loop.

From the evidence of the Kuo-kuo grave, a plain mirror of the type which evolved from the bronze button of the northern Scytho-Siberian Culture was found with an animal design mirror (Fig. 95); after the Warring States Period, these types merged into the mirror with the single attachment loop. At some point in the Late Bronze Age, these mirrors must have been used for seeing one's image. On the other hand, the mirror must also have had supernatural power to judge from its circular shape, which resembles that of the sun.

Two more questions remain. The first concerns the origin of the slender bronze daggers found in the Maritime Province of the Soviet Union. The second question concerns the origins of the antenna-shaped dagger handle head.

## THE ORIGIN OF THE BRONZE CULTURE OF THE SOVIET MARITIME PROVINCE

A long time ago, Ryuzo Torii introduced a slender bronze dagger and a mirror with geometric decoration and multiple attachment loops from Shtokova. In more recent times, a group of artifacts, including slender bronze daggers and mirrors with geometric decoration from the Yeswestov site in the Maihe River Basin, have been reported. The Shtokova site is located on the left bank of the Maihe River, while the Yeswestov site is 5 to 6 kilometers upstream on the right bank of the Maihe. On the summit of a limestone hill at Yeswestov, remains were found of a kind of fortification which was made by piling up pieces of sandstone and granite.

The Yeswestov site was found during road construction at the eastern foot of the hill in 1959. Once again, the site was destroyed immediately and we have only the verbal accounts of those who were on the spot. Apparently it consisted of a stone cist coffin, from which 2 slender bronze daggers of Type IIBa, 1 mirror with rough geometric decoration and two attachment loops, 1 bronze spear (Fig. 89:1), 1 bronze chisel, 1 bronze short spear, 1 stone adze (Fig. 89:4), 1 unidentifiable stone artifact (Fig. 89:5), and the lower jaw of a human were found.

The reverse side of the mirror with geometric decoration and multiple attachment loops (Fig. 89:6) was divided by double concentric bands, and the inner area was again divided by two concentric belts; thus, three major zones of decoration were created. Both the inner and outer areas were decorated with sawtooth motifs created by alternating triangles which were filled with short parallel fine lines. The same geometric motif was applied in the central circle. The attachment loops were placed slightly above the center. The rim of the mirror had a triangular cross section and the reverse side was slightly concave. Having all of the diagnostic characteristics of the mirror with rough geometric decoration, it was almost of the same style as the mirror from Koejŏng-dong.

Figure 95. Bronze mirror with multiple attachment loops and animal decoration from the Kuo-kuo site, Shang-ts'un-ling, San-men-hsia City

While the Yeswestov site shares the same general mirror and dagger types with other sites in the Korean peninsula, it seems to be later in time period than Koejŏng-dong site. The types of remains unearthed from Yeswestov, such as the bronze dagger, bronze mirror, bronze spear, bronze short spear, and bronze chisel, were the same as those found in the Korean peninsula. The bronze in the daggers and mirrors also contained nickel in the same way as artifacts from the Korean peninsula. Naoshi Hirai stated that the bronze objects from this site seemed actually to have been obtained from Liaoning or Korea. However, the type of bronze dagger found is restricted to Korea, as we have previously discussed. Moreover, the mirror with the rough geometric decoration and two attachment loops—with the design field divided into inner and outer areas by circles—is not known from Liaoning. The source must therefore be Korea. The Yeswestov mirror is definitely related to the small mirror from Koejŏng-dong.

There are many problems concerning the migration of ethnic groups and ideas into the Maritime Province. But at this point we are considering only two artifact types—the slender bronze dagger and the mirrors with geometric decoration.

It is strange that from the eastern area bordering Foushun, on the eastern side of the Liao River, no bronze daggers have yet been found. Probably this area did not have the kind of native social complexity which would allow it to receive this culture. It seems that the Yeswestov artifacts are products of diffusion along the seacoast from Korea.

According to the archaeological reports by Andreyev and Okladnikov of the Soviet Union, the ceramics from the shell mounds of the Maritime Province show the same decorative patterns and vessel shapes as the Geometric or Plain Pottery from sites in North Hamgyŏng Province. Again, a diffusion route along the east coast of the Korean peninsula from the late Neolithic to the Bronze Age seems to have been most likely.

## THE ORIGIN OF THE KOREAN ANTENNA DAGGER

The blade of this type of dagger is attached to the handle, which has two "feelers," like the antennae of insects, on the top.

From Pisan-dong, a bronze dagger classified as Type IIC had a duck-shaped handle top (Plate 86; Fig. 80:1). The ducks, which were realistically portrayed, were placed tails together with their heads on their backs. The dagger blade, handle, and handle head were separately cast. Since a Type III dagger was associated with this site, it seems that it should be placed at the end of the Bronze Age. The blade of the dagger axe from the site became larger and slightly non-functional, which suggests the period just mentioned.

Another example of this same kind of realistic duck-headed handle top is assumed to have come from P'yŏng-yang (Fig. 96:6). If we look for Japanese equivalents for the more simplified duck-shaped decoration in Korea, the closest one is that from Takamatsu-no-dan, Mine, Tsushima (Fig. 96:3). The process of change of style can be seen in the examples from Mine village, and Kashiwazaki, Karatsu City, Saga (Fig. 96:2) and the example in the Keio University collection (Fig. 96:1). A specimen in the British Museum (Fig. 96:5) looks almost like the ones from Kashiwazaki and the Keio University collection in the simplified style of the head design and the small circle design on the handle.

The most realistic prototypes of the antenna daggers are the examples from the Korean peninsula. The process of simplification can be seen as one moves from Tsushima to Kashiwazaki. The change occurs over geographical distance.

The dagger in the British Museum is labelled "Scythian-style dagger, Chou Dynasty," probably because the exact provenience is unknown. However, there was no such dagger in the Chung Yuan area in the Chou Dynasty. The specimen has clear indentations, although they are shallow, and there is a ridge from the tip to the base. There are grooves on both sides of the center as well. The blade, handle, and handle-head decoration appear to have been cast at the same time, and this same characteristic is seen in the example from Kashiwazaki. Although these examples were cast in one piece, they maintained a number of stylistic features, such as the small holes pierced on both sides of the blade guard, which show that this style was originally developed from the separately cast form.

An example of the separately cast, duck-shaped handle-head decoration was recently found in the collection of the

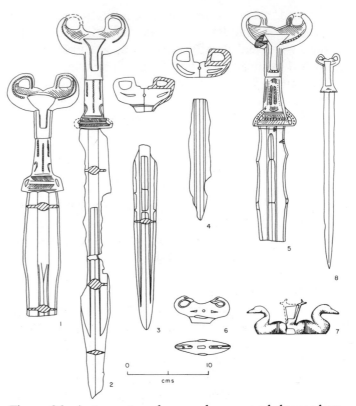

Figure 96. Antenna-type bronze daggers and dagger handle ornaments

1. Provenience not clear (collection of Kyonghi University)
2. From Kashiwazaki, Saga Prefecture, Japan
3. From Takamashinodan, Mine, Tsushima, Nagasaki Prefecture, Japan
4. From Mine, Nagasaki Prefecture, Japan
5. Provenience not clear (British Museum collection)
6. Said to come from P'yŏngyang
7. Provenience unclear (Songjŏn University Museum collection)
8. From Hsi-ch'a-kou, Hsi-feng-hsien, Liaoning, China

Songjŏn University Museum (Fig. 96:7). Of unknown provenience, it is extremely similar to an example from Shige-no-dan, Toyotama-mura, Tsushima. The figures on the Songjŏn University specimen are more realistic than those on the Tsushima example.

Only one example is known from Liaoning, from the cemetery at Hsi-ch'a-kou, Hsi-feng-hsien; since iron weapons and horse equipment were abundant from this site, it appears to belong to a much later period. The antenna portion seemed to be more simplified than the earlier examples. Before establishing the origins of the antenna dagger, we will need a great deal more research. However, the occurrence of very realistic examples in P'yŏngyang and Taegu, along with more simplified forms in Japan and Liaoning, would seem to indicate that the Korean peninsula was the center for this type.

## CONCLUSIONS

I have tried to look at the cultural characteristics of each area, and to establish a chronology through the discussion of type sites from each period. As the diagnostic remains of the Early Period of the Bronze Age, the bronze button, the bronze knife, and the bronze axe were selected. These artifacts are contemporary with the Early Period of Plain Pottery. The sites which yielded these artifacts also produced many stone artifacts; thus, bronze and stone tools coexisted.

The next step was the construction of a typology of bronze daggers and the discussion of sample sites to give their context. I hope that by using the total site assemblages it has been possible to avoid some of the errors which might have been created by using only the daggers. However, typical sites could not be found for some of the types, such as IA. In this case, sites such as Shih-erh-t'ai-ying-tzu or Kang-shang in the Liaoning area were used. For Type IB, the Yonghŭng-ni site was cited as a typical example, even though it was not scientifically excavated. The most typical example of Type IC was an example in the Kyŏngbuk University Museum. Type IIA was best represented by a dagger from Koejŏng-dong, Taejŏn, which was found with a wide range of artifacts. The burial forms and the characteristics of the artifacts would prove that this site belonged to the tradition of the cultures of northern Asia. The Plain Pottery and black pottery which occurred with the bronze artifacts from this site show its relative chronological position. Yonghŭng-ni and Koejŏng-dong are important for showing the relationship between iron and bronze technology in Korea.

Type IIB daggers, which are the most numerous of the slender bronze daggers, were subdivided into two types, depending on whether the ridge extended from the tip to the area of indentation, or whether it extended the full length of

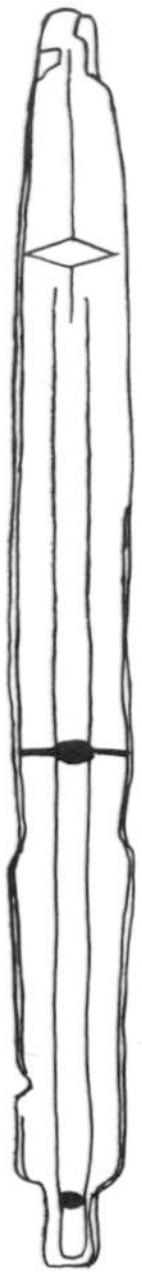

Figure 97.
Bronze dagger
(Type IV) from
Namhyǒngje-san,
P'yongyang City

the blade. Type IIBa was found from a number of locations both during and after the Japanese occupation.

The Pujo Yegun grave provided a representative example of the Type IIBb dagger. The context of this site can be considered to be reliable, judging from the Chinese documents and the seals which were recovered. Its dating seems to be rather secure.

The grave which produced the seal of Pujo Chang provides a reliable context for Type IIC, which seems to date to the first century B.C. The relative dating of the types and sites can be determined by using this datum point. With the limited material we have at hand, this chronology can only be a working hypothesis.

Type IIC and Type III overlapped chronologically, as we can see from the sites of Pisan-dong and Manch'on-dong. Type III is a further variation of the slender bronze dagger which still has a vestige of indentation on the blade.

A new style finally emerged which lacked the indentations, grooves, and ridges. This type is exemplified by a specimen from T'osǒng-ni, Kangnam-gun, one in the Songjǒn University Museum collection (Plates 40, 78), and one from Namhyǒngje-san (Fig. 97). This type can be seen in the collection of daggers from the groups of stone cist coffins at Lou-shang, Liaoning, as well. It appears to have been influenced by the Chinese bronze daggers. No representative site is known from the Korean peninsula; I would, however, classify this as Type IV.

The dagger from T'osǒng-ni had two indented portions on each side of the blade and a short stem portion. It appears that the blade, the handle, and the handle top were separately cast, as was the case for other bronze daggers in the Korean peninsula. The first century B.C. appears to be the latest date for Types III and IV.

We have discussed the origin of the Bronze Culture in Korea, extending our consideration to the Bronze Culture of northern Eurasia. In recent years, materials from Liaoning and also from the Caucasus allow us to trace the origins of some forms found in Korea and to trace the diffusion route of bronze technology in general to the Eurasian area.

The method of casting separately the body and handle of bronze daggers in Liaoning and Korea was surely the tradition of the oldest style of daggers in northern Eurasia. The prototypes of these daggers can be found in such places as northern Iran or the northern Caucasus. Bronze axes from these areas have flaring blades like those from Korea, although the method of hafting was different.

The prototype of the bronze spear was also found in northern Iran and the Caucasus. It reflects the basic type from northern Europe and Siberia. The bronze spear which appeared in the late Shang Dynasty can also be regarded as the product of diffusion of the northern Bronze Culture, since those from northern Iran and the northern Caucasus areas are more primitive typologically and also have chronological precedence. The bronze spear and dagger axe appeared in the Late Bronze Age of the Chung Yuan.

However, the important point in this discussion is that the origins of the Early Bronze Culture of the Korean peninsula can be sought in the cultures of the north rather than in those of the Chung Yuan.

At this point it is very difficult to draw conclusions about the beginning date of the Bronze Culture. Although it seems that the bronze buttons and knives are quite early—as old, in fact, as the Early Period of Plain Pottery—there are as yet no materials which would allow us to establish an absolute date.

It would seem, however, that the oldest *pip'a*-shaped or Liaoning daggers may have existed in the early part of the first millennium B.C. The terminal date for these bronze artifacts must be around the first century B.C., judging from the occurrence of the slender bronze dagger in the grave of Pujo Chang. Depending on the area, bronze daggers and spears seem to have persisted as late as the first century A.D. In some areas, however, the full Iron Age seems to have developed by the first century A.D., judging from the western slope of the Kimhae shell mound or the Ungch'ŏn shell mound. Vessels used for steaming grain have been found in the Ungch'ŏn shell mound (Plate 107). It seems that the first century A.D. is probably a suitable boundary date.

Iron technology was first diffused to the Korean peninsula during the fourth and third centuries B.C., but bronze artifacts were in wider use even up to the first century B.C. (Plate 108.) For simplicity, I would accept the view that the Bronze Age in China lasted until the beginning of the Han, with the Iron Age beginning in the Han—even though the manufacture of iron artifacts began as early as the Chou.

# Postscript

From the foot of Pibong-san (Mountain) of Taegong-ni in Hwasun-gun, South Chŏlla Province, 3 slender bronze daggers, 2 mirrors with fine-line geometric decoration and multiple attachment loops, 2 bridles with bells on each end, 2 eight-headed bell fixtures, 1 socketed axe, and 1 scraper—a total of 11 bronze objects—were found by accident in 1971 (Plates 109–115). The bronze daggers were Type IIBb, which proved that this site belongs to the second or third century B.C. The mirror had two attachment loops, and the field of decoration was divided into inner and outer areas by concentric circles. The bridle had the same characteristics as northern examples. A rectangular hole was perforated in the center of the bit portion between the two bells on the bridles, and the bells were round with four long openings. On the long-bit portion there were two rows of short slanting lines. The eight-headed bell fixture had a central portion decorated with dot patterns, short slanting lines, and triangular shapes, and can be considered typical of the bronze artifacts of Korea. On the back was a loop attachment, suggesting that the object might have been used as a horse ornament. The specimen is similar to one which, together with a bridle, was thought to have come from the Naktong Basin.

# Glossary of Characters for Personal and Place Names

The characters for city districts (*kuyok*) and small rural divisions like townships (*myŏn*) for Figures 5 and 55 are not included.

Amsa-dong 岩寺洞
Amsa-ri 岩寺里
An, Yŏng-jun 安永俊
Anak-gun 安岳郡
Annam-dong 岩南洞
Arimitsu, Kyoichi 有光教一
Asan-gun 牙山郡
Chaeryong-gun 載寧郡
Cha'gang 慈江
Chia-ke-chuang 賈各莊
Chang 長
Chang, Kwang-chih 張光直
Chang-chia-chia-tzu 鄭家佳子
Chang-shih 長史
Changbong-do 長峯島
Changch'on-ni 將泉里
Changhae 蒼海
Changhyŏn-ni 蔣峴里
Changki 長鬐
Changsŏng-dong 長城洞
Changwŏn-gun 昌原郡
Changpin 長浜
Chao Ti 昭帝
Chao-wu-ta-meng 昭烏達盟
Chao Yang 朝陽
Ch'echŏn-gun 堤川郡
Chekiang 浙江
Ch'eng 丞
Cheng-tzu-yai 城子崖
Ch'ien-shan-yang 錢山洋
Chih 陞
Ch'imat'ae 馳馬台
Chinhan 辰韓
Chinp'a-ri 真坡里
Chisan-dong 馳山洞
Chit'am-ni 智塔里

Chiyong-ni 芝英里
Ch'obu-ri 草芙里
Ch'o-do 草島
Ch'oe Suk-kyong 崔淑卿
Chŏlla 全羅
Chŏmam-dong 点岩洞
Chon, Chu-nong 田疇農
Ch'ŏnan 天安
Chong, Paek-un 鄭白雲
Chŏngbaeng-ni 貞柏里
Chŏngbaengsan 正方山
Ch'ongho-ri 清湖里
Chongjin 清津
Chongju-gun 定州郡
Chŏngo-dong 貞梧洞
Ch'ŏngong-ni 泉谷里
Ch'onjŏn-ni 泉田里
Chŏnju 全州
Chŏnju-ri 大柱里
Ch'opo-ri 草浦里
Chqsan-dong 造山洞
Choson ryŏ 朝鮮令
Chou 周
Chuam-ni 舟岩里
Ch'un Ch'iu 春秋
Chung-ni 中里
Chung Yuan 中原
Chunggang-gun 中江郡
Ch'ungch'ŏng 忠清
Chungdok-ni 中德里
Chungheung-dong 中興洞
Chunghwa-gun 中和郡
Ch'unjin-dong チュンジンドン
Ch'ungnam 忠南
Ch'ungung-ni 春宮里
Dŏkp'ung-ni 德豊里

Egami, Namio 江上波夫
Esaka, Teruya 江坂輝彌
Fou-shun 撫順
Fujita, Ryosaku 藤田亮策
Fukuoka 福岡
Funin 富任
Haeju 海州
Haesangumi 海山九味
Haeun-myŏn 海雲面
Hakgok-ni 鶴谷里
Haksŏng-gun 鶴城郡
Hamada, Kosaku 浜田耕作
Hamaguri 蛤
Hamgyŏng 咸鏡
Hamhŭng 咸興
Hamju-gun 咸州郡
Hamnam 咸南
Han, P'il-dong 韓弼東
*Han Shu* 漢書
*Han Yuan* 翰苑
Hasang-myŏn 下廂面
Hasŏ-dong 下瑞洞
Hirai, Naoshi 平井尚志
Hoam 湖巖
Hochyŏl-li 会峴里
Hoeryŏng 会寧
Hogok 虎谷
Hongwŏn-gun 洪原郡
Hopei 河北
Hŏsan 許山
Hosan-dong 湖上洞
*Hou Han Shu* 後漢書
Hsi-ch'a-kou 西岔溝
Hsi-feng hsien 西豊県
Hsiung-nu 匈奴
Hsu, Ping-ku 徐秉琨

Hu 胡
Huang, Shih-ch'ang 黃士強
Hŭkku-bong 黑狗峯
Hŭkkyo-ri 黑橋里
Huo-mu-ch'eng-i 后牧城驛
Hungnam-gun 興南郡
Hwang-Ki-dŏk 黃基德
Hwanghae 黃海
Hwangju-gun 黃州郡
Hwangsŏng-ni 黃石里
Hwasun-gun 和順郡
Hyonnae-myŏn 県内面
Hyŏnt'o (Hsüan t'u) 玄菟
Ichida, Jiro 市田次郎
Ikcuchi, Hiroshi 池內宏
Iksan-gun 益山郡
Im, Pyong-t'ae 林炳泰
Insan-gun 隣山郡
Ipsil-ni 入室里
Ipsong-ni 立石里
Itatsuke 板付
Jehol 熱河
Kaech'ŏn-gun 价川郡
Kagok 歌谷
Kamno-ri 삼모리
Kalhyŏn-ni 葛峴里
Kang, Tong-in 姜德仁
Kang-shang 崗上
Kanggye-gun 江界郡
Kanghwa-do 江華島
Kangnam-gun 江南郡
Kangnŭng 江陵
Kangsang-ni 江上里
Kangsŏ 江西
Kangsŏ-gun 江西郡
Kangwŏn 江原

Kapsŏng-gun 亀城郡
Karak-dong 可楽洞
Karak-ni 可楽里
Karatsu 唐津
Kasahara, Ugan 笠原烏丸
Kashiwazaki 柏崎
Kasi-dong 加柴洞
Kasuya-gun 糟屋郡
Kayamoto, Kamejiro
　　榧本亀次郎
Kayamoto, Kameo 榧本亀生
Kim, Che-won 金載元
Kim, Chŏng-mun 金正文
Kim, Jeong-hak 金廷鶴
Kim, Ki-ung 金基雄
Kim, Wŏn-yong 金元龍
Kim, Yang-sŏn 金良善
Kim, Yong-gan 金用玕
Kim, Yong-ki 金竜基
Kim, Yong-nam 金勇男
Kim, Yŏng-u 金永祐
Kimhae 金海
Kirin 吉林
Ko 戈
Ko, Sang-hyŏn 高常賢
Kodŏng-ni 高德里
Koejŏng-dong 槐亭洞
Koejŏng-il-dong 槐亭一洞
Koejŏng-i-dong 槐亭二洞
Kohung-gun 高興郡
Koguryŏ 高句麗
Kombok-ni 檢卜里
Kongju 公州
Koryŏng-gun 高靈郡
Kosŏng-gun 高城郡
Koyang-gun 高陽郡
Kujŏng-ni 九政里
Kŭksŏng-gun 極星洞
Kulp'o-ri 屈浦里
Kŭm-gang 錦江
Kŭmgok-dong 金谷洞
Kŭmho 琴湖
Kŭmt'al-li 金灘里
Kungsan 弓山
Kungsal-li 弓山里
Kunsan 群山
Kunsu 郡守
Kunyang-ni 軍粮里
Kuo-kuo 虢国
Kup'yŏng-ni 旧坪里
Kureungsan 九陵山
Kusan 亀山
Kusumi-cho 久住町
Kwangju 広州
Kwangsan-gun 光山郡
Kwanmo 冠帽
Kyo-dong 校洞
Kyŏngbuk 慶北
Kyongheung-gun 慶興郡

Kyŏngju 慶州
Kyŏnggi 京畿
Kyŏngsang 慶尙
Kyŏngsŏng-gun 鏡城郡
Li, I-yu 李逸友
Li, Kwang-chou 李光周
Li-chang hsien 歴城県
Liao 遼
Liao-ho 遼河
Liaoning 遼寧
Liaotung 遼東
Lien, Chao-mei 連照美
Ling 令
Lou-shang 楼上
Lu Shun 旅順
Lu-shun-k'ou-ch'u 旅順口区
Lu Ta 旅大
Lungshan 竜山
Lungshan Chen 龍山鎮
Ma-tao-kou 馬道溝
Mahan 馬韓
Mangu-ri 忘憂里
Manch'on-dong 晚村洞
Man'gyŏngdae-ri 万景台里
Miao-ti-kou 廟底溝
Miju-gun 美州郡
Mikami, Tsugio 三上次男
Miryang 密陽
Mine 三根
Ming-tao-ch'ien 明刀錢
Mirim-ni 美林里
Misa-ri 渼沙里
Misong-ni 美松里
Monggeum-p'o 夢金浦
Mori, Tamezo 森為三
Morimoto, Rokuji 森本六爾
Muan-gun 務安郡
Mugye-ri 茂渓里
Mukpang-ni 墨房里
Mumun 無文
Munjŏng-ni 文井里
Muryong-ni 舞龍里
Musan 茂山
Myŏngil-li 明逸里
Myongju-gun 溟州郡
Nabong-ni 羅福里
Nagato 長門
Najin 羅津
Naktong 洛東
Nambong-ni 南峰里
Namhyŏngje-san 男兄弟山
Namnyŏ 南閭
Namsan-dong 南山洞
Nan-shan-ken 南山根
Nangmin-dong 樂民洞
Ning-ch'eng hsien 寧城県
Nishitani, Tadashi 西谷正
Nongp'o-dong 農圃洞
Nongso-ri 農所里

Nonhyŏn-ni 論峴里
Nonsan 論山
Obuja-dong 五富子洞
Ogura, Takenosuke 小倉武之助
Oikawa, Tamijiro 及川民次郎
Oita ken 大分県
Ŏji-dong 御池洞
Okazaki, Takashi 岡崎敬
Okchŏ 沃沮
Oksŏng-ni 玉石里
Okŭm-san 五金山
Oluanpi 鵝鑾鼻
Onch'on 温泉
Ŏroe-myŏn 漁雷面
Ŏŭn-dong 漁隱洞
Oya-dong 梧野洞
Paeban-ni 排盤里
Paek, Yon-haeng 白鍊行
Paek, Yong-gyu 白容奎
Paeksŏng-ni 白石里
Paektu 白頭
Pak, Kyŏng-wŏn 朴敬源
Pak, Son-hun 朴善薰
Pal-li 磻里
Pallyong-san 盤竜山
Panch'ŏn-ni 反川里
Pang, Sŏn-o 方善梧
Pangdong-ni 方洞里
Pangwon-dong 防垣洞
P'ano-ri 板五里
Pan P'o ts'un 半坡村
Pao-shen-miao 雹神廟
Pip'a 琵琶
Pibong-san 飛鳳山
Pisang-dong 飛山洞
P'onam-dong 浦南洞
Pongam-ni 鳳岩里
Pongilch'on-ni 奉日川里
Pongsan-gun 鳳山郡
Pongui 鳳儀
Pongyong-dong 鳳龍洞
Puch'on-gun 富川郡
Pujo 夫租
Pujo Chang 夫租長
Pujo Chang In 夫租長印
Pujo Sŭ 夫租丞
Pukch'ŏn 北青
P'ungnyong-ni 豊竜里
Punyŏng-gun 富寧郡
Pusan 釜山
Puyŏ-gun 扶余郡
Pyegok-ni 柿谷里
P'yŏng-ni 坪里
P'yŏngan 平安
P'yŏngyang 平壤
Pyŏnhan 弁韓
Sa-dong 寺洞
Sach'on-gun 泗川郡
Saeul-dong 沙乙洞

Saga 佐賀
Sagi-ri 沙器里
Sajik-dong 社稷洞
San-yung 山戎
San Kuo Chih 三国志
San-men-hsia 三門峽
Sang-ni 上里
Saro-ri 四老里
Sato, Tatsuo 佐藤達夫
Sawa, Shun'ichi 沢俊一
Sejung-ni 細竹里
Shan-chu-tzu 山咀子
Shang 商
Shang-fang-ching 尙方鏡
Shang-ts'un-ling 上村嶺
Shen-yang 瀋陽
Shensi 陝西
Si-do 矢島
Shiga-jima 志賀島
Shih-erh-t'ai-ying-tzu
　　十二台営子
Shih Yuan 始元
Shui-tung-kou 水洞溝
Sihŭng-gun 始興郡
Sillyŏng 新寧
Simch'ol-li 沈村里
Sinam-ni 新岩里
Sinch'ang-gun 新昌郡
Sinch'ang-ni 新昌里
Sindae-dong 新大洞
Sin-do 信島
Sinhŭng-dong 新興洞
Sinuiju 新義州
So, Kuk-t'ae 徐国泰
Sŏbyŏn-dong 四辺洞
Sŏch'ŏn-gun 舒川郡
Sŏg'am-ni 石巖里
Sohn, Pow-key 孫宝基
Sŏhŭng-gun 瑞興郡
Sŏkchang-ni 石壮里
Soksa-dong 碩士洞
Sŏkt'al-li 石灘里
Sokung-san 小弓山
Somae-dong 小梅洞
Son-ni 船里
Sŏnch'ŏn 宣川
Sŏngch'ŏn 成川
Sŏngjin 城津
Sŏngju 星州
Sŏngmun-ni 城門里
Songnim 松林
Songp'yŏng-dong 松坪洞
Songsan-ni 松山里
Sŏngtong-ku 城東区
Sop'ohang 西浦項
Sŏp'o-myŏn 西浦面
Sop'o-ri 西浦里
Sorok-to 小鹿島
Sosaeng-myŏn 西生面

Soya-do 蘇爺島
Ssu-erh-pao 寺児堡
Ssu-wei-shan-tzu 西囲山子
Suan-gun 遂安郡
Sugup'o 水口浦
Sui Yuan 綏遠
Sun, Shou-tao 孫守道
Sung-che 崧泽
Sung, Wen-hsun 宋文薰
Sungari 松花
Sungbong-do 昇鳳島
Sungjŏn 崇田
Susŏng-ni 水石里
Suyŏk-dong 水駅洞
Ta-huo-fang 大伙房
Ta-yin 大尹
Tadep'o-dong 多大浦洞
Taedong 大東
Taedong-gun 大同郡
Taegong-ni 大谷里
Taegu 大邱
Taejŏn 大田
T'aesŏng-ni 台城里
T'ai-shou 太守
Talsŏ 達西
Tang-ch'on 唐村
T'ang-shan 唐山
Tangdong-ni 堂洞里
Tangjin 唐津
Tam-ni 塔里
Tateyashiki 立屋敷
Tayul-li 多栗里
To, Yu-ho 都宥浩
T'oegewon-ni 退溪院里
Tojang-ni 道場里
Toksŏ-ri 讀書里

Tŏkŭn-ni 德隱里
Tokunaga, Shigeyasu 德永重康
Tongdaewŏl-li 東大院里
Tongmak-dong 東幕洞
Tongmak ni 東幕里
Tongmyŏng Wang 東明王
Tongnae 東萊
Tongsam-dong 東三洞
Tonggwan-jin 潼関鎮
Torii, Ryuzo 鳥井竜藏
T'osŏng-ni 土城里
Toyotama-mura 豊玉村
Tsao-ta-kou 騷達溝
Tso Chuan 左傳
Tsushima 対島
Tujŏng-ni 斗井里
Tuman 豆満
Tung-chia-ying-tzu 東家営子
Tung, Chu-chen 佟柱臣
Tung-hu 東胡
Tung-i 車吏
Tung-i Chang 東琉長
Tung-i Chuan 東夷傳
Tung-pu-tu-wei 東部都尉
Tunp'o-ri 屯浦里
Tŭronän 드러난
Uiju-up 義州邑
Ukikunden 宇木汲田
Ulsan 蔚山
Umehara, Sueji 梅原末治
Ungbong 鷹峯
Ungch'ŏn 熊川
Undae-ri 雲垈里
Unggi 雄基
Ungok-ni 雲谷里
Unp'o-ri 雲浦里

Unsŏng-ni 雲城里
Unyon-ni 雲淵里
Ŭnyul-gun 殷栗郡
Waryong-san 臥竜山
Wei 尉
Wei Chih 魏志
Wiwŏn-gun 渭原郡
Wonam-ni 猿岩里
Wŏnbong-ni 円峯里
Wŏnsudae 元師臺
Wonsu-dong 元水洞
Wu Shu 五銖
Wu Ti 武帝
Yangdo-ri 艮道里
Yangdong-ni 艮洞里
Yangju 楊州
Yangsan-gun 梁山郡
Yang Shao 仰韶
Yangtze 揚子
Yangyang 襄陽
Yayoi 弥生
Ye Maek 濊貊
Ye Wang 濊王
Yegun 薉君
Yen-kuo 燕国
Yi, Chin-hui 李進煕
Yi, Pyong-son 李炳善
Yi, Sun-jin 李淳鎮
Yi, Un-chang 李殷昌
Yi, Wŏn-kŭn 李元根
Yijin-dong 梨津洞
Yin 殷
Yokoyama, Shozaburo
　横山将三郎
Yŏksam-dong 駅三洞
Yŏndo-ri 燕島里

Yŏngdong 嶺東
Yongam 靈岩
Yongang-myŏn 龍岳面
Yŏnbaek-gun 延白郡
Yŏngbyŏn-gun 寧辺郡
Yŏngch'ŏn 永川
Yongch'ŏn-gun 龍川郡
Yongdang-ni 龍塘里
Yongdang-p'o 龍塘浦
Yŏngdo 影島
Yongdong-ni 龍東里
Yŏngdŭng-p'o 永登浦
Yonggang-gun 龍岡郡
Yonghŭng-gun 龍興郡
Yonghŭng-ni 龍興里
Yŏnghŭng-up 永興邑
Yŏn'gi-gun 燕岐郡
Yŏngil 迎日
Yongin-gun 龍仁郡
Yongjin-ni 鎔津里
Yŏngsŏn-dong 瀛仙洞
Yongsu-dong 龍水洞
Yongyŏn-dong 龍淵洞
Yŏnhwa-ri 蓮華里
Yŏnsei 延世
Yŏnt'ae-bong 煙臺峯
Yu, Myŏng-jun 柳明俊
Yuan-shuo 元朔
Yun, Mu byŏng 尹武炳
Yung Shih 永始
Yup'an 油坂
Yusu 佚臼

# Bibliography

PUBLICATIONS IN KOREAN

An, Yŏng-jun. 1961. "The Site of Chung-ni, Pukch'ŏng-gun." *Kogo Minsok* 3.

_____. 1966. "Concerning Newly Unearthed Bronze Dagger Remains from a Site in South Hamgyŏng Province." *Kogo Minsok* 4:33 37.

Archaeology Laboratory (P'yŏngyang). 1957. "The Excavation of a Prehistoric Site at Nongp'o-ri, Ch'ŏngjin." *Munhwa Yusan* 4.

Choe, Suk-kyŏng. 1960. "The Study of Korean Chipped Stone Knives." *Yoksa Hakpo* 13:23–53.

_____. 1962. "Prehistoric Sites of Hyŏnnae-myŏn, Kŏsong-gun." *Publications of the Institute for Korean Culture* 3.

Chon, Chu-nong. 1963. "Concerning Objects from Ko Chosŏn Unearthed at Tŭrŏnan, Hasŏ-dong, Sinchang-gun." *Kogo Minsok* 1.

Chŏng, Paek-un. 1958. "Report of the Excavation of the Prehistoric Site of Wŏnam-ni, Kangnam." *Munhwa Yusan* 1.

Chosŏn Minjujuŭi Inmin Konghwaguk Kwahagwŏn Kogohak Kŭp Minsokhak Yon'guso. 1956. "The Prehistoric Site of Ch'odo, Najin." *Yujok Palgul Pogo* 1. P'yŏngyang.

_____. 1957. "Report of the Excavations of the Kungsan Prehistoric Site." *Yujok Palgul Pogo* 2. P'yŏngyang.

_____. 1958. "Report on the Excavation of the Group of Burial Mounds at T'aesong-ni." *Yujok Palgul Pogo* 5. P'yŏngyang.

_____. 1959. "Report on the Excavations of Primitive Remains at Konggui-ri, Kanggye City." *Yujok Palgul Pogo* 6. P'yŏngyang.

————. 1960. "Excavation Report of the Prehistoric Site of O-dong, Hoeryŏng." *Yujok Palgul Pogo* 7. P'yŏngyang.

————. 1961. "Report of the Excavation of the Chit'am-ni Site." *Yujok Palgul Pogo* 8. P'yŏngyang.

————. 1965. "Report of the Excavation of the Kumt'al-li Prehistoric Site." *Yujok Palgul Pogo* 10. P'yŏngyang.

Han, Pyong-sam. 1968. "A Bronze Sword and Associated Artifacts from the Yonghŭng-ni Site, Kaech'on: An Investigation Concerning the Slender Bronze Sword." *Kogohak* 1:61–76.

Hwang-Ki-dŏk. 1959. "A Brief Report on Sites Found in the Construction of Irrigation Facilities in the Area of Oji-dong." *Munhwa Yusan* 1:38–52.

————. 1960. "Interim Report on the Excavation of the Prehistoric Site of Hogok-dong, Musan-up." *Munhwa Yusan.* 1:52–76.

————. "The Neolithic Culture of the Tuman River Basin." *Munhwa Yusan* 1:1–32.

Hwang-Ki-dŏk and Yi, Wŏn-kun. 1966. "Report on the Excavation of the Bronze Age Site of Simch'ol-li, Hwangju-gun." *Kogo Minsok* 3:32–42.

Im, Hyo-jai. 1968. "The Appliqué-Decorated Pottery from Sŏsaeng-myŏn, Tongnae-gun, South Kyŏngsang Province." *Kogohak* 1:115–125.

Kim, Che-wŏn and Yun, Mu-byŏng. 1967. *The Study of Korean Dolmens.* National Museum, Report of Investigations, vol. 6.

Kim, Chŏng-mun. 1964. "Interim Report of the Sejung-ni Site (1)." *Kogo Minsok* 2:44–54.

Kim, Jeong-hak. 1958. "Problems of the Palaeolithic Culture in Korea." *Collected Papers of Korea University* 3:1–25.

————. 1962. "Report of the Excavation of the Prehistoric Dwelling Sites from Myŏngil-li, Kwangju." *Komunhwa* 1:26–30.

————. 1963. "Report on Dwelling Sites from Karang-ni, Kwangju." *Komunhwa* 2:11–25. Translated into Japanese by Tadashi Nishitani in *Kodaigaku Kenkyu* 49:11–25.

————. 1967. "The Origins of the Korean Race as Seen from Archaeology." *Paeksan Hakpo* 1:133–151.

————. 1967. "Problems Regarding the Black Pottery of Korea." *Taedong Munhwa Yongu* 4:117–267.

————. 1967. "The Study of the Plain Pottery of Korea." *Paeksan Hakpo* 3:1–98.

————. 1968. "The Study of the Geometric Pottery of Korea." *Paeksan Hakpo* 4:1–100.

————. 1969. "The Origins of Korean Culture as Seen from Archaeology." *Korean Cultural Anthropology* 2:2–6.

Kim, Ki-ung. 1961. "Preliminary Report on the Excavations at Mukpang-ni, Kaech'ŏn-gun." *Munhwa Yusan* 2:45–54.

Kim, Wŏn-yong. 1952. "Associated Stone and Metal Objects from Kujŏng-ni, Kyŏngju." *Yoksa Hakpo* 1:3–14.

_____. 1959. "Pottery and Stone Tools from Changhyŏn-ni, Hasang-myŏn, Ulsan-gun," in "Essays Presented to Professor Hwang Ui-ton on his 70th Birthday," *Haewon.*

_____. 1961. "The Bronze Dagger Burial of Shih-erh-t'ai-ying-tzu; Problems Concerning the Origin of the Bronze Culture of Korea." *Yoksa Hakpo* 16:109–122.

_____. 1961. "Comb-Pattern Pottery from Misa-ri, Kwangju." *Yoksa Hakpo* 14:133–145.

_____. 1962. "Pottery and Stone Artifacts from the Amsa-ri Site." *Yoksa Hakpo* 17, 18:355–383.

_____. 1963. "Artifacts from the Cist Coffin at Mugye-ri, Kimhae." *Tonga Munhwa* 1:139–158.

_____. 1964. *The Jar Burial Site of Sinch'ang-ni.* Publications of the Department of Archaeology and Anthropology, Seoul National University, no. 1.

_____. 1965. "Prehistoric Short-Necked Pottery from the Tongnae Site." *Ajia Yongu* 18, 2:309–313.

_____. 1966. "Report of the Investigations of House Sites in the Prehistoric Village of Susŏng-ni." *Misul Charyo* 11:1–16.

_____. 1967. "A Bronze Mirror with Fine Decoration and a Slender Sword from Yangyang-gun, Kangwŏn Province, Korea." *Shirin* 50, 2:150–157.

_____. 1970. "Problems Concerning the Bronze Dagger with Bird Form Handle." *Paeksan Hakpo* 8:1–28.

Kim, Yang-sŏn. 1962. "Reconsideration of the Typology of Stone Swords." *Komunhwa* 1:7–25.

Kim, Yang-sŏn and Im, P'yŏng-t'ae. 1960. "Report on the Excavations of the Dwelling Site of Yŏksam-dong, Kwangju." *Sahak Yongu* 20:23–51.

Kim, Yong-gan. 1961. "Interim Report of the Cave Excavations of Misong-ni." *Munhwa Yusan* 1, 2:45–57.

_____. 1964. "The Archaeological Position of the Misong-ni Site." *Chosen Gakuho* 26. Translated into Japanese by Chin-hŭi Yi as "The Chronological Position of the Misong-ni Site as Seen from Archaeology." *Kokogaku Zasshi* 50, 1.

Kim, Yong-gan and Hwang-Ki-dŏk. 1967. "Ko Choson Culture in the Latter Part of the First Millennium B.C." *Kogo Minsok* 2:1–17. Translated into Japanese by Tadashi Nishitani and Kimichika Nagashima in *Kodaigaku* 14; 3, 4:245–263.

Kim, Yong-gan and Yi, Sun-jin. 1966. "Report of the 1965 Excavations of the Sinam-ni Site." *Kogo Minsok* 3:20–31.

Kim, Yong-ki. 1965. "Report on the Excavation of the Nongso-ri Shell Mound, Kimhae." *Komunhwa* 4:17–26.

Kim, Yong-nam. 1961. "Interim Report of the Sŏp'ohang Shell Mound." *Munhwa Yusan* 3:42–59.

――――. 1963. "Report on the Excavations of the Shell Mound at Yongdang-ni, Haeju City." *Kogo Minsok* 1:49–54.

Kim, Yong-u. 1964. "Interim Report of the Sejung-ni Site (2)." *Kogo Minsok* 4:40–50.

――――. 1964. "Summary Report of the Excavations at the Kamno-ri Site, Chungwha-gun." *Kogo Minsok* 1:55–57.

National Museum (compiler). n.d. *An Illustrated Collection of Bronze Artifacts Collected After August 15, 1945*. Seoul.

Paek, Yŏn-haeng. 1962. "Concerning the Seal of Pujo Yegun." *Munhwa Yusan* 4:58–70. Translated into Japanese by Kimichika Nagashima and Tadashi Nishitani in *Kokogaku Kenkyu* 14, 4:86–90.

――――. 1965. "Objects from Ko Choson Found at Sŏg'am-ni. *Kogo Minsok* 4:63–64.

――――. 1966. "A Brief Report of the Excavation of the Prehistoric Site of Chuam-ni, Insan-gun." *Kogo Minsok* 2:21–23.

――――. 1966. "On the Relics from Ko Choson Unearthed at Sŏg'am-ni." *Kogo Minsok* 1:27–28.

Pak, Kyŏng-wŏn. 1958. "Report on the Investigation of Dolmens from Sŏngmun-ni, Ch'angwŏn-gun." *Yoksa Hakpo* 10:323–327.

――――. 1962. "Recent Finds from Southern Kyŏngsang Province." *Kogo Misul* 3, 8:233–237.

――――. 1970. "Bronze Objects from the Kimhae Region." *Kogo Misul* 106, 107:1–5.

Pak, Sŏn-hun and Yi, Wŏn-kŭn. 1965. "Interim Report of the Excavations of the Prehistoric Site at Sŏktal-li." *Kogo Minsok* 3:28–39.

Pang, Son-o. 1968. "Some Problems Concerning Korean Megaliths," in "Collected Papers on History Dedicated to Professor Kim Yang-sŏn," *Sahak Yongu* 20:61–86.

Report of the Excavation of Burial Mounds of the Taedong and Chaeryŏng Rivers. 1959. *Kogohak Charyo* 2.

Sŏ, Kuk-t'ae. 1964. "A Top-Shape Pottery Site at Sinhŭng-dong." *Kogo Minsok* 3:35–45.

Sohn, Pow-key. 1967. "Newly Excavated Stratified Palaeolithic Remains in Korea." *Yoksa Hakpo* 35/36:1–25.

_____. 1968. "Pebble Chopping Tool Industry of the Stratified Cultures of Sŏkchang-ni, Korea." *Hanguk Sa Yongu* 1:1–62.

To, Yu-ho. 1960. *The Archaeology of Prehistoric Korea.* P'yŏngyang.

_____. 1964. "Problems of the Kulp'o Palaeolithic Culture in Korea." *Kogo Minsok* 2:3–7. Translated into Japanese by Han-dŏk Chŏng in *Kokogaku Zasshi* 50, 3:53–59.

To, Yu-ho and Hwang-Ki-dŏk. 1957. "An Interim Report of the Excavation of Chit'am-ni." *Munhwa Yusan* 5, 6.

To, Yu-ho and Kim, Yong-nam. 1965. "Later Information on the Kulp'o Culture." *Kogo Minsok* 1:54–57. Translated into Japanese by Han-dŏk Chŏng in *Kokogaku Zasshi* 53, 1.

Yi, Nan-yŏng. 1964. "Prehistoric Relics Excavated at P'onam-dong, Kangnŭng City." *Yoksa Hakpo* 24:119–140.

Yi, Pyŏng-sŏn. 1961. "Interim Report of the Excavation of the Ancient Site of T'osŏng-ni. Chungang-gun." *Munhwa Yusan* 5:46–63.

_____. 1962. "Report of the Excavations in the Vicinity of Yŏng-ch'ŏn-gun and Chongju-gun." *Munhwa Yusan* 1:50–59.

Yi, Sun-jin. 1964. "The Grave of Pujo Yegun." *Kogo Minsok* 4:34–39. Translated into Japanese by Kimichika Nagashima and Tadashi Nishitani. *Kokogaku Kenkyu* 14, 4:78–85.

_____. 1965. "Interim Report of the Excavation of the Sinam-ni Site." *Kogo Minsok* 3:40–49.

Yi, Un-ch'ang. 1968. "Remains of the Bronze Age Excavated at Koejŏng-dong, Taejŏn." *Journal of Asiatic Studies* 11, 2:75–95.

Yi, Wŏn-kün. 1964. "Report of the Prehistoric Sites of Wonbong-ni, Sonch'on-gun, and Sŏksan-ni, Chŏngju-gun." *Kogo Minsok* 1:51–53.

Yu, Myong-jun. 1957. "A Ming-tao-ch'ien Coin from Sŏngch'ŏn, Cha'gang Province." *Munhwa Yusan* 1.

Yun, Mu-byŏng. 1963. "The Pit Dwelling Site of Tujŏng-ni, Chŏnan." *Misul Charyo* 8:17–22.

_____. 1966. "Typology and Distribution of Korean Bronze Daggers." *Chintan Hakpo* 29, 30:41–50.

PUBLICATIONS IN JAPANESE

Akiyama, Shingo. 1964. "Chariot Fittings from Early Lolang." In *Various Problems in Japanese Archaeology.* Okayama: Kokogaku Kenkyukai.

_____. 1968, 1969. "Various Aspects of the Early Metal Culture of Northeast China, Parts I, II, III—from the Point of View of

Archaeological Materials, Particularly Bronze Daggers.'' *Kokogaku Zasshi* 53, 4:1–29; 54, 1:1–24.

Arimitsu, Kyoichi. 1935. ''On the Saddle Querns of the Stone Age of Korea.'' *Shirin* 35, 4:1–23.

———. 1936. ''On the Shell Mound of Yŏngsŏn-dong, Pusan.'' *Jinruigaku Zasshi* 51, 2:59–67.

———. 1941. ''A Box-Style Stone Slab Tomb and Its Funerary Objects Unearthed at Ohyang-myon, Kanggye-gun, North P'yŏngan Province.'' *Kokogaku Zasshi* 31, 3:167–168.

———. 1959. *The Study of Korean Polished Stone Daggers.* Kyoto Daigaku Bungakubu Kokogaku Sosho, no. 2.

———. 1962. *The Study of Comb Pattern Pottery of Korea.* Kyoto Daigaku Bungakubu Kokogaku Sosho, no. 3.

———. 1965. ''Ceramics of the Annam-dong Shell Mound, Pusan.'' *Chosen Gakuho* 36:13–24.

———. 1965. ''An Introduction and Inquiry into New Materials Relating to the Initial Metal Culture of Korea. *Shirin* 48, 2:120–132.

Chong, Han-dok. 1966. ''The Top-Shaped Pottery of the Megalithic Period of Northwest China and Its Associated [Material] Culture.'' *Kokogaku Zasshi* 52, 2:1–16.

Chŏng, Paek-un. 1960. ''Concerning the Beginning of the Use of Ironware in Korea.'' Translated by Mun-guk Pak. *Chosen Gakuho* 17:171–182.

Egami, Namio. 1936. ''Ancient Bronze Mirrors from the Sui Yuan Area: Thoughts Relating to the Origin of the Bronze Mirror with Fine Line Decoration.'' *Kokogaku Zasshi* 26, 7:395–404.

Egami, Namio, and Mizuno, Seiichi. 1935. *Nai Chia Ku Ch'ang Ch'eng Chih Tai.* Archaeologia Orientalis Series B, vol. 7. Tokyo, Kyoto: Far Eastern Archaeological Society.

Fujita, Ryosaku. 1931. ''The Investigation of Songpyong-dong, Unggi.'' *Seikyu Gakuso.*

———. 1941. ''Report on the Investigation of Hsiao-ying-tzu, Yen-chi.'' *Report on the Investigations of Antiquities in Manchuria.*

———. 1948. ''The Investigation of a Stone Cist Coffin at Taebongdong, Taegu.'' In *The Study of Korean Archaeology.* Kyoto: Kodo Shoin.

———. 1948. ''Ming-tao-ch'ien Coins Found in Korea, and Their Sites.'' In *The Study of Korean Archaeology.* Kyoto: Kodo Shoin.

Fujita, Ryosaku and Umehara, Sueji. 1947. *A New Synthesis of Korean Ancient Culture,* vol. 1. Kyoto: Yotoku Sha.

Hamada, Kosaku, and Mizuno, Seiichi. 1938. *Ch'ih Feng Hung-*

*Shan-Hou*. Archaeologia Orientalis Series A, vol. 6. Far Eastern Archaeological Society: Tokyo and Kyoto.

Harada, Yoshito and Komai, Kazuchika. 1931. *Mu-yang-ch'eng*. Archaeologia Orientalis Series A, vol. 2. Far Eastern Archaeological Society: Tokyo and Kyoto.

Hirai, Naoshi. 1960. "A Mirror with Fine Geometric Decoration and Associated Artifacts from the Soviet Maritime Province." *Kokogaku Zasshi* 46, 3:68–77.

———. 1961. "Concerning the Polished Stone Daggers from the Soviet Maritime Province—A Comparative Study of Korean Examples." *Chosen Gakuho* 18:32–45.

Kanaseki, Takeo. 1966. "Problems Concerning the Origins of the Japanese as Seen from Physical Form." *Minzokugaku Kenkyu* 30, 4:274–276.

Kanaseki, Takeo; Miyake, Soetsu; and Mizuno, Seiichi. 1942. *Yung-t'ou-wa*. Archaeologia Orientalis. Far Eastern Archaeological Society: Tokyo and Kyoto.

Kasahara, Ugan. 1936. "Remains of Comb Pattern Pottery from Ch'ŏngho-ri, North Korea." *Jinruigaku Zasshi* 51, 2:183–197.

Kayamoto, Kamejiro. 1934. "Report on the Investigation of the Sang-ni Site, Yongak-myŏn, Taedong-gun, South P'yŏngan Province." Chosen Sotokufu Hakubutsukan Report No. 6. Seoul.

———. 1938. "Jar Burials from the Shell Mound of Hoehyŏl-li, Kimhae." *Kokogaku* 9, 1:40–45.

Kayamoto, Kameo. 1932. "Bronze Weapons and Bronze Tools with Handles from Taedong-myŏn." *Kokogaku Zasshi* 23, 3:133–142.

———. 1935. "A Bronze Mirror with Plural Knobs and Fine-Line Decorations Found at Sorok Island, Southern Korea." *Kokogaku* 6, 3:110–114.

———. 1936. "Concerning A Bronze Object from a Shell Mound at Hoehyŏl-li, Kimhae." *Kokogaku* 7, 6:284–252.

Kayamoto, Nobuto. 1952. "Dolmens from Taebong-dong, Taegu." *Kokogaku Zasshi* 38, 4:34–51.

———. 1957. "The Jar Burials and Box-Shaped Coffins from the Kimhae Shell Mound: A Re-examination of the Kimhae Shell Mound." *Kokogaku Zasshi* 43, 1:1–20.

———. 1957. "The Process of Change in the Historic Burial Mounds of Korea and Its Chronology." *Kokogaku Zasshi* 43, 2:1–23.

Kim, Jeong-hak. 1968. "New Materials from Korea." In Eiichiro Ishida and Seiichi Izumi, eds., *Symposium on the Origins of Japanese Horticulture*. Tokyo: Kadokawa Shoten.

Kokubu, Naoichi. 1971. *The Study of Japanese Ethnographic Culture*. Tokyo: Keiyusha.

Komai, Kazuchika. 1938. "Bronze Mirrors with Fine-Line Geometric Decoration Unearthed in Manchuria." *Kokogaku Zasshi* 28, 2:84–92.

Mikami, Tsugio. 1959. "The Culture of the Decorated Pottery of Korea and Its Spread." *Chosen Gakuho* 14:309–321.

———. 1961. *The Study of Primitive Burial Mounds in Manchuria and Korea*. Tokyo: Yoshikawa Kobunkan.

Miki, Fumio. 1941. "New Materials on Bronze Age Objects Found in Korea." *Kokogaku Zasshi* 31, 2:124–126.

Mizuno, Seiichi; Higuchi, Takayasu; and Okazaki, Takashi. 1953. *Archaeological Survey of Tsushima Island in the Korea Strait Carried Out in 1948*. Archaeologia Orientalis Series B, vol. 6. Far Eastern Archaeological Society: Tokyo and Kyoto.

Mohr, A.; Chard, C. S.; and Sample, L. L. 1966. "New Materials Relating to the Ceramic Chronology of the Early Neolithic of Korea." Translated by Hiroaki Okada. *Chosen Gakuho* 41:71–82.

Mori, Teijiro. 1968. "Concerning the Diffusion of the Slender Bronze Dagger in the Yayoi Period." In *The Japanese Race and Southern Culture*.

Mori, Teijiro and Okazaki, Takashi. 1960. "The Itazuke Site, Fukuoka Prefecture." In *The Formation of the Horticultural Culture of Japan*. Tokyo: Tokyodo.

Morimoto, Rokuji. 1927. "Bronze Age Burial Mounds in Funin, Nagato." *Kokogaku Kenkyu* 2:87–100.

———. 1943. "Concerning Bronze Mirrors with Fine-Line Decoration." In *A Study of Japanese Archaeology*. Kyoto: Kuwana Bunseido.

Nishitani, Tadashi. 1966. "Concerning Bronze Planing Tools Found in Korea." *Kodaigaku Kenkyu* 46:1–8.

———. 1966. "The So-Called Pit Chamber Tombs and Early Metal Artifacts in Korea." *Kokogaku Kenkyu* 13, 2:10–30.

———. 1967. "Problems Relating to the Origins of Metal Artifacts in Korea." *Shirin* 50, 6:85–109.

———. 1968. "Bronze Artifacts Found at Manch'on-dong, Taegu City, North Kyŏngsang Province." *Kodaigaku Kenkyu* 51:29–35.

———. 1968. "Japanese-Korean Relations as Seen from Bronze Artifacts with Special Reference to Yayoi Culture." *Publications of the Society for the Study of Korean History,* no. 4:1–25.

———. 1968. "A Newly Discovered Example of a Bronze Mirror

with Fine-Line Geometric Decoration Found in Korea." *Kokogaku Zasshi* 53, 4:69–74.

———. 1969. "Bronze Artifacts from Iksan-gun, North Chŏlla Province." *Kokogaku Zasshi* 54, 4:98–105.

Oikawa, Tamijiro. 1933. "The Tongsam-dong Shell Mound of Maki-no Shima [Yŏng-do]." *Kokogaku* 4, 5:139–148.

Okazaki, Takashi. 1956. "Early Iron Implements in Japan, with Special Reference to the Finds at Karakami, Harunotsugi on Iki Island." *Kokogaku Zasshi* 42, 1:14–29.

———. 1968. "Materials Concerning the Earliest Rice Cultivation in Japan, and Its Relation to the Korean Peninsula." *Chosen Gakuho* 49:67–88.

———. 1968. "Problems Concerning the Seal of Pujo Yegun." *Chosen Gakuho* 46:45–60.

Reisen, E. 1930. "Archaeological and Palaeontological Contributions of the Tientsin Pei ch'iang Museum." *Kokogaku Ronso* 2.

Saito, Tadashi. 1935. "Comb Pattern Pottery Sherds from Sosaeng-myŏn, Ulsan. South Kyŏngsang Province." *Kokogaku Zasshi* 25, 6:362–384.

Sawa, Shun'ichi. 1937. "Two Sites Which Have Produced Stone Molds." *Kokogaku* 8, 4:189–196.

Sekino, Takeshi. 1963. "A Consideration of North Chinese Ceramics—Particularly the Grey and Black Wares." In *The Study of Chinese Archaeology*. Tokyo: Tokyo Daigaku Toyo Bunka Kenkyusho. pp. 1–62.

Serizawa, Chosuke. 1965. "A Lower Palaeolithic Industry from the Sozudai Site, Oita Prefecture, Japan." In *Reports of the Research Institute for Japanese Culture, Tohoku University,* no. 1:1–120.

Shimada, Sadahiko. 1938. "Concerning Bronze Swords from Near Lao T'ieh Kuo-chia-t'un, Southern Manchuria." *Kokogaku Zasshi* 28, 2:109–118.

Sugihara, Sosuke. 1960. *Yayoi Period*. World Archaeology Series, vol. 2. Tokyo: Heibonsha.

———, ed. 1965. *Preceramic Period*. Archaeology of Japan, vol. 1. Tokyo: Kawade Shobo Shinsha.

———. 1972. *Studies in the Bronze Objects of Japan*. Tokyo: Chuo Koron Bijutsu Shuppan.

Sugihara, Sosuke and Kobayashi, Yukio. 1964. *A Compilation of Yayoi Pottery*. Kyoto.

Sugihara, Sosuke and Serizawa, Chosuke. 1957. *The Earliest Jōmon Period Shell Mounds of Natsushima, Kanagawa Prefecture*. Tokyo: Meiji University Bungaku Kenkyusho.

Takahashi, Kenji. 1928. "A Newly Found Bronze Mirror with Fine-Line and Sawtooth Decoration." *Kokogaku Zasshi* 19, 3:202–211.

Tamura, Koichi. 1964. "The So-Called Pit Tomb: A Re-examination of the Grave Area at T'aesong-ni." *Kokogaku Zasshi* 50, 3:60–73.

Tokunaga, Shigeyasu and Mori, Tamezo. 1939. "Report of Archaeological Excavations at Tonggwan-jin on the Shore of the Tuman River." *Reports of the First Manchurian Research Expedition,* vol. 2, part 4.

Tokunaga, Shigeyasu and Naora, Nobuo. 1934. "Report on Studies of Materials Excavated from Ku-hsiang-t'un, Kirin, Manchuria." *Reports of the First Manchurian Research Expedition,* vol. 2, part 4.

———. 1939. "Specimens of Ancient Man Excavated from Ku-hsiang-t'un, Kirin, Manchuria." *Reports of the First Manchurian Research Expedition,* vol. 2, part 4.

———. 1940. "Palaeolithic Specimens Excavated from Tonggwan-jin, Korea." *Reports of the First Manchurian Research Expedition,* vol. 6, part 3.

Torii, Ryuzo. 1925. "Northern and Southern Korea in the Prehistory of Korea." In *Prehistoric Japan.*

———. 1929. "Bronze Swords and Mirrors Found In Easternmost Siberia." *Kokogaku Kenkyu* 3, 1.

Umehara, Sueji. 1927. "A New Example of the Narrow Bronze Sword—Miscellaneous Notes from Europe—Part Three." *Kokogaku Zasshi* 17, 9:616, 617.

———. 1930. "Bronze Swords, Halberds, and Related Items Newly Found in Korea." *Jinruigaku Zasshi* 45, 3:301–318.

———. 1934. "Reconsideration on the Bronze Mirrors with Plural Knobs and Fine-Line Decoration." In "Papers Presented to Professor Oda." *Chosen Ronshu.* Osaka: Yago Shoten.

———. 1943. "A New Specimen of the Mirror with Fine-Line Geometric Decoration—A Fragment Found at Yŏng-am, South Chŏlla Province." *Jinruigaku Zasshi* 58, 9:360–361.

———. 1944. "The Prehistoric Culture of Southern Manchuria, with Special Reference to the Kwantung State." In *An Outline of East Asian Archaeology.* Kyoto: Hoshino Shoten.

———. 1968. "Multi-Knobbed, Fine-Patterned Mirrors Reinvestigated." *Chosen Gakuho* 46:1–24.

Wajima, Seiichi, ed. 1966. *Yayoi Period.* Archaeology of Japan, vol. 3. Tokyo: Kawade Shobo Shinsha.

Yi, Chin-hŭi. 1959. "Developments in Postwar Korean Ar-

chaeology: The Earliest Period of the Metal Culture."
*Kokogaku Zasshi* 45, 1:46–54.

_____. 1960. "The Development of Korean Archaeology After
Liberation." *Kokogaku Kenkyu* 6, 2:21–35.

_____. 1960. "Excavation of the Chit'am-ni Site, North Hwang-
hae Province." *Shundai Shigaku* 10:229–237.

_____. 1961. "A Newly Discovered Pit Tomb." *Kokogaku Zasshi*
47, 1:43–57.

Yokoyama, Shozaburo. 1930. "Report of the Site of Ungbong."
*Shizengaku Zasshi* 2, 5:7–18.

_____. 1933. "The Tongsam-dong Shell Mound of Yŏng-do Is-
land, Pusan City." *Shizengaku Zasshi* 5, 4:1–49.

_____. 1934. "On the Yup'an Shell Mound." In "Papers
Presented to Professor Oda." *Chosen Ronshu.* Osaka: Yago
Shoten.

_____. 1953. "Prehistoric Sites of the Eastern Suburbs of Seoul."
*Aichi University, Bulletin of the Arts Association,* nos. 6, 7.


PUBLICATIONS IN ENGLISH AND OTHER WESTERN LANGUAGES

Andersson, J. G. 1934. *Children of the Yellow Earth: Studies in
Prehistoric China.* London: Kegan, Paul, Trench, and Trub-
ner.

_____. 1943. "Semi-lunar and Rectangular Knives." In *Re-
searches into the Prehistory of the Chinese.* The Museum of
Far Eastern Antiquities, bulletin no. 15, pp. 223–229, plates
163–165.

_____. 1947. "Prehistoric Sites in Honan." The Museum of Far
Eastern Antiquities, bulletin no. 19, pp. 1–124, maps I–IV,
plates 1–149.

Chang, K. C. 1961. "Neolithic Cultures of the Sungari Valley,
Manchuria." *Southwestern Journal of Anthropology* 17,
1:56–74.

_____. 1963. *The Archaeology of Ancient China.* New Haven:
Yale University Press.

_____. 1964. "Prehistoric Ceramic Horizons in Southeastern
China and their Extension into Formosa." *Asian Perspectives*
8;1, 2:195–202.

Chard, C. 1958. "An Outline of the Prehistory of Siberia. Part 1.
The Pre-Metal Periods." *Southwestern Journal of Anthropology* 14, 1:1–33.

Chase, D. 1961. "A Limited Archaeological Survey of the Han
River Valley in Central Korea." *Asian Perspectives* 4; 1,
2:141–149.

Flint, R. F. 1955. *Glacial Geology and the Pleistocene Epoch*. New York: John Wiley & Sons.

Gaul, J. H. 1943. "Observations on the Bronze Age in the Yenisei Valley, Siberia." In *Studies in the Anthropology of Oceania and Asia*. Papers of the Peabody Museum of American Archaeology and Ethnology, Harvard University, vol. 20, pp. 149–188.

Gimbutas, M. 1953. "The Earliest Culture History of the Northern Part of the U.S.S.R.—A Review Article." In *Proceedings of the Prehistoric Society for 1953*, part 1, paper no. 4.

_____. 1956. *The Prehistory of Eastern Europe: Part 1. Mesolithic, Neolithic, and Copper Age Cultures in Russia and the Baltic Area*. American School of Prehistoric Research, Peabody Museum, Harvard University, bulletin no. 20.

_____. 1958. "Middle Ural Sites and Chronology of Northern Eurasia." In *Proceedings of the Prehistoric Society for 1958*, new series vol. 24, pp. 120–157.

Griffin, J. B., ed. 1952. *Archaeology of the Eastern United States*. Chicago: University of Chicago Press.

Jettmar, K. 1951. "The Altai Before the Turks." The Museum of Far Eastern Antiquities, bulletin no. 23, pp. 135–223, plates I–XXXVI.

_____. 1951. "The Karasuk Culture and Its Southeastern Affinities." The Museum of Far Eastern Antiquities, bulletin no. 22, pp. 83–126, plates 1–16.

Karlgren, B. 1945. "Some Weapons and Tools of the Yin Dynasty." The Museum of Far Eastern Antiquities, bulletin no. 17, pp. 101–144, plates 1–40.

Kokubu, Naoichi. 1964. "The Prehistoric Southern Islands and East China Sea Areas." *Asian Perspectives* 7; 1, 2:224–242.

Lautensach, H. 1945. *Korea, eine Landeskunde auf Grund Eigenes Reisen der Literture*. Leipzig: K. F. Koehler Verlag.

Levin, M. G. and Potapov, L. P., eds. 1964. *The Peoples of Siberia*. Chicago: University of Chicago Press.

Mongait, A. L. 1959. *Archaeology in the U.S.S.R.* Translated from the Russian by David Svinsky. Moscow: Foreign Languages Publishing House.

Movius, H. L., Jr. 1949. "The Lower Palaeolithic Cultures of Southern and Eastern Asia." *American Philosophical Society, Transactions*, new series no. 38, part 4, pp. 329–420.

_____. 1959. "Old World Prehistory; Palaeolithic." In A. L. Kroeber, ed., *Anthropology Today*. Chicago: University of Chicago Press.

Okladnikov, A. P. 1950. "The Neolithic and Bronze Age of the

Baikal Region, Parts I and II.'' Translated into English by O. Frink. Ms Peabody Museum, Harvard University.

_____. 1964. ''Ancient Population of Siberia and Its Culture.'' In M. G. Levin and L. P. Potapov, eds., *Peoples of Siberia.* Chicago: University of Chicago Press.

_____. 1968. *The Soviet Far East in Antiquity; an Archaeological and Historical Study of the Maritime Region of the U.S.S.R.* Arctic Institute of North America. Anthropology of the North: Translation from Russian Sources, no. 6. Toronto: University of Toronto Press.

Pearson, R. J. 1969. *Archaeology of the Ryukyu Islands: A Regional Chronology from 3000 B.C. to the Historic Period.* Honolulu: University of Hawaii Press.

Solheim, W. G. 1963. ''Formosan Relationships with Southeast Asia.'' *Asian Perspectives* 8, 1/2:251–260.

Tolstoy, P. 1953. ''Some Amerasian Pottery Traits in North Asian Prehistory.'' *American Antiquity* 19, 1:25–39.

Ward, L. 1954. ''The Relative Chronology of China through the Han Period.'' In R. Ehrich, ed., *Relative Chronologies in Old World Archaeology.* Chicago: University of Chicago Press.

## PUBLICATIONS IN CHINESE

An, Chih-min. 1953. ''Report on the Excavations from T'ang Shan City, Hopei Province.'' *K'ao Ku Hsueh Pao* 6:57–116.

_____. 1954. ''Artifacts from the Stone Coffins of T'ang Shan.'' *K'ao Ku Hsueh Pao* 7:77–87.

Chin-chou City Museum. 1960. ''Report on an Eastern Chou Grave from Wu-chin-t'ang, Chin-hsi-hsien, Liaoning.'' *K'ao Ku* 5:7–9.

Chu, Kuei. 1960. ''Bronze Dagger Tombs from Shih-crh-t'ai-ying-tzu, Liaoning.'' *K'ao Ku Hsueh Pao* 1:63–72.

Institute of Archaeology, Academia Sinica. 1959. ''Chou Dynasty Graves from Shang-ts'un-ling, Kuo-kuo.'' *K'ao Ku Hsueh K'an, Ting Chung* 10.

Kirin Ta-hsueh Li-shih-shi Wen-wu Ch'en-lieh-shih. 1960. ''Report on the Excavations of Stone Slab Coffins at Ssu-wei-shan-tzu in Kirin.'' *K'ao Ku* 4:35–38.

Li, Chi. 1963. ''The Historical Position of Chinese Black Pottery.'' *Kuo-li Taiwan Ta-hsueh K'ao-ku Jen-jui-hsueh Kan* 21, 22:1–12.

Li, I-yu. 1959. ''Investigation of Bronze Artifacts Unearthed at Chao-wu-ta-meng, Inner Mongolia.'' *K'ao Ku* 6:277.

Lu Shun Museum. 1959. ''Report on Graves of the Warring States

Period at Huo-mu-ch'eng-i of Lu-shun-k'ou-ch'u.'' *K'ao Ku* 8.

Shen-yang City Survey Group for Cultural Objects. 1964. "Materials Related to Bronze Daggers from the Area of Shen-yang City." *K'ao Ku* 1:44–45.

Sun, Shou-tao and Hsu, Ping-ku. 1964. "Bronze Daggers from Ssu-erh-pao, Liaoning, and the Stone Cist Coffins at Ta-huo-fang." *K'ao Ku* 6:277–285.

Sung, Wen-hsun; Huang, Shih-chang; Lien, Chao-mei; and Li, Kuang-chou. 1967. "Oluanpi: A Prehistoric Site at the Southern Tip of Taiwan." *Annual Bulletin of the China Council for East Asian Studies,* no. 6:1–46. Taipei.

Sung, Wen-hsun. 1969. *Changpinian: A Newly Discovered Preceramic Culture from the Agglomerate Caves on the East Coast of Taiwan.* Taipei: Chung-kuo Tung-ah Hsueh-shih Yen-chiu Chi-hua Wei-yuan-hui.

Tung, Chu-chen. 1955. "The Neolithic Cultures of Kirin." *K'ao Ku T'ung Hsin* 2:5–12.

Plates

1

2

1,2. Pottery vessels, Geometric Pottery Period, from the Amsa-dong (formerly Amsa-ri) site, Seoul City. Neolithic Period. Songjŏn University Museum, Seoul.

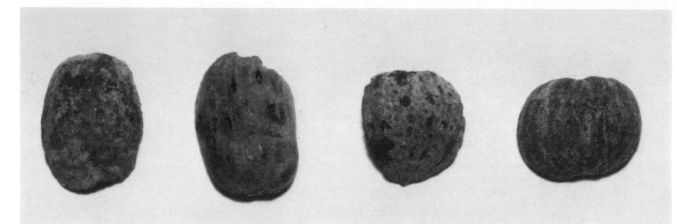

3. Seeds of *Aesculus turbinata* (horse chestnut) from the Amsa-dong site, Seoul City. Neolithic Period. Korea University Museum, Seoul.

4. Bases of Geometric Pottery vessels from the Amsa-dong site, Seoul City. Neolithic Period. Korea University Museum, Seoul.

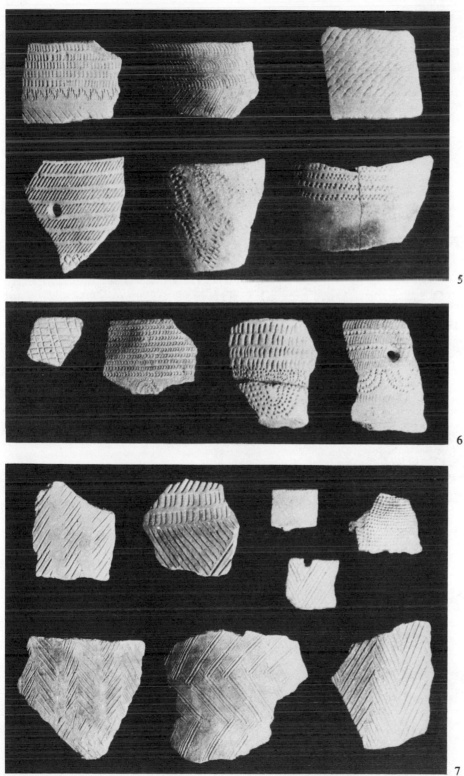

5,6,7.  Decoration motifs on Geometric Pottery from the Amsa-dong site, Seoul City. Neolithic Period. Korea University Museum, Seoul.

8. Mortar and pestle from the Amsa-dong site, Seoul. Neolithic Period. Korea University Museum, Seoul.

9

10

9. Stone tools from Amsa-dong, Seoul. Neolithic Period. Korea University Museum.

10. Hearth from the Amsa-dong site. Neolithic Period. Seoul City.

11

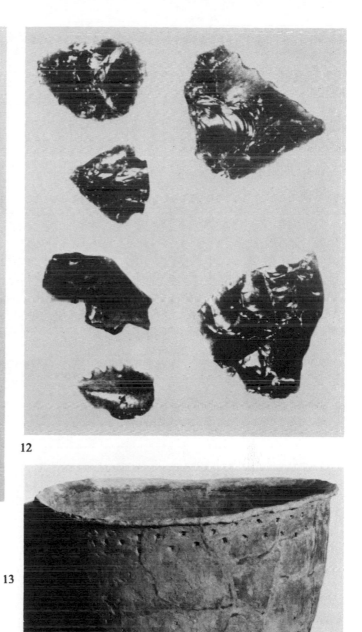

12

13

11. Shell and bone tools from the Tongsam-dong shell
mound, Yŏngdo, Pusan City. Neolithic Period. Pusan
University Museum, Pusan.

12. Obsidian artifacts from the Tongsam-dong shell
mound, Yŏngdo, Pusan City. Neolithic Period. Pusan
University Museum, Pusan.

13. Plain Pottery vessel said to be from the North
Hamgyŏng area. Bronze Age. National Museum of Korea,
Seoul.

14,15,16. Plain Pottery vessels, from Karak-ni, Seoul City. Bronze Age. Korea University Museum, Seoul.

14

15

16

17. Stone tools from the Karak-ni site, Seoul City. Bronze Age. Korea University Museum, Seoul.

18. Plain Pottery vessel, Yŏksam-dong site, Seoul City. Bronze Age. Songjŏn University Museum, Seoul.

19. Plain Pottery vessel from Dolmen C, Hwangsŏng-ni site, Chech'on-gun, North Ch'ungch'ŏng Province. Bronze Age. National Museum of Korea, Seoul.

17

19

18

20. Red-painted and burnished pottery vessel from Dolmen C, Hwangsŏng-ni, Chech'on-gun, North Ch'ungch'ŏng Province. Bronze Age. National Museum of Korea, Seoul.

21. Semilunar stone knife from Dolmen B, Hwangsŏng-ni site, Chech'on-gun, North Ch'ungch'ŏng Province. Bronze Age. National Museum of Korea, Seoul.

22. Ring-shaped adze from Dolmen A, Hwangsŏng-ni site, Chech'on-gun, North Ch'ungch'ŏng Province. Bronze Age. National Museum of Korea, Seoul.

23. Stone adze collected near Dolmen 10, Hwangsŏng-ni site, Chech'on-gun, North Ch'ungch'ŏng Province. Bronze Age. National Museum of Korea, Seoul.

24. Stone arrowheads and dagger from Dolmen No. 7, Hwangsŏng-ni site, Chech'on-gun, North Ch'ungch'ŏng Province. National Museum of Korea.

20

21

23

22

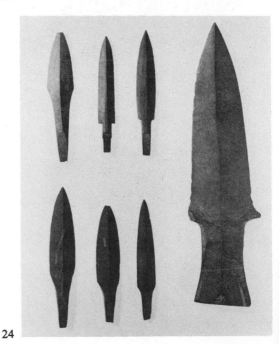

24

25. Plain Pottery vessel from Sajik-dong, Tongnae, Pusan City. Bronze Age. Pusan University Museum, Pusan.

27. Red-painted and burnished pottery vessel from Koejŏng-i-dong site, Pusan City. Bronze Age. Pusan University Museum, Pusan. (See Figure 51.)

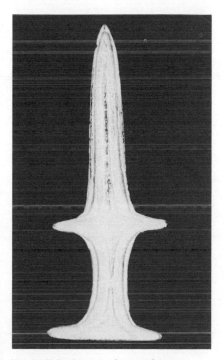

26. Polished stone dagger from Sajik-dong, Tongnae, Pusan City. Pusan University Museum, Pusan.

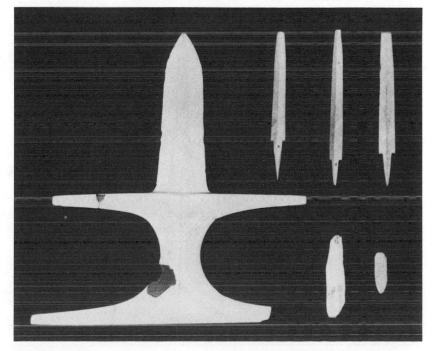

28. Stone dagger, stone arrowheads from the Koejŏng-i-dong site, Pusan City. Bronze Age. Pusan University Museum, Pusan. (See Figure 51.)

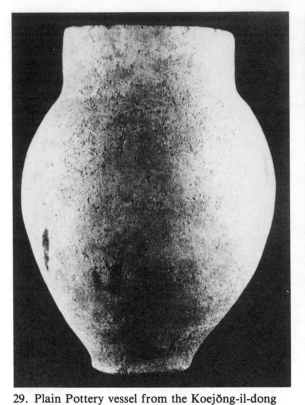

30. Paddle impressed pottery vessel from the Koejŏng-dong shell mound. Bronze Age. Pusan University Museum, Pusan.

29. Plain Pottery vessel from the Koejŏng-il-dong site, Pusan City. Bronze Age. Pusan University Museum, Pusan. (See Figure 52.)

31. Painted pottery vessel from Sach'on, South Kyŏngsang Province. Kaya Culture. Pusan University Museum, Pusan.

32. Red-painted and burnished pottery vessel from Sach'on, South Kyŏngsang Province. Kaya Culture. Pusan University Museum, Pusan.

35          36         33             34

33. Black Pottery from Koejŏng-dong, Taejŏn City, South Ch'ungch'ŏng Province. Bronze Age. National Museum of Korea, Seoul.

34. Plain Pottery vessel from Koejŏng-dong, Taejŏn City. South Ch'ungch'ŏng Province. Bronze Age. National Museum of Korea, Seoul.

35. Bronze dagger with handle attached, excavation site unclear. Bronze Age. National Museum of Korea.

36. Bronze dagger (and handle ornament) from P'yŏngyang, South P'yŏngun Province. Bronze Age. Songjŏn University Museum, Seoul.

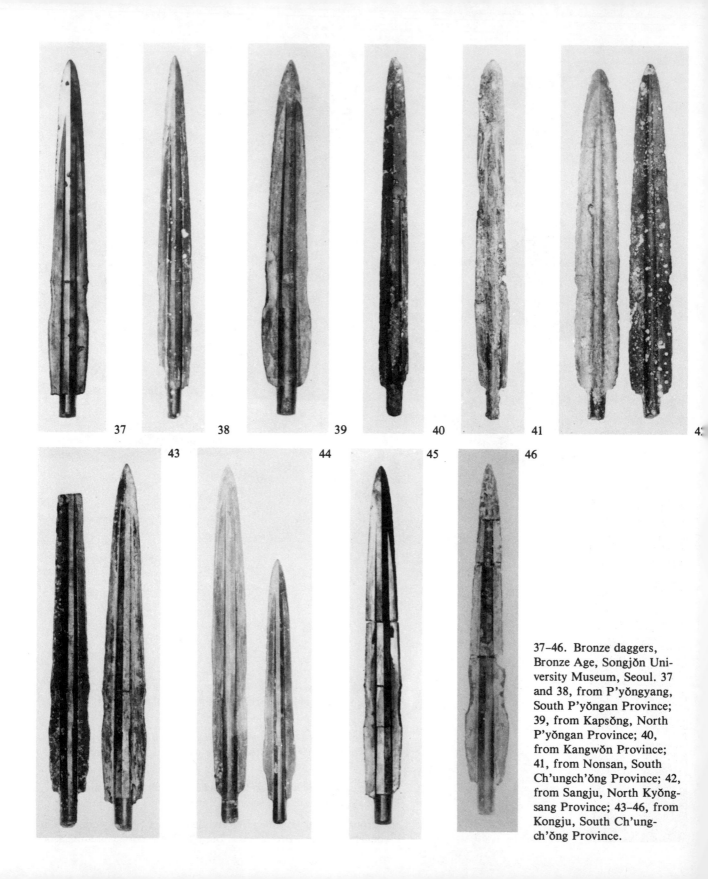

37–46. Bronze daggers, Bronze Age, Songjŏn University Museum, Seoul. 37 and 38, from P'yŏngyang, South P'yŏngan Province; 39, from Kapsŏng, North P'yŏngan Province; 40, from Kangwŏn Province; 41, from Nonsan, South Ch'ungch'ŏng Province; 42, from Sangju, North Kyŏngsang Province; 43–46, from Kongju, South Ch'ungch'ŏng Province.

47      48          49

47. Long knife with ring handle from P'yŏngyang, South P'yŏngan Province. Bronze Age. Songjŏn University Museum, Seoul.

48. Bronze spearheads from Kongju, North Kyŏngsang Province. Bronze Age. Songjŏn University Museum, Seoul.

49. Bronze socketted spear from Kyŏngju, North Kyŏngsang Province. Bronze Age. Songjŏn University Museum, Seoul.

50. Bronze chisel, adze, socketted spear fragments from Kongju, South Ch'ungch'ŏng Province. Bronze Age. Songjŏn University Museum, Seoul.

51. Bronze planing tool from Kongju, South Ch'ungch'ŏng Province. Bronze Age. Songjŏn University Museum.

52. Molds for bronze daggers from Ch'obu-ri, Yongin-gun, Kyonggi Province. Bronze Age. National Museum of Korea, Seoul.

51        52

50

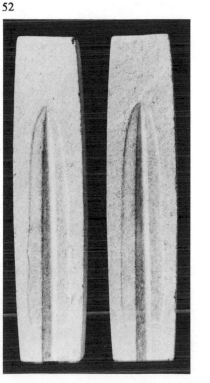

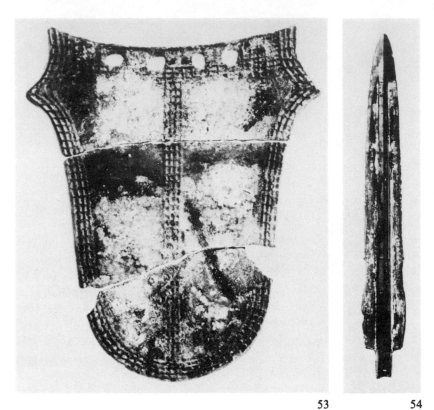

53

54

53. Shield-form bronze object (horse nose guard) from Koejŏng-dong, Taejŏn City, South Ch'ungch'ŏng Province. Bronze Age. National Museum of Korea, Seoul.

54. Bronze dagger from Koejŏng-dong, Taejŏn City. South Ch'ungch'ŏng Province. Bronze Age. National Museum of Korea, Seoul.

55. Stone arrowheads from Koejŏng-dong, Taejŏn City, South Ch'ungch'ŏng Province. Bronze Age. National Museum of Korea, Seoul.

56. Jade ornaments from Koejŏng-dong, Taejŏn City, South Ch'ungch'ŏng Province. Bronze Age. National Museum of Korea, Seoul.

57. Bronze mirror with single attachment loop, from Koejŏng-dong, Taejŏn City, South Ch'ungch'ŏng Province. Bronze Age. National Museum of Korea, Seoul.

55

56

57

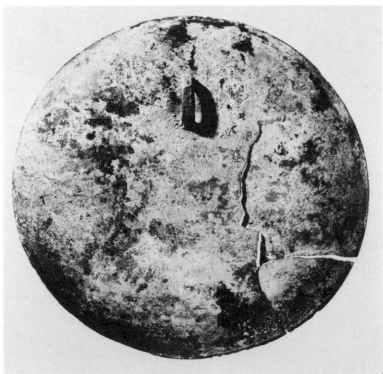

58,59. Bronze hand bells from Koejŏng-dong, Taejŏn City, South Ch'ungch'ŏng Province. Bronze Age. National Museum of Korea, Seoul.

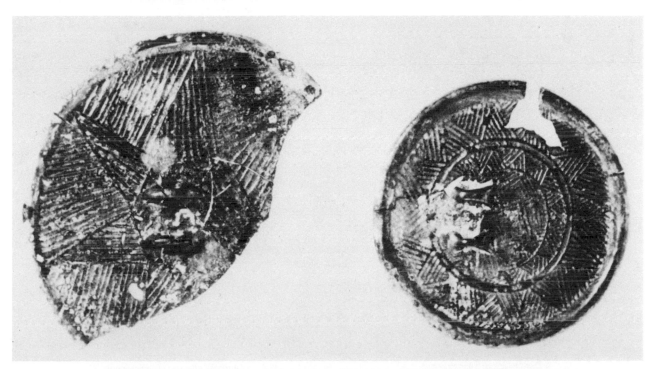

60,61.Mirrors with fine-line geometric decoration from Koejŏng-dong, Taejŏn City, South Ch'ungch'ŏng Province. Bronze Age. National Museum of Korea, Seoul.

62,63,64. Bronze objects in the shape of dagger handles, possibly shin guards, from Koejŏng-dong, Taejŏn City, South Ch'ungch'ŏng Province. Bronze Age. National Museum of Korea, Seoul.

65,66,67. Bronze objects in Plates 62, 63, 64—reverse side.

68. Bronze daggers, fragments of mirrors with fine-line Geometric decoration, and jade ornament from Yŏnhwa-ri, Puyŏ-gun, South Ch'ungch'ŏng Province. Bronze Age. National Museum of Korea, Seoul.

69. Bronze daggers from Yŏngam, South Chŏlla Province. Bronze Age. Songjŏn University Museum, Seoul.

70. Bronze halberds (dagger axes) from Yŏngam, South Chŏlla Province. Bronze Age. Songjŏn University Museum, Seoul.

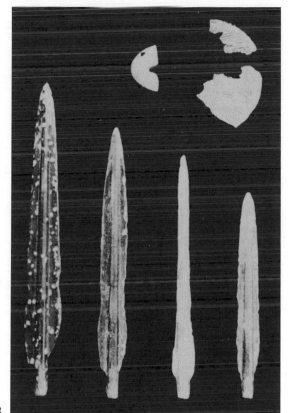

68

69

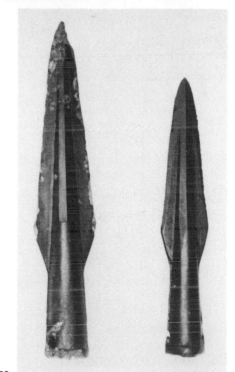

70

71

72

73

71. Stone molds for bronze adzes from South Chŏlla Province. Bronze Age. Songjŏn University Museum, Seoul.

72. Stone molds for bronze chisels, needles, adzes, and halberds, from Yŏngam, South Chŏlla Province. Bronze Age. Songjŏn University Museum, Seoul.

73. Stone molds for bronze daggers, halberd, from Yŏngam, South Chŏlla Province. Bronze Age. Songjŏn University Museum, Seoul.

74. Bronze mirror with fine-line Geometric decoration from Yŏngam, South Chŏlla Province, Bronze Age. Songjŏn University Museum, Seoul.

75. Mirror with fine-line geometric decoration from Yŏngam, South Chŏlla Province. Bronze Age. Songjŏn University Museum.

74

75

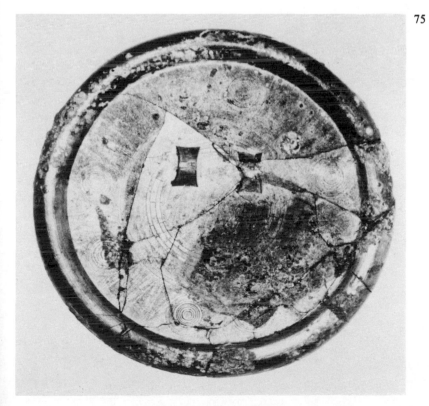

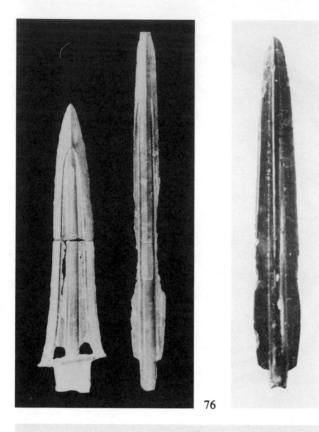

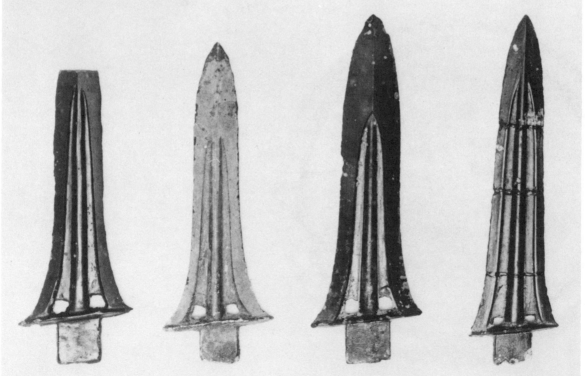

76. Bronze halberd or dagger axe, and dagger, from Pongam-ni, Yŏn'gi-gun, South Ch'ungch'ŏng Province. Bronze Age. National Museum of Korea, Seoul.

77. Bronze halberds. From left: Kongju; Sog'am-ni, P'yŏngyang; Yoi-do, Yŏngdŭng p'o; P'yŏngyang. Songjŏn University Museum, Seoul.

78. Bronze dagger from the ruins of T'osŏng, Yangyang-gun, Kangwŏn Province. Bronze Age. National Museum of Korea, Seoul.

76

78

77

79

79. Bronze hand bells. Upper row, from P'yŏng-ni, Kyŏngju City; lower left, right, from P'yŏng-ni; lower center, from Ipsil-ni, Kyŏngju City. Songjŏn University Museum, Seoul.

80. Bronze hand bells from Ipsil-ni, Kyŏngju City, North Kyŏngsang Province. Bronze Age. Songjŏn University Museum, Seoul.

81. Bronze handle ornament from Koryŏng-gun, North Kyŏngsang Province. Bronze Age. Songjŏn University Museum, Seoul.

80          81

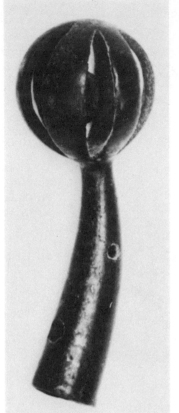

82

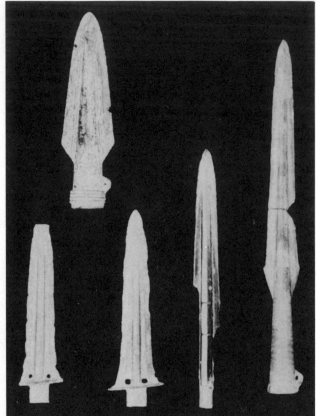

83

84

85

82. Bronze ornament from Ipsil-ni, Kyŏngju City, North Kyŏngsang Province. Bronze Age. Songjŏn University Museum, Seoul.

83. Bronze dagger, halberds, spearheads from P'yŏng-ni, Kyŏngju City, North Kyŏngsang Province. Bronze Age. National Museum of Korea, Seoul.

84. Top portions of dagger handles, from left: Kyŏngju City; provenience unclear; Kongju City. Songjŏn University Museum, Seoul.

85. Bronze handle grip decoration, from Kongju City, North Ch'ungch'ŏng Province. Bronze Age. Songjŏn University Museum, Seoul.

86. Bronze dagger from Pisan-dong, Taegu City, North Kyŏngsang Province. Bronze Age. Collection of Byŏng-ch'ŏl Yi.

87,88,89,90. Bronze daggers from Pisan-dong, Taegu City, North Kyŏngsang Province. Bronze Age. Collection of Byŏng-ch'ŏl Yi.

91. Bronze halberd from Pisan-dong, Taegu City, North Kyŏngsang Province. Bronze Age. Collection of Byŏng-ch'ŏl Yi.

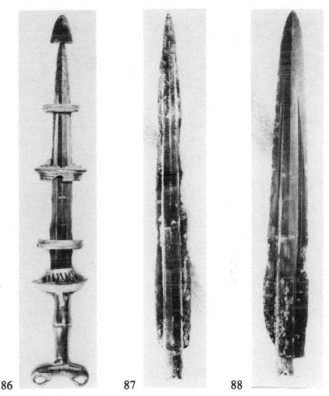

86        87        88

89        90        91

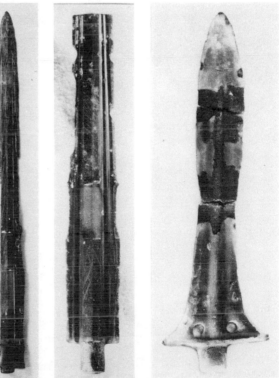

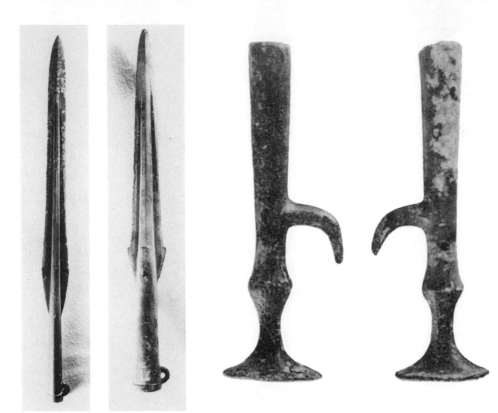

92  93  94

92,93. Bronze spearheads from Pisan-dong, Taegu City, North Kyŏngsang Province. Bronze Age. Collection of Byŏng-ch'ŏl Yi.

94. Bronze chariot fittings, for holding poles of canopy from Pisan-dong, Taegu City, North Kyŏngsang Province. Bronze Age. Collection of Byŏng-ch'ŏl Yi.

95. Bronze belt hook in the form of a tiger from Pisandong, Taegu City, North Kyŏngsang Province. Bronze Age. Collection of Byŏng-ch'ŏl Yi.

96. Bronze belt hook in Plate 87—reverse side.

95

96

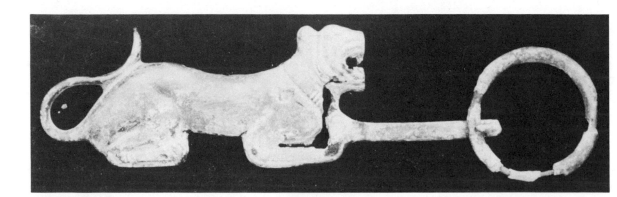

97,98. Bronze belt hooks from Sangju, North Kyŏngsang Province. Bronze Age. Songjŏn University Museum, Seoul.

99. Bronze daggers with attachments for the handle, sheath, and tip from Manch'on-dong, Taegu City, North Kyŏngsang Province. Bronze Age. National Museum of Korea, Seoul.

100. Bronze halberd from Manch'on-dong, Taegu City, North Kyŏngsang Province. Bronze Age. National Museum of Korea, Seoul.

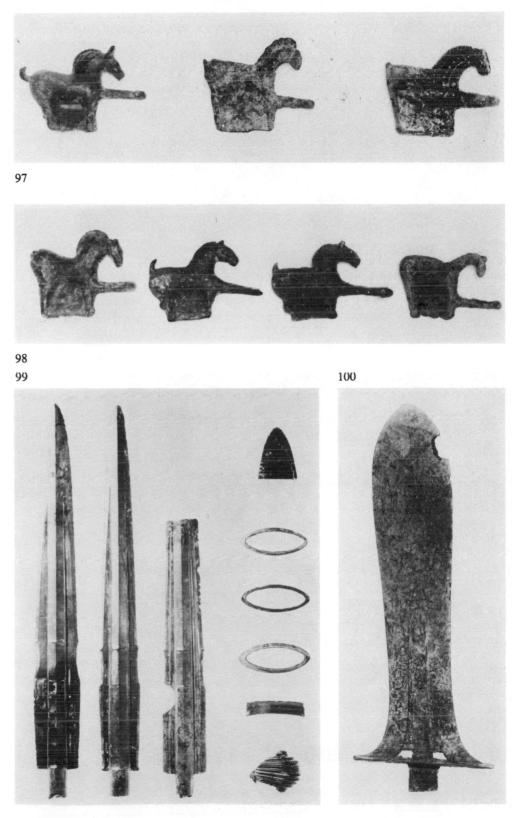

97

98

99

100

101. Bronze dagger handle ornament from Yangdong-ni, Kimhae-gun, South Kyŏngsang Province. Bronze Age. Collection of Tong-in Kang.

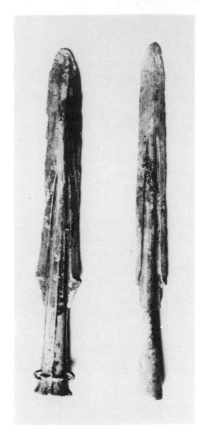

103. Bronze socketted spearhead from Yangdong-ni, Kimhae-gun, South Kyŏngsang Province. Bronze Age. Collection of Tong-in Kang.

102. Bronze mirror with square decoration motif and four deities from Yangdong-ni, Kimhae-gun, South Kyŏngsang Province. Bronze Age. Collection of Kyong-won Pak.

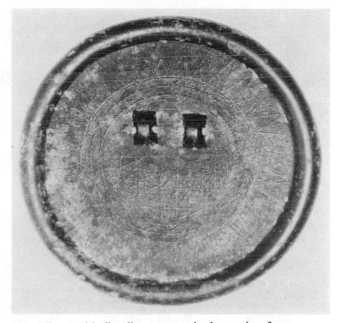

104. Mirror with fine-line geometric decoration from southern Korea (provenience uncertain). Bronze Age. Song-jŏn University Museum, Seoul.

105. Mirror with fine-line geometric decoration from southern Korea (provenience uncertain). Bronze Age. Song-jŏn University Museum.

106. Mirror with fine-line Geometric decoration from the ruins of T'osŏng, Yangyang-gun, Kangwŏn Province. Bronze Age. National Museum of Korea, Seoul.

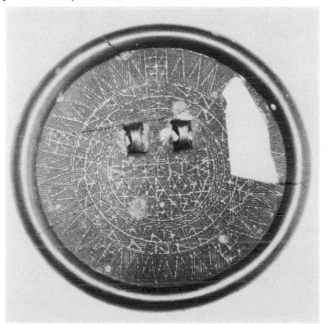

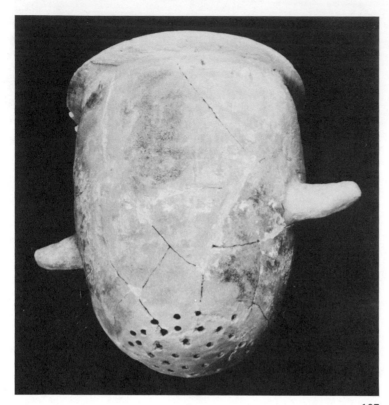

107

107. Pottery steamer vessel from the Masan shell mound, Ungch'ŏn, Ch'angwŏn-gun. Circa first century B.C. Pyŏn Han. Korea University Museum, Seoul.

108. Iron daggers from Hwayon-dong, Taegu City, North Kyŏngsang Province. Circa first century B.C. Collection of P'il-dong Han.

109. Eight-headed bronze bell from Taegong-ni, Hwasun-gun, South Chŏlla Province. Bronze Age. Korea Culture Information Center.

108

109

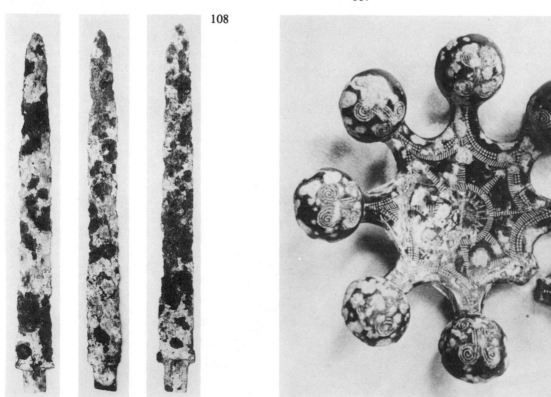

110,111,112. Bronze daggers from Taegong-ni, Hwasun-gun, South Chŏlla Province. Bronze Age. Korea Culture Information Center.

113,114. Double bronze horse bells from Taegong-ni, Hwasun-gun, South Chŏlla Province. Bronze Age. Korea Culture Information Center.

115. Bronze mirror with fine-line geometric decoration from Taegong-ni, Hwasun-gun, South Chŏlla Province. Bronze Age. Korea Culture Information Center.

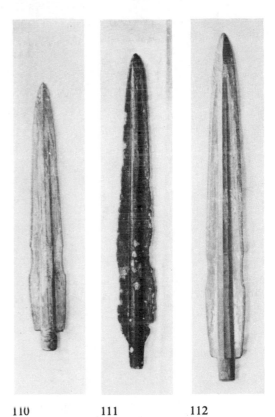

| 113 | 114 | 115 | 110 | 111 | 112 |

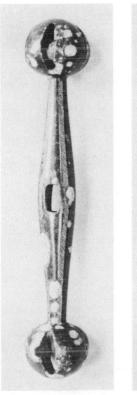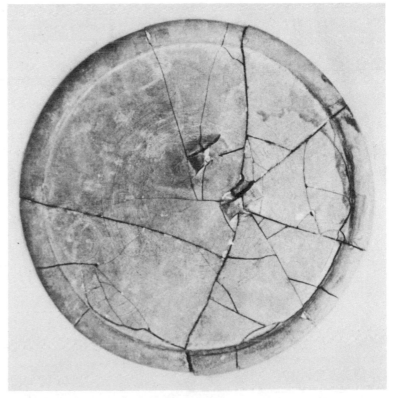

# Index

# About the Author

Jeong-hak Kim was professor at Pusan National University and director of the University Museum. He is currently director of the Pusan City Museum. He has done research at Harvard University and is the author of *The Formation of Korean People* and a coauthor of *The Origin of Agriculture in Japan*.

# About the Translators

Richard J. Pearson is professor of anthropology at the University of British Columbia. He is the author of *Archaeology of the Ryukyu Islands* and has contributed articles to numerous journals. He has spent sixteen years doing research and fieldwork in East Asian archaeology.

Kazue Pearson was educated at Doshisha University and received her master's degree in library science at Simmons College.

## Ⅹ Production Notes

This book was designed by Roger J. Eggers and typeset on the Unified Composing System by the design and production staff of The University Press of Hawaii.

The text typeface is English Times. The display face is Serif Gothic.

Offset presswork and binding were done by Halliday Lithograph. Text paper is Glatfelter P & S Hi Opaque Offset, basis 55.